AN

AUTHENTIC AND COMPREHENSIVE

HISTORY OF BUFFALO,

WITH SOME ACCOUNT OF

ITS EARLY INHABITANTS BOTH SAVAGE AND CIVILIZED,

COMPRISING

HISTORIC NOTICES OF THE SIX NATIONS OR IROQUOIS INDIANS, INCLUDING A SKETCH OF THE LIFE OF SIR WILLIAM JOHNSON, AND OF OTHER PROMINENT WHITE MEN, LONG RESIDENT AMONG THE SENECAS.

ARRANGED IN CHRONOLOGICAL ORDER,

IN TWO VOLUMES.

BY WILLIAM KETCHUM.

VOL. I.

BUFFALO, N. Y.
ROCKWELL, BAKER & HILL, PRINTERS.

1864.

TO THE

HON. MILLARD FILLMORE,

PRESIDENT OF THE

BUFFALO HISTORICAL SOCIETY,

THESE VOLUMES ARE RESPECTFULLY DEDICATED,

BY THE

AUTHOR.

BUFFALO, December, 1864.

CONTENTS.

CHAPTER I.

CHAPTER II.

CHAPTER III.

CHAPTER IV.

CHAPTER V.

CHAPTER VI.

CHAPTER VII.

CHAPTER VIII.

CHAPTER IX.

CHAPTER X.

CHAPTER XVIII.

CHAPTER XIX.

CHAPTER XX.

CHAPTER XXI.

CHAPTER XXII.

CHAPTER XXIII.

CHAPTER XXIV.

CHAPTER XXV.

PREFACE.

The historical notice of the Six Nations of Indians, the last remnant of whom now linger among us, which was at first expected to form only an introduction to the History of Buffalo, has unavoidably grown upon the hands of the author, until its dimensions are sufficient to fill a volume, almost the size originally contemplated for the whole work. This has necessarily compelled a division of the work, into two parts. The first volume, embracing the period from the first authentic records of European intercourse with the Iroquois or Five Nations, down to the final overthrow of their confederacy during our own revolution.

To do justice to this part of our History, has required a much greater amount of research, than was anticipated, for the reason, that the Indian history has never been written—at least their own version of it. In the fable of the lion and the man, the lion said, if lions had been sculptors, the man would have been represented in a very different attitude. Had the Indians been historians, many of the events of their history, would have presented a very different aspect. They have been represented as destitute of all the feelings of humanity, and the barbarous treatment of their prisoners of war has been cited as evidence of this. But it should be remembered that this barbarity had a different origin than in any want of the natural feelings of humanity in their nature; and this inhumanity was exercised from a far different motive, than has generally been supposed. The Iroquois considered themselves superior to all other men. And they took great pains not only to impress this idea upon all with whom they came in contact, but they taught it to their children. Their cruelties were practiced only against their enemies, or prisoners taken in war. They recognized courage, as the highest trait of character. In the practice of the cruelties they inflicted upon their prisoners, they made an exhibition not only of their own superiority over them, but they put the courage and fortitude of those who had essayed to cope with them in battle, to the test, by compelling them to quail under the infliction of these tortures. They gloried in submitting to the same trial of their own courage and fortitude, if captured in war, and their old men have voluntarily submitted to, nay, even courted, the infliction of these barbarous cruelties upon themselves. It was a part of their education, a part of their system of war. Colden in his history of the Five Nations written early in the eighteenth century, says:

"Our Indians have refused to die meanly, or with but little pain, when they thought their country's honor would be at stake by it; but have given their bodies willingly to the most cruel torments of their enemies, to show, as they said, that the Five Nations consisted of men, whose courage and resolution could not be shaken."

The torture of Father Jogues and others by the Mohawks, in 1643, has been referred to by some writers as evidence of their cruelty, he being a Jesuit Priest, or Missionary. But it should be remembered that he was taken in battle. He was found with weapons of war in his hands, fighting by the side of the Hurons, the "sworn enemies of the Iroquois." He had taken the sword, and could expect nothing else but to "perish by the sword." He had undertaken to act the warrior's part, could he expect to escape the warrior's fate?

At the same time when Father Jogues was a prisoner in the hands of the Mohawks, the Dutch Domine of the Collegiate Reformed Protestant church in New York, writes thus of the Iroquois: "though they are so very cruel to their enemies, they are very friendly to us, and we have no dread of them. We go with them into the woods, we meet with each other sometimes at an hour or two's walk from any houses, and think no more about it than if we met with christians. They sleep by us too, in our chambers before our beds. I have had eight at once, who laid, and slept upon the floor near my bed."*

It has been represented that in the conduct of their wars, the Iroquois were actuated by a spirit of revenge. But it may be doubted whether they were influenced by any baser motives in this respect, than those civilized nations who do the same things under the more specious name of "retaliation." At the first introduction of fire-arms among the Iroquois, they did not readily adopt their use in war. They did not consider it brave, or honorable, to shoot an adversary while at a distance; but, chose to meet him at close quarters, with the tomahawk and scalping knife; and when they first began to use fire-arms, they usually threw them away after the first fire, and rushed in, with tomahawk in hand; they could not

*See a short sketch of the Mohawks by Johannes Megapolensis Jr., New York Historical Society's collections, 2d series, vol. 3, page 156.

wait to reload. Fighting by shooting at each other at a distance, to them was no fighting at all, and the best armed and best disciplined soldiers, were no match for them at close quarters.

Their social habits and moral character have been equally misrepresented, and misunderstood. Before they had became contaminated by their intercourse with Europeans, they might in many respects have served as patterns for our imitation. "The hospitality of these Indians," (says Colden) "is no less remarkable, than their virtue; as soon as any stranger comes, they are sure to offer him victuals. If there be several in company, and come from afar, one of their best houses is cleaned, and given up for their entertainment. Their complaisance on these occasions, goes even farther than christian civility allows of, as they have no other rule for it, than the furnishing their guest with everything they think will be agreeable to him."

And if the person be one of distinction, every inducement was offered to prolong his visit, or to make his permanent abode with them; and it was esteemed an honor for the young women to become the chosen partners of such, and "perform all the duties of a fond wife, during the strangers stay," and this was from no base, or sordid motive. These associations often became lasting, and as in the case of the Jonciares and the Montours, among the French, the Johnsons, Abeels, and others among the English, became permanent, and of mutual obligation. Indeed there were weightier objects underlying these associations. The intermarriage with other nations or individuals, was encouraged, and practiced from motives of state policy, as much as in European governments. The union thus formed, though wanting in the formality required by our customs and laws, was the most solemn and binding known to them. It was not coercive, but entirely optional on both sides.

Greenhalgh, who visited the Senecas as early or earlier than any other white man of whom we have any account, says: they invited him and his party to choose from their maidens, not such as we liked, but "such as liked us." That these alliances were often of great political consequence to the Six Nations, there is abundant proof in the instances, which have been already mentioned.

The Iroquois were equally remarkable in regard to their civil polity; and it is utterly impossible to account for their superiority in this respect, over all the other Indian Nations, upon any other hypothesis, than that they must have obtained their ideas on this subject, from Europeans.

"The Five Nations, (says Colden) have such absolute notions of liberty, that they allow of no kind of superiority one, over an other; and banish all servitude from their territories. They never make any prisoner a slave, but, it is customary among them, to make a compliment of naturalization into the Five Nations; and considering how highly they value themselves above all others, this must be no small compliment."

And although there was no power to punish for crimes, they were less frequent than in civilized society. They had also a high sense of honor. "After their prisoners were secured (we again quote from Colden) they never offered them the least mal-treatment, but on the contrary will rather starve themselves, than to suffer them to want; and I have been always assured, that there is not one instance of their offering the least violence to female chastity." The following is the testimony of Mrs. Rebecca Gilbert, who with her family was a prisoner two years among the Senecas, in 1781-2:

"The Indians were remarkable on all occasions for their modesty, their chaste reserve, and their deference and respect for their female captives, Insomuch, that no forwardness, no insult, no curiosity, or impropriety of conduct, or expression, was ever manifested, towards any of the female prisoners, during the time of their captivity among them."*

This has been the uniform testimony of all female prisoners on this subject, and speaks volumes in praise of the Indians. The Iroquois have been distinguished for their orators, and it has been a subject of remark, as well as surprise, how they should be able to attain such proficiency in this art, without apparent means for studying, and perfecting themselves in so high an accomplishment. In no age of their history, as it has come down to us, have they been destitute of men possessing very high qualifications as public speakers. In all their public business, they use great deliberation, and it would be considered a breach of decorum, to reply to a speech, on the same day; and when the reply is made, it is done with the strictest observance of order, and deliberation. Every sentence or topic under discussion, is first repeated, almost verbatim, in the words of the first speaker; and then answered in their regular order, with a directness, and precision, that might be imitated with great propriety by orators, who boast of a higher cultivation, and training in the schools. So remarkable is this trait in the character of the Iroquois, as to lead to the conjecture that this too, must have been learned from intercourse with cultivated Europeans; how, or at what period of their history, even tradition does not inform us.

It is to be considered that most of the Indian speeches which have come

*Narrative of the captivity of the Gilbert family, p 218.

down to us, were interpreted by illiterate, or uneducated persons; and their force, and beauty have not been preserved; so that it is not fair to judge, in all cases, by these imperfect specimens. That the Iroquois possessed intellectual qualities of a superior order, there is abundance of evidence, and under favorable circumstances, that they might have attained high distinction in literature, art, and science, there is no doubt. But we have known them only in their degradation; after their contact with the white man had transformed all the high, ennobling qualities of his original character, into those of the lowest, and vilest of the race he strove to imitate; it has been true of the history of the intercourse of the Indians with the whites, that they readily learned to practice the vices of the whites, but rarely to imitate their virtues. The introduction of spiritous liquors among them, was probably the most prolific source of evil. As early as 1641, it was said of the Mohawks, (and it was measurably true of all the other Five Nations.)

"There is one vice, which the Indians have all fallen into, since their acquaintance with the christians, and of which they could not be guilty, before that time; that is drunkenness.

"It is strange how all the Indian nations, and almost every person among them, male and female, are infatuated with the love of strong drink, they know no bounds to their desire. * * * They have never been taught to conquer any passion, but by some contrary passion; and the traders with whom they chiefly converse, are so far from giving them an abhorrence of this vice, that they encourage it all they can, not only for the profit of the liquor they sell, but that they may have an opportunity to impose upon them; and this, as they chiefly drink spirits, has destroyed greater numbers, than all their wars, and disease put together."

The most fruitful source of difficulty between the whites and the Indians, has been their lands. This began almost with the first settlement at New York by the Dutch, and has continued with occasional intermission, down almost to our own times. No impartial observer can fail to discover, that in these controversies the Indians were almost always, the aggrieved party. Nor can the means resorted to, even by those acting in an official capacity to accomplish their purposes, be always justified. Sir William Johnson himself did not escape censure in this respect. The history of these transactions is in general a history of wrongs done to the Indians, by which they were made to suffer in other ways besides being dispossessed of their lands, without adequate compensation.

There is another respect in which great injustice has been done to the Indians. The avidity with which the public mind has received every story of Indian barbarity, come from what quarter it might, without investigation as to its truth, or probability, has caused some of the most extravagant and absurd fictions, to be copied into histories, as veritable facts. The celebrated scalp letter, ingeniously written in 1781, by Dr. Franklin for political purposes no doubt, has been repeatedly copied into books, as veritable history. The scalp certificate pretended to have been found on the person of the celebrated Seneca Chief, Sayenquaraghta, as it is pronounced in the Mohawk, or Gui-yah-gwaah-doh as it is in the Seneca, or "smoke-bearer," as it is literally in English, or "old smoke," or "old King," as he was familiarly called by the whites. This certificate, which bears on its face evidence of its spurious character, has passed into history as genuine; when the least investigation, or the slightest knowledge of contemporaneous history, would have proved its absurdity.

The imposition practiced upon the poor Indians, early attracted the attention of philanthropists, particularly the Quakers. Although efforts to christanize them, had been made by the disciples of St. Francis, the Jesuits, and the Moravians, at an early period, protestant missionaries met with very little success among the Six Nations, until the time of the celebrated missionary Kirkland, who established himself permanently with the Oneidas, over whom he gained great influence, which was felt more or less through all the other Nations of the confederacy.

Notwithstanding these efforts to avert, or mitigate the evils to which they were exposed, and under which they suffered, very little was accomplished to arrest their downfall. It is true, there were individual cases of conversion to the christian faith among them, and in the judgment of charity, there were many examples of real christian piety, exhibited in the life, and death, of these sons of the forest; but nothing could avert the doom of the great mass.

During the latter years of the French supremacy over the Six Nations, it had been their settled policy to scatter them; and induce them to settle upon the line of the frontier posts the French had established from Quebec to New Orleans. Through the exertions and influence of the Jonciares, father and son, and others, the French were able to accomplish their purpose to some extent, and considerable numbers of the Six Nations were settled upon the frontiers of Maryland, and Virginia, where they became allied to the Shawnese, and other nations residing there, by marriage and otherwise, forming what were denominated the Mingoes; it is said this was the name by which the Six Nations called themselves.

After the surrender of Canada by the French, to the English, they endeavored to persuade the Six Nations to withdraw their people from the

Ohio and its tributaries, and to concentrate them upon their own lands, within the boundaries of New York. Sir William Johnson had directed his efforts and influence to accomplish this object, for several years before his death, in which he was seconded by many of the leading chiefs of all the Six Nations, with perhaps the exception of the Senecas, who, by their proximity to these settlements, had become more intimately connected with them.

The encroachments of the English from Maryland and Virginia, upon the Indian settlements on the Ohio river, soon involved the Indians in difficulty with the settlers, in which the Five Nations, particularly the Senecas, became involved. Sir William Johnson had the sagacity to foresee these troubles, but neither he, nor his successors, although they made strenuous efforts to this end, were able to avert the impending storm, and by the most natural process in the world, the Senecas became engaged with their allies, and dependents, in the wars, which, with varying success, desolated that region.

There is little doubt that had the colonists, on the breaking out of the Revolution, had the means of furnishing the Indians with the supplies they had been for a long time accustomed to receive, first, from the French, and then from the English, the friendship, or at least the neutrality of the Six Nations, with perhaps the exception of the Mohawks, might have been secured. The influence of the Johnsons and Brant, secured the adherence of the Mohawks to the cause of the Crown, and the Senecas living so remote from Albany, were almost inaccessible to the colonists, while they were easily reached by the British, who were established at Fort Niagara; and from this period we may date the disruption of the confederacy of the Six Nations, which hitherto had withstood every effort to break the golden chain which bound it together. Although some efforts were made to preserve their national existence after the war of the Revolution, these efforts were feeble, and only showed how they had fallen from their once proud position.

The Mohawks removed permanently to Canada; the other nations, or the small remnant of them, remained within the territory of the United States; but were scattered far and wide. The Oneidas alone had remained true to the cause of the colonists, or at least observed a strict neutrality, for which, they suffered at the hands of their own brethren, the Mohawks, and from the British tories, during the progress of the war. After the peace, the Senecas, disheartened, dispirited, driven from their homes, without the means of subsistence, sued for peace and protection, which was granted, and the small remnant of them. are now enjoying the fruit of that protection, upon lands assigned them upon the Tonawanda, Cattaraugus and Alleghany Reservations, where many of them have attained to a measure of civilization, which secures to them all the comforts of life, by means of agriculture, which is successfully pursued by them, and it should be mentioned to the credit of their patriotism, that they have furnished several hundred warriors to our present army, inferior to none in the field.

I should do injustice to my own feelings, and to the liberality and kindness of the gentlemen who have given me free access to, and use of, their libraries, in aid of the execution of this work. From the extensive library of the Hon. Geo. R. Babcock, rich in all that relates to early American history, I have derived much that is valuable in this department. The choice collection of early French publications in regard to the history of this country, in Canada and upon the lakes, in the library of O. H. Marshall, Esq., have furnished valuable aid in regard to the early history of our Indians, and I am also indebted to L. K. Haddock, Esq., for several rare publications in regard to the history of the same period. Much the largest portion of the facts connected with the history of the Six Nations, from about the middle of the eighteenth century, has been derived from the Johnson manuscripts, or the Colonial Documents, published by the government of the State of New York, edited by Mr. O'Callaghan. These documents are a mine of wealth to the historian, and the difficulty has been to abridge the extracts so as to bring them within reasonable limits. To the Buffalo Historical Society, I am indebted for the use of this work, as well as that of other valuable books, papers, and manuscripts, relating to the history of our city and its vicinity—deposited in their fire proof vaults.

If these pages shall contribnte, in any degree, to throw light upon the true character of the Six Nations, and serve to correct some of the errors into which the public mind has fallen, in respect to them, one of the principal objects of the author will be accomplished.

Buffalo, December, 1864.

CHAPTER I.

A history of Buffalo that did not contain some account of its aboriginal inhabitants would be incomplete. In attempting to give a full, complete and authentic history of Buffalo, its settlement, growth, and extraordinary commercial, mechanical, and manufacturing development, it will be necessary to give such facts as have come down to us, both traditional and historical, of the race who preceded us in the occupation and ownership of our present inheritance—a people now nearly extinct, but whose fading glory ushered in a new era of civilization and enterprise scarcely paralleled in the history of our race.

The territory once exhibited on the map as the "Country of the Iroquois," comprising almost the entire state of New York, is now the seat of a highly intelligent, christian civilization, teeming with populous cities, beautiful villages, highly cultivated farms, mills, manufactories, schools, churches, and everything that denotes enterprise, intelligence and universal prosperity.

When it is considered that this change in western New York has been wrought within the space of less than one hundred years—yes, within the life-time of many now living, it will be admitted that the change is most extraordinary, wonderful.

Beginning with the earliest authentic accounts of this country, and of its inhabitants, the history of events will be given in their regular chronological order, with such notice of prominent individuals who were connected with contemporaneous events, as history or recollection shall furnish.

This will involve the necessity of resorting to the Indian traditions for information in regard to events which occurred prior to the advent of European settlement on this continent. But these will be used only so far as they are confirmed by the evidence and observation of the earliest visitors to this locality, and from sources of unquestionable authenticity.

The first visits of Europeans to this locality, the records of which have come down to us, were made early in the 17th century.

In a report made to Father L'Allemant, dated 1640, it is said "Jean Brebeuf and Joseph Marie Chaumonot, two Fathers of our company which have charge of the mission to the Neutre Nation, set out on the 2d day of November, A. D. 1640, to visit that people;" after speaking of the superior qualifications of these men for such an embassy, he says: "altho' many of our French traders have visited that people for purposes of trade, we have no knowledge of any who have been there to preach the gospel, except Father De La Roche Daillon, a Recollect, who passed the winter there in the year 1626." He then proceeds to describe very minutely the route and distances to reach the place of their residence, and fixes it "at the foot of the lake of the *Erigh* or *Cat Nation*"—"most of their villages being on the west side of the river, our French who first discovered this people, named them the

Neutre Nation, their country being the ordinary passage by land between some of the Iroquois and the Hurons, who were sworn enemies, while they remained at peace with both. The people of both nations remained in peace and safety in the wigwams of the villages of that nation." It is not improbable that the Kaw-quaws—an alien tribe residing among the Senecas, were a remnant of the Neutre Nation, altho' Mr. Schoolcraft thinks the Kaw-quaws are a remnant of the Eries. But the whole current of history, both written and traditional, is against this theory.

In the endeavor to maintain a strict neutrality between the Iroquois on one side, and the western nations with whom they were constantly at war on the other, the Neutre Nation were alternately the prey of both, until they were themselves ultimately nearly destroyed. At the period of the visit of the first French missionaries, soon after A. D. 1600, they were settled in several villages about the foot of lake Erie, upon both sides of the Niagara River, or rather the lake, as at that period it was not their custom to make their permanent residence upon any navigable water. It is not likely that these villages occupied the site of our present city, but were some miles away from the water, in order that they might not be exposed to surprise, or the sudden attacks of their enemies. "According to the estimate of the Fathers who have been there, the Neutre Nation at the period of their first visit computed about 12000 souls, in all their villages upon both sides of the river," or rather the lake.

The early maps place their villages upon both sides, at some distance from the lake, and river; none, so far as is remembered, place them upon the immediate shore of either the lake or river.

At the period of which we now speak, the Iroquois or Five Nations, were engaged in a war with the Hurons, who resided in the vicinity of the lake of that name. The Iroquois were the terror of all the surrounding nations. Father Hennepin, who visited their five villages or cantons, as he calls them, in 1678, says of them: "The Iroquois, whom the Sweedes, then the Dutch, the English, and French, have furnished with fire-arms, are reckoned at present, the most warlike of all the savages yet known. They have slain the best warriors among the Hurons, and forced the rest of the nations to join with them to make war together against all their enemies situated five or six hundred leagues distant from their five cantons. They have already destroyed above two millions of men, (Martin D. Valiries, one of the first of the order of St. Francis to visit North America, says: Fort Cataraqui, (Kingston,) was built for a defence against the incursions of the Iroquois. The Iroquois are a barbarous and insolent nation, that has shed the blood of more than two millions of souls, and are now actually at war with the inhabitants of Canada;" p. 17,) all accounts agree in representing the Iroquois or Five nations as the most powerful and formidable of all the known Indian Nations upon this Continent at the period of the first permanent settlement of Europeans—at the period of which we are now speaking, say 1658–9, they had driven away or destroyed all the nations who claimed any jurisdiction over the territory now embraced in the states of New York, Pennsylvania, a great part of Ohio, and Canada; and the terror of their name had extended westward, and southward, beyond the Mississippi.

From their own traditions, confirmed by the earliest records of history, their most powerful enemies and rivals were the *Eries*, or the *Cat Nation*, living upon the south side of the lake which bears their name. It is not likely that the permanent habitations of the Eries were upon or near the shore of the lake for reasons already stated. The terrible conflicts between the Eries and the Iroquois occurred for the most part before the settlement of Europeans. But the fact is mentioned by all the early writers, and the period of the final overthrow of the Eries, is pretty definitely fixed at about 1654–5. Father Le Moine went on an embassy to the Iroquois villages in 1654, and although he describes his journey very minutely, it does not appear that it extended further west than Onondaga, where a great council was held, at which all the Iroquois Nations were fully represented.

In a lengthy and formal speech which he made to them, he said he had "presents to be given to the five Iroquois, a hatchet each for the new war waging against the Cat Nation; also, a present to wipe away the tears of all the young warriors for the death of their great Chief Annencraos, a short time prisoner with the Cat Nation." In some observations made upon a journey of two Jesuit Missionaries, Fathers Chaumont and Dablon, to the country of the Iroquois, they say—"so soon as they become masters of their enemies—having crushed all the nations who attacked them—they glory of triumphing over Europeans, as well as Americans, so that the very moment they saw the dreaded *Cat Nation* subjected by their arms, and by the power of the Senecas, their allies, they would have massacred all the French at Onontague, were it not that they pretended to attract the Hurons, and to massacre them as they had done before."

Subsequent events which are minutely recorded in the

reports made by different officers of the French government, show that the fears entertained of the bad faith of the Iroquois, were not groundless.

The following Indian Tradition was written out by the author and furnished to the Buffalo Commercial Advertiser, and published in that paper July, 1845. It is the Indian account of some of the last great battles of the Iroquois with the Eries, the last of which was fought near this city, probably not far from the period of Father LeMoine's visit or embassy in 1654—to which allusion has already been made. This tradition was current among the Indians when the French missionaries first visited them, and has been ever since. The main features of it are corroborated by facts and history. After the period named the Eries are not mentioned in history, except as having been exterminated by the Iroquois. One of the French missionaries relates it in substance, and says that the account of it had only a parallel in the account: II. Samuel, chap. II., verses 14, 15, 16, 17, &c. "And Abner said to Joab: Let the young men now arise and play before us. And Joab answered: Let them arise. Then there arose and went over by number twelve of Benjamin, which pertained to Ishbosheth the son of Saul, and twelve of the servants of David. And they caught every one his fellow by the head, and thrust his sword in his fellow's side, so they fell down together: wherefore that place was called Helkathhazzurrim, which is in Gibeon. And there was a very sore battle that day, and Abner was beaten before the servants of David."

CHAPTER II.

INDIAN TRADITION

The Eries were among the most powerful and warlike of all the Indian tribes. They resided on the south side of the great Lake which bears their name, at the foot of which now stands the city of Buffalo. The Indian name for which was Te-osah-wa.

When the Eries heard of the confederation which had been formed between the Mohawks, (who subsequently resided in the valley of the river of that name,) the Oneidas, the Onondagas, the Cayugas, and the Senecas, who also resided for the most part upon the shores and outlets of the Lakes bearing their names respectively, (called by the French the Iroquois Nation,) they imagined it must be for some mischievous purpose. Altho' confident of their superiority over any one of the tribes inhabiting the countries within the bounds of their knowledge, they dreaded the power of such combined forces. In order to satisfy themselves in regard to the character, disposition, and power of those they considered their natural enemies, the Eries resorted to the following means:

They sent a friendly message to the Senecas, who were their nearest neighbors, inviting them to select one hundred of their most active, athletic young men, to play a game of ball against the same number to be selected by the Eries, for a wager that should be considered worthy the occasion, and the character of the great nation in whose behalf the offer was made.

The message was received and entertained in the most respectful manner. A council of the "Five Nations" was called, and the proposition fully discussed, and a messenger in due time despatched with the decision of the council respectfully declining the challenge.

This emboldened the Eries, and the next year the offer was renewed, and after being again considered, again formally declined.

This was far from satisfying the proud lords of the "Great Lake," and the challenge was renewed the third time. The blood of the young Iroquois could no longer be restrained. They importuned the old men to allow them to accept the challenge, and the wise counsels that had hitherto prevailed at last gave way, and the challenge was accepted. Nothing could exceed the enthusiasm with which each tribe sent forward its chosen champions for the contest. The only difficulty seemed to be, to make a selection where all were so worthy. After much delay, one hundred of the flower of all the "Five Nations" were finally designated, and the day for their departure fixed. An experienced chief was chosen as the leader of the party, whose orders the young men were strictly enjoined to obey. A grand council was called, and in the presence of the assembled multitude the party was charged in the most solemn manner to observe a pacific course of conduct towards their competitors, and the nation whose guests they were to become, and to allow no provocation, however great, to be resented by any act of aggression on their part, but in all respects to acquit themselves in a manner worthy the representatives of a great and powerful people, anxious to cultivate peace and friendship with their neighbors. Under these injunctions the party took up its line of march for Te-os-ah-wa.

When the chosen band had arrived in the vicinity of the point of their destination, a messenger was sent forward to notify the Eries of their arrival, and the next day was to be set apart for their grand entree.

The elegant and athletic forms, the tasteful yet not cumbrous dress, the dignified, noble bearing of their chief, and more than all, the modest demeanor of the young warriors of the Iroquois party, won the admiration of all beholders. They brought no arms. Each one bore a bat, used to throw or strike the ball, tastefully ornamented—being a hickory stick about five feet long, bent over at the end, and a thong netting wove into the bow. After a day of refreshment all things were ready for the contest. The chief of the Iroquois brought forward and deposited upon the ground a large pile of costly belts of wampum, beautifully ornamented moccasins, rich beaver robes, and other articles of great value in the eyes of the sons of the forest, as the stake or wager, on the part of his people. These were carefully matched, article by article, by the chief of the Eries, tied together and again deposited in a pile. The game began, and although contested with desperation and great skill by the Eries, was won by the Iroquois, and they bore off the prize in triumph. Thus ended the first day.

The Iroquois having now accomplished the object of their visit, proposed to take their leave. But the chief of the Eries, addressing himself to the leader said, their young men, though fairly beaten in the game of ball, would not be satisfied unless they could have a foot race, and proposed to match ten of their number against an equal number of the Iroquois party, which was assented to, and the Iroquois were again victorious.

The Kaw-Kaws, who resided on or near the Eighteen Mile Creek, being present as the friends of the Eries, invited the Iroquois to visit their village before they returned home, and thither the whole company repaired.

The chief of the Eries, evidently dissatisfied with the result of the several contests already decided, as a last and final trial of the courage and prowess of his guests, proposed to select ten men, to be matched by the same number to be selected from the Iroquois party to wrestle, and that the victor should dispatch his adversary on the spot by braining him with a tomahawk, and bearing off his scalp as a trophy.

This sanguinary proposition was not at all pleasing to the Iroquois. They however concluded to accept the challenge with a determination—should they be victorious—not to execute the bloody part of the proposition. The champions were accordingly chosen. A Seneca was the first to step into the ring, and threw his adversary amidst the shouts of the multitude. He stepped back and declined to execute his victim who lay passive at his feet. As quick as thought, the chief of the Eries seized the tomahawk and with a single blow scattered the brains of his vanquished warrior over the ground. His body was dragged out of the way and another champion of the Eries presented himself. He was as quickly thrown by his more powerful antagonist of the Iroquois party, and as quickly dispatched by the infuriated chief of the Eries. A third met the same fate. The chief of the Iroquois party seeing the terrible excitement which agitated the multitude, gave a signal to retreat. Every man obeyed, and in a moment they were out of sight.

In two hours they arrived at Te-osah-wa, gathered up the trophies of their victories, and were on their way home.

The visit of the hundred warriors of the Five Nations, and its results, only served to increase the jealousy of the Eries, and to convince them that they had powerful rivals to contend with. It was no part of their policy to cultivate friendship and strengthen their own power by cultivating peace and friendly alliance with other tribes. They knew of no mode of securing peace to themselves, but by exterminating all who opposed them. But the combination of several powerful nations, any one of which might be almost an equal match for them, and of whose personal prowess they had witnessed such an exhibition, inspired the Eries with the most anxious forebodings. To cope with them collectively, they saw was impossible. Their only hope therefore was in being able, by a vigorous and sudden movement, to destroy them in detail. With this view a powerful war party was immediately organized to attack the Senecas, whose principal residence was at the foot of Seneca lake, near the present cite of the village of Geneva. It happened that at this period there resided among the Eries a Seneca woman, who in early life had been taken prisoner, and had married a husband of the Eries. He died and left her a widow without children, a stranger among strangers. Seeing the terrible note of preparation for a bloody onslaught upon her kindred and friends, she formed the resolution of apprising them of their danger.

As soon as night set in, taking the course of the Niagara river, she traveled all night, and early next morning reached the shore of lake Ontario. She jumped into a canoe she found fastened to a tree and boldly pushed out into the open lake. Coasting down the south shore of the lake, she arrived at Oswego river in the night, near which a large settlement of her nation resided. She directed her steps to the house of the head chief and disclosed to him the object of her visit. She was secreted by the chief, and runners were dispatched to all the tribes, summoning them immediately to meet in council. When all were convened, the chief arose and in the most solemn manner rehearsed a vision, in which he said a beautiful bird had appeared to him and told him that a great war party of the Eries was preparing to make a secret and sudden descent upon them to destroy them, that nothing could save them but an immediate rally of all the warriors of the Five Nations, to meet the enemy before they had time to strike the meditated blow. These solemn announcements were heard in breathless silence. When the chief had finished and sat down, there was one terrific yell of menacing madness, and the earth fairly shook when the frenzied mass stamped the ground with fury, and brandishing high in the air the war clubs, demanded to be led against the invaders. No time was to be lost, delay might be fatal. A body of five thousand warriors was formed, with a corps of reserve of one thousand young men who had never been in battle. The bravest chiefs from all the tribes were put in command, and spies immediately sent out in search of the enemy; the whole body taking up a line of march in the direction from whence they expected an attack.

The advance of the war party was continued for several days, passing through successively the settlements of their friends, the Onondagas, the Cayugas, and the Senecas. But they had scarcely passed the last wigwam near the foot of Can-an-da-gua lake, when their scouts brought in intelligence of the advance of the Eries, who had already crossed the Chin-isse-o (Genesee) river in large force.

The Eries had not the slightest suspicion of the approach of their enemies. They relied upon the secrecy and celerity of their movements to surprise and subdue the Senecas almost without resistance.

The two parties met about midway between Canandaigua lake and the Genesee river, and near the outlet of two small lakes, near the foot of one of which (the Honeyoye,) the battle was fought. When the two parties came in sight of each other, the outlet of the lake only intervened between them. The entire force of the Iroquois was not in view of the Eries. The reserve corps of one thousand young men had not been allowed to advance in sight of the enemy. Nothing could exceed the impetuosity of the Eries at the first sight of an opposing force on the opposite side of the stream. They rushed through it and fell upon them with tremendous fury.

Notwithstanding the undaunted courage and determined bravery of the Iroquois warriors, they could not withstand such a terrible onslaught, and they were compelled to yield the ground on the bank of the stream. The whole force of the Iroquois, except the corps of reserve, now became engaged ; they fought hand to hand,

and foot to foot; the battle raged horribly, no quarter was asked or given on either side. As the fight thickened and became more and more desperate, the Eries, for the first time became sensible of their true situation. What they had long anticipated had become a fearful reality. *Their enemies had combined for their destruction*, and they now found themselves engaged suddenly and unexpectedly in a fearful struggle, which involved not only the glory, but the very *existence* of their nation. They were proud, and had been hitherto victorious over all their enemies. Their power was felt, and their superiority acknowledged by all the surrounding tribes. They knew how to *conquer*, but not how to *yield.* All these considerations flashed upon the minds of the bold Eries, and nerved every arm with almost superhuman power.

On the other hand, the united forces of the weaker tribes, now made strong by union, fired by a spirit of emulation, excited to the highest pitch among the warriors of the different tribes, brought for the first time to act in concert; inspired with zeal and confidence by the counsels of the wisest chiefs, and led on by the most experienced warriors of all the tribes, the Iroquois were *invincible.*

Though staggered at the first desperate onslaught of the Eries, the Iroquois soon rallied and made a stand, and now the din of battle rises higher and higher; the war club, the tomahawk and the scalping knife, wielded by herculean arms, do terrible deeds of death.

During the hottest of the battle, which was fierce and long, the corps of reserve consisting of one thousand young men, were by a skillful movement under their experienced chief and leader, placed in rear of the Eries on the opposite side of the stream in ambush.

The Eries had been driven seven times across the stream, and had as often regained their ground, but the eighth time, at a given signal from their leader, the corps of reserve in ambush rushed upon the almost exhausted Eries with a tremendous yell, and at once decided the fortunes of the day. Hundreds disdaining to fly, were struck down by the war clubs of the vigorous young warriors, whose thirst for the blood of the enemy knew no bounds. A few of the vanquished Eries escaped to carry the news of the terrible overthrow to their wives and children, and their old men who remained at home. But the victors did not allow them a moment's repose, but pursued them in their flight, killing without discrimination all who fell into their hands. The pursuit was continued for many weeks, and it was five months before the victorious war party of the Five Nations returned to their friends in celebrating their victory over their last and most powerful enemy, the Eries.

Tradition adds that many years after, a powerful war party of the decendents of the Eries came from beyond the Mississippi, ascended the Ohio river, crossed the country, and attacked the Senecas. A great battle was fought near this city, in which the Eries were again defeated and slain to a man, and their bodies were burned and the ashes buried in a mound which is still visible near the old Indian Mission Church, a monument at once of the indomitable courage of the terrible Eries, and their brave conquerors, the Senecas.

CHAPTER III.

The arrival and permanent settlement of Europeans on this continent, seriously affected not only the aboriginal inhabitants, their habits, modes of thought, and of action, but also wrought a great change in the face of the country, particularly in our own State. The earliest records and observations of those who visited the coasts of New England, before any permanent settlement of Europeans was made, represent the country for the most part as an open prairie—produced by the periodical burning over, of immense tracts of country by the native inhabitants—and this was a custom persisted in from time immemorial. The reason assigned for this by Thos. Morton, in 1636, was, that it was for the purpose of keeping down the growth of trees, shrubs, vines, and vegetation, which would otherwise grow so rank as to become impenetrable and obstruct the vision, as well as the passage through it. But subsequent observation assigned a better and more probable reason for these periodical burnings. The inhabitants subsisted almost entirely by the chase; agriculture as a means of subsistence was entirely unknown to them. They lived almost entirely upon fish, and the flesh of the animals they were able to kill by the means they then employed, which would now be considered very inadequate to accomplish the purposes designed. They found it necessary to adopt some method to entice the graminivorous animals into the vicinity of their settlements, and by burning the dried vegetation every spring, they not only kept down the growth of timber and shrubs, but stimulated the growth of a tender nutricious grass, eagerly sought for by the deer, the elk, the moose, and the buffalo. These not only sought the luxuriant pastures for food, but they soon learned that these open plains afforded protection against their enemies of the carnivorous race of animals which prey upon them. These stealthy marauders of the feline and canine species, exercised their vocation in the dense forests, or in the darkness of the night. They seldom ventured into the open plain; hence the harmless, defenceless animals which furnished food for man, roamed almost unmolested over the grassy plains kept in perrennial verdure by his superior sagacity.

All the regions of country which are usually denominated "oak openings," are to be considered as once open prairies, like the vast prairies of the west, whose origin is to be ascribed to the same cause. These prairies extended over a great portion of what is now New England, a large portion of the states of New York, New Jersey, Pennsylvania, Ohio, Kentucky, Tennessee, &c. A large portion of Upper Canada, particularly that part of it bound by the lakes Ontario, Erie and Huron, may also be included in the once prairie region, for it will be observed that "oak openings" prevail to a large extent in all the territory named. What are called the "*plains*," in our own vicinity, are a striking example of the change which has taken place within less than two hundred years.

President Theodore Dwight, who visited Buffalo (or as it was then called Buffalo Creek,) in 1803, has the following observations: "From Batavia there are two roads to Buffalo Creek, and a third which passes directly to Queenstown, seven miles below the Falls of Niagara. The last is the nearest route to the Falls, but being lately and imperfectly made, and passing through a country scarcely at all inhabited, presents to a traveller a disagreeable path, and wretched accommodations. The new road to Buffalo Creek, is five miles shorter than the old, but is of recent date, and stretches out in no less than thirteen miles of mud, before it becomes reunited. The old road, which I suppose to have been the ancient military route, contains from eight to nine miles of mud out of twenty-three. We chose this, by advice of a gentleman acquainted with both, and soon entered upon the first of three mirey expansions, lying in this part of our journey. Here, however, we had the advantage of daylight, and the mire was less deep, than on the preceding evening, yet it was sufficiently tedious. We dined at Dunham's, five miles from Batavia. After leaving Dunham's, and passing through another maple swamp, we entered upon the second of the *plains*, above mentioned.

"From the appellation of plains, usually given to these tracts, you will naturally think as I did, that they are level grounds. This however, is a mistake. They are generally elevated, and every where present a surface rolling easily, without any sudden declivity except on the borders of streams or swamps. The variations of the surface are however continual, and some of the eminences rise considerably above the common level. These grounds, are also termed *openings*, as being in a great degree destitute of forests. The vegetation with which they are covered consists of grass, weeds and shrubs, of various kinds. The grass, resembles a species sometimes seen on the intervales of Connecticut, and named perhaps locally, *thatch*. The stalk is single, from three to five feet in height, tinted in various parts with a brown hue, and topped with a spreading ear, generally resembling that of spear grass. Besides the shrubs, which have nothing remarkable in them, there are, on all these plains some, and on some of them many, young trees, particularly near the Genesee. * * * The soil of these plains is loam of a light brown hue, mingled with gravel, and covered by a very thin vegetable mould, the residum chiefly of shrubs and herbage. * * * The origin of the peculiar appearance of these grounds is probably this: the Indians annually and sometimes oftener, burned such parts of the North American forests, as they found sufficiently dry. In every such case the fuel consists chiefly of the fallen leaves, which are rarely dry enough for an extensive combustion except on uplands, and on these only, when covered with a dry soil. * * * The object of these conflagrations was to produce fresh and sweet pasture for the purpose of alluring the deer to the spots on which they had been kindled. Immediately after the fire, a species of grass springs up, sometimes called fire grass, because it usually succeeds a conflagration. Whether it is a peculiar species of grass, I am unable to say, not having seen it since the days of childhood. Either from its nature or the efficacy of the fire, it is remarkably sweet, and eagerly sought by deer. All the underwood is at the same time consumed, so that these animals are easily discovered at considerable distances, a thing impracticable where the forests have not been burned. * * Thus in time these plains were deforested to the degree in which we now see them, and were gradually converted into pasture grounds. It ought to be observed that they were in all probability burnt over for ages after they were deforested, I presume down to a very late period. In a dry season the grass would furnish ample fuel for this purpose."*

It is not likely that a tree upon the whole tract could be found, giving evidence of an age beyond that period, say two hundred and fifty years, with the exception perhaps, of localities protected from the annual conflagrations by water. The evidences that large tracts of country, particularly in western New York, were formerly covered by water, are abundant. The high ground upon which a large portion of our own city is built, gives evidence of the gradual subsidence of the waters of Lake Erie. The same appearances are equally visible upon the shores of Lake Ontario, that the waters of that lake formerly stood much above their present level, a fact which has attracted the notice of all observant travellers as well as residents.

The following is an extract from the journal of an English traveller (Weld,) who visited this locality in 1796, and employed an Indian guide to conduct him through the unbroken wilderness, from the Indian settlement on Buffalo Creek to the Genesee river, at or near Mount Morris: "We found the country as we passed along, interspersed with open plains of great magnitude. Some of them, I should suppose, not less than fifteen or twenty miles in circumference. The trees on the borders of these

*Travels in New England and New York, by Timothy Dwight, in 1804.

having ample room to spread, were luxuriant beyond description, and shot forth their branches with all the grandeur and variety which characterise the English timber, particularly the oak. The woods around the plains were indented in every direction with bays and promontories, as Mr. Gilpin terms it, whilst rich clumps of trees interspersed here and there, appeared like so many clusters of beautiful islands. * * * These plains are covered with long coarse grass, which at a future day will probably afford feeding to numerous herds of cattle; at present they are totally unfrequented. Throughout the North Western territory of the United States, and even beyond the head waters of the Mississippi, the country is interspersed with similar plains, and the further you proceed to the westward, the more extensive and general are they. Amidst those to the westward are found numerous herds of buffalos, elks, and other wild graminivorous animals; and formerly animals of the same description were found on the plains of the State of New York, but they have all disappeared long since, owing to their having been so constantly pursued both by the Indians and the white people."

This state of comparative quiet and peace was interrupted by the introduction of a new element; we call it "christian civilization." Man in his normal condition is the same every where. He was found here exhibiting the usual traits of his character, warring upon his own species. But the harmless peaceful animals, who had not yet learned that man was his enemy, were destined to be driven from these peaceful haunts. The pastures that had been for long ages prepared and kept for his use, no longer received the periodical fertilising preparation necessary to the production of their coveted food. Man, hitherto his friend, was not only diverted from this work to other pursuits, but was transformed into an enemy.

Father La Moine, who visited the Onondagas in 1634, says: "Traveling through vast prairies we saw in divers quarters immense herds of wild bulls and cows, their horns resemble in .some respects the antlers of a stag. Our game does not leave us; it seems that venison and game follow us every where. Droves of twenty cows plunge into the water as if to meet us. Some were killed for sake of amusement by blows of an axe." Again he says: "I never saw so many deer, but we had no inclination to hunt. My companion killed three as if against his will. What a pity, for we left all the venison there, reserving the hides and some of the most delicate morsels." We can have but very inadequate conception of the rapidity with which animals will increase when all the circumstances are favorable; neither have we probably any conception of the multitude of animals that existed in the region we have designated, before they were disturbed by advancing civilization. All the prairie region, extending westward, and southward, almost indefinitely, abounded with vast multitudes of herbaceous animals; while the hilly, mountainous, timbered regions extending through several of the States known as the Alleghany or Apalachian Ridge, swarmed with multitudes of carnivorous animals. These, driven by hunger to seek for prey, sometimes descended to the plains, but returned to their native haunts as soon as their hunger was appeased.

All the descriptions we have of the great numbers of wolves, bears, panthers, wild cats, &c., &c., which the early settlers encountered, are comparatively of recent date, extending back only eighty, or at most one hundred years; still these accounts seem almost fabulous. La Salle and his party in their journey through the region lying south of Lake Erie, in the winter of 1680, encountered the wolves in such numbers, as to be in danger of being overpowered and devoured by them, notwithstanding that the party was well armed with guns, and had abundance of ammunition. The extraordinary multitude of game of all kinds upon the south shore of Lake Erie, is spoken of by several of the early travellers from 1680 to 1724; and is by some, attempted to be accounted for, by the fact, that since the terrible war between the Eries and the Iroquois, no one resided there. It was not considered safe to even pass through the country. It is stated as a well authenticated fact, that over four hundred bears were killed in a single season upon Point Pelee, on the north shore of Lake Erie, where it appeared these animals crossed the lake at certain seasons of the year in great numbers; passing from island to island, thus making the crossing easy upon the ice in winter, and by swimming in summer.

As late as 1804, it is stated by a traveller, (Rev. Mr. Harris,) that it was not safe to leave a horse hitched alone, particularly after dark, in North Eastern Ohio, as he would be in danger of being devoured by wolves, who infested that region of country at that time in great numbers. Deer, and the buffalo, were found in great numbers upon the prairies and bottom lands in Ohio, by the early settlers, in what was then the North Western Territory. The use of fire arms in hunting, infused a terror among the animals they never experienced before. The mode of killing animals before the introduction of fire arms, did not excite in them but little fear of man. Bears were usually killed by a kind of deadfall or trap, ingeniously formed of logs. The deer were sometimes killed with the bow and arrow, but this was without noise or any thing to frighten or alarm, like the noise, fire, and smoke of a gun. Indeed, the animals were not killed for any other purpose except to furnish food from their flesh, or clothing from their skins. But when both hide and flesh, became articles of sale in great quantities to Europeans, they began to be hunted for a far different motive, and to a much greater extent. And with the new weapons furnished by the traders, who early became eager to obtain the skins of all the furred animals, the destruction of the animals became greatly increased, while their propagation from the same causes was proportionally diminished. An early English traveller speaks of the perfectly wanton manner in which the deer were destroyed at the time he wrote, 1806. He said it was sufficient excuse for a man to leave his business, however urgent, if a deer came in sight, and a whole neighborhood has been known to be aroused and join in the pursuit, regardless of everything else; and if during the winter season a deep snow should become crusted over by a freezing rain upon its surface, it would be a signal for multitudes to sally out with dogs, and murder the poor helpless creatures by scores, at a season of year too, when neither the flesh or skins were of any, or little value.

CHAPTER IV.

The date, or occasion of the formation of the confederation of the Five Nations, has not been settled, with any degree of certainty. The attempts which have been made at different times, and by different persons, seem to end in mere conjecture or vague speculation. Tradition places it about 1539, upon what authority is not so clear. The Indian legends make it more obscure, from the great variety of extravagant and absurd superstitions connected with it. Nearly all accounts agree in assigning the ancient seat of the Five Nations in the North, or at least upon the banks of the St. Lawrence.

Champlain, on his first arrival in that river, soon after 1600, found them engaged in a war of extermination against the Hurons, who inhabited the shores of the lake bearing their name. The Franciscan Missionaries, who were the first to visit the Hurons, became interested in their behalf, and Champlain was induced to join the Hurons in two or three expeditions against the Iroquois, across lake Ontario, then called the lake of the Iroquois. One of these expeditions, which was undertaken in 1615, proved disastrous to the French. They were repulsed in an attack upon one of the Castles of the Onondagas; Champlain was severely wounded, and came nigh falling into the hands of the savages. His army was dispersed, his own men making their way as best they could to Quebec, where they reported that he was killed. He was, however, carried off by his Huron warriors, in a rude wicker basket into their own country, where he remained through the winter. The next spring he was able to return to Quebec, where he was received with great joy and surprise by the inhabitants, who had given him up as dead.

The following brief history of this transaction is from Champlain's own account, translated by O. H. Marshall, Esq., and furnished the New York Historical Society, in 1849. See proceedings, page 100, &c.

"On the 10th of October (1615,) we arrived before the fort of the enemy. Some skirmishing ensued among the Indians, which frustrated our design of not discovering ourselves until the next morning. The impatience of our savages, and the desire they had of witnessing the effects of our fire arms on the enemy, did not suffer them to wait. When I approached with my little detachment, we showed them what they had never before seen or heard. As soon as they saw us, and heard the balls whistling about their ears, they retired quickly into the fort, carrying with them their killed and wounded. We also fell back upon the main body, having five or six wounded, one of whom died. The Indians now retired out of sight of the fort, and refused to listen to the advice of Champlain as to the best mode of conducting the siege.

"He continued to aid them with his men, and in imitation of the ancient mode of attack, planned a kind of moveable tower, sufficiently high when advanced to the fort to overlook the palisades. It was constructed of pieces of wood placed one upon another, and was finished in a night. The village (says Champlain,) was enclosed by four rows of interlaced palisades thirty feet high, near a body of unfailing water. Along these palisades the Iroquois had placed conductors to convey water to the outside to extinguish fire. Galleries were constructed on the inside of the palisades, protected by a ball proof parapet of wood, garnished with double pieces of wood. When the tower was finished, two hundred of the strongest men advanced it near to the palisades. I stationed four marksmen on its top, who were well protected from the stones and arrows which were discharged by the enemy.

"The French soon drove the Iroquois from the galleries, but the undisciplined Hurons, instead of setting fire to the palisades as directed by Champlain, consumed the time in shouting at the enemy, and discharging harmless showers of arrows into the fort. Without discipline, and impatient of restraint, each one acted as his fancy pleased him. They placed the fire on the wrong side of the fort, so that it had no effect.

"When the fire had gone out, they began to pile wood against the palisades, but in such small quantities that it made no impression. The confusion was so great that nothing could be heard. I called out to them and pointed out as well as I could the danger they incurred by their imprudent management, but they heard nothing by reason of the great noise that they made.

"Perceiving that I should break my head in calling—that my remonstrances were in vain—and that there were no means of remedying the disorder, I resolved to effect with my own people what could be done, and to fire upon those we could discover.

"In the mean time the enemy profited by our disorder. They brought and threw water in such abundance, that it poured in streams from the conductors, and extinguished the fire in a very short time. They continued without cessation to discharge flights of arrows, which fell on us like hail. Those who were on the tower killed and wounded a great number. The battle lasted about three hours. Two of our chiefs, some head men, and about fifteen others were wounded. The unsuccessful issue of the assault induced the besiegers to think of retiring until they should be joined by a reinforcement of five hundred men that was daily expected. Champlain was twice severely wounded by arrows; the first time in the leg, the second in his knee.

"They remained before the Onondaga fort until the 16th day of October, when, in opposition to the remonstrances of Champlain and their chiefs, they raised the siege and began their homeward march. Champlain being unable to walk, was placed in a basket of wicker work, and so doubled up and fastened with cords that he was unable to move. Thus bound and confined, he was carried by the Indians on their backs for several days. The Iroquois pursued them for half a league, in hopes of cutting off some stragglers, but their arrangements for the retreat were such, that they suffered no loss. The wounded were placed in the centre, and the front and rear and wings were protected by chosen warriors. When they arrived on the borders of lake Ontario, they were rejoiced to find their canoes had not been discovered and broken up by the enemy.

"Champlain was now desirous of returning to Quebec by way of the St. Lawrence—a route yet untraversed by the white man—but the Indians refused him a canoe or guides. He was thus compelled to accompany them home and pass a long and dreary winter in the Huron country. He did not reach Quebec until the following June, when he was received as one risen from the grave, the Indians having reported his death a long time previous."

Soon after, the Iroquois invaded Canada, and defeated the Hurons in a great battle, almost in sight of Quebec, having previously bound the French to a strict neutrality by a treaty, which they did not dare to violate by an open interference. The Iroquois were not only brave in battle, but wise and politic in council. One of the early French writers speaking of the visit of a deputation which came to Quebec from the upper Iroquois, (the Senecas,) says: "The first of these embassadors who came from the upper Iroquois, were presented to M. de Tracy, in the month of December, 1665, and the most influential among them was a famous Captain called Garacontie; who always signalized his zeal for the French, and employed the credit which he has among all these tribes, in extricating our prisoners from their hands, as he has liberated very recently Seur Le Moine, an inhabitant of Montreal, who had been captured three months ago by these barbarians. M. de Tracy having notified him by the usual presents that he would give him friendly audiance, he pronounced a harangue full of good sense, and an eloquence, evincing no trace of the barbarous. It contained nothing but courtesies, and offers of friendship, and service, on the part of his tribe, wishes for a new Jesuit

Mission, and expressions of condolence on the death of the late Father Le Moine, the intelligence of which he had just received."

President Dwight, who possessed greater means both for observation and information than others, whose highly cultivated, vigorous mind, was exercised in investigating everything that related to their history.

Of the Iroquois or Six Nations (as they were called, after the incorporation of the Tuscaroras, who fled from North Carolina to them for protection in 1712 according to historical record,) he says :

"The Iroquois have certainly been a most extraordinary people. Had they enjoyed the advantages possessed by the ancient Greeks and Romans, there is no reason to believe they would be at all inferior to those celebrated Nations. Their minds appear to have been equal to any efforts within the reach of man. Their conquests, if we consider their numbers, and their circumstances, were little inferior to those of Rome itself. In their harmony, the unity of their operations, the energy of their character, the vastness, vigor and success of their enterprises, and the strength and sublimity of their eloquence, they may be fairly compared with the Greeks. Both the Greeks and the Romans before they began to rise into distinction had already reached the state of society in which men are able to improve, the Iroquois had not. The Greeks and Romans had ample means for improvement, the Iroquois had none."

Gov. Dewitt Clinton in a Discourse on the History of the Six Nations delivered in 1811, says:

"There is a striking similarity between the Romans and the Confederates, not only in their martial spirit, and rage for conquest, but in their treatment of the conquered. Like the Romans, they not only adopted individuals, but incorporated the remnant of their vanquished enemies in to their nation; by which they continually recruited their population, exhausted by endless and wasting wars, and were able to continue their career of victory, and desolation. If their unhappy victims hesitated or refused, they were compelled to accept the honors of adoption."

Speaking of the manner in which they conducted their public affairs, he observes:

"Their exterior relations, general interests, and national affairs, were conducted and superintended by a great council, assembled annually in Onondaga, the central canton, composed of the chiefs of each republic, and eighty Sachems were frequently convened at this national assembly. It took cognisance of the great questions of war and peace, of affairs of tributary nations, and their negociations with the French and English colonies; all their proceedings were conducted with great deliberation, and were distinguished for order, decorum, and solemnity. In eloquence, in dignity, and in all the characteristics of personal policy, they surpassed an assemblage of feudal Barons, and were perhaps not far inferior to the great Amphyctionic Council of Greece." In regard to their military powers and skill, he says: "Whatever superiority of force the Iroquois might have, they never neglected the use of stratagems; they employed all the crafty ideas of the Carthagenians; the cunning of the fox, the ferocity of the tiger, and the power of the lion, were united in their conduct. They prefered to vanquish their enemy by taking him off his guard, by involving him in an ambuscade, by falling upon him in the hour of sleep; but where emergencies rendered it necessary for them to face him in the open field of battle, they exhibited a courage and contempt of death, which have never been surpassed. * * The conquests and military achievements of the Iroquois were commensurate with their martial ardor, their thirst for glory, their great courage, their invincible perseverance, and their political talents. Their military excursions were extended as far north as the Hudson Bay. The Mississippi did not form their western limits, their power was felt in the most southern and eastern extremities of the United States. * * * To describe the military enterprises of this people would be to delineate the progress of a tornado or earthquake. Destruction followed their footsteps, and whole nations exterminated, rendered tributary, exiled from their country, or merged in their conquerors, declare the superiority and terror of their arms."

When Champlain arrived in Canada in 1603, he found them at war with the Hurons or Algonkins. He took part, and headed three expeditions against them, in two of which he was successful, but in the last he was repulsed. This unjust and impolitic interference laid the foundation of continual wars between the French and the Confederates. * * * The conquests of the Iroquois previous to the discovery of America, are only known to us through the imperfect channels of tradition; but it is well authenticated that since that memorable era they exterminated the nation of the Eries or Erighs on the south side of Lake Erie, which has given a name to that Lake. They nearly extirpated the Andastez, and the Chauanons. They conquered the Hurons and drove them and their allies, the Ottawas, among the Sioux on the head-waters of the Mississippi, "where they separated into bands and proclaimed wherever they went the terror of the Iroquois." They also subdued the Illinois, the Miamis, the Algonkins, the Delawares, the Shawnees, and several tribes of the Abenaquis. After the Iroquois had defeated the Hurons in a dreadful battle fought near Quebec, the Neperceneans who lived upon the St. Lawrence fled to Hudson's Bay to avoid their fury. In 1649 they destroyed two Huron villages and dispersed the nation; and afterwards they destroyed another village of six hundred families. Two villages presented themselves to the confederates and lived with them. "The dread of the Iroquois," says the Historian, "had such an effect upon all the other nations that the borders of the river Outaouis which were long thickly peopled became almost deserted, without its ever being known what became of the greater part of the inhabitants."—(Herriott p. 70.)

"The Illinois fled to the westward after being attacked by the Iroquois, and did not return until a general peace, and were permitted in 1760 by the confederates to settle between the Wabash and Sciota rivers. The banks of Lake Superior were lined with Algonkins who sought an assylum from the Five Nations. They also harrassed all the northern Indians as far as Hudson's Bay, and they even attacked the nations on the Missouri. When La Salle was among the Natches in 1683 he saw a party of that people who had been on an expedition against the Iroquois. Smith the founder of Virginia in an expedition up the Bay of Chesepeake, in 1608, met a war party of the confederates then going to attack their enemies. They were at peace with the Cowetans or Creeks, but they warred against the Catawbas, the Cherokees, and almost all the Southern Indians. The two former sent deputies to Albany where they effected a peace through the mediation of the English. In a word, the confederates were with few exceptions the conquerors of all the Indian nations east of the Mississippi. Such was the terror of the nations that when a single Mohawk appeared on the hills of New England, the fearful spectacle spread pain and terror, and flight was the only refuge from death. Charlevoix mentions a singular instance of this terrific ascendancy. Ten or twelve Ottawas being pursued by a party of Iroquois, endeavored to pass over to Goat Island on the Niagara River in a canoe, and were swept down the cataract, and what it appeared, they preferred it to the tender mercies of their enemies.

> "The vast immeasurable Abyss,
> Outrageous as a Sea, dark, wastful, wild,
> Up from the bottom turned."*

"In consequence of their sovereignty over the other nations the confederates exercised a proprietary right in their lands. In 1742 they granted to the province of Pennsylvania certain lands on the west side of the Susquehannah, having formerly done so on the east side. In 1744 they released to Maryland and Virginia certain lands claimed by them in those Colonies, and they declared at this treaty that they had conquered the several nations living on the Susquehannah and Potomac Rivers and on the back of the great Mountains in Virginia. In 1754 a number of the inhabitants of Connecticut purchased of them a large tract of land west of the Delaware River, and from thence spreading over the east and west branches of the Susquehannah River. In 1768 they gave

*Milton's Paradise Lost.

a deed to William Trent and others for land between the Ohio and Monongahela Rivers. They claimed and sold the land on the north side of the Kentucky river. In 1768 at a treaty held at Fort Stanwix, with Sir William Johnson, 'line of property' as it was commonly denominated was settled, marking out the boundary between the English Colonies and the territories of the confederates. The vicinity of the confederates was fortunate for the colony of New York. They served as an effectual shield against the hostile incursions of the French and their savage allies. Their war with the French began with Champlain and continued with few intervals, till the treaty of Utrecht, which confirmed the surrender of Canada, Nova Scotia, and Acadia to Great Britain. For near a century and a half they maintained a war against the French possessions in Louisiana and Canada; sometimes alone and sometimes in conjunction with the English colonies. During this eventful period they often maintained a proud superiority, always an honorable resistance, and no vicissitude of fortune or visitation of calamity, could ever compel them to descend from the elevated ground which they occupied in their own estimation, and in the opinion of the nations. * * *

"The confederates were as celebrated for their eloquence as for their military skill and political wisdom. Popular or free governments have in all ages been the congenial soil of oratory, and it is indeed all important in institutions merely advisory, where persuasion must supply the place of coercion, when there is no magistrate to execute, no military to compel, and where the only sanction of law is the controling power of public opinion; eloquence being therefore conceded so essential, must always be a great standard of personal merit, a certain road to popular favor, and a universal passport to public honors. These combined inducements operated with powerful force on the mind of the Indian, and there is little doubt but that oratory was studied with as much care, and application, among the confederates as it was in the stormy democracies of the eastern hemisphere. I do not pretend to assert, that there were as at Athens, and Rome, established schools and professional teachers for the pu pose, but I say it was an attainment, to which they devoted themselves, and to which they bent the whole force of their faculties. Their models of eloquence were to be found in no books, but in the living orators of their local and national assemblies. Their children, at an early period of life attended their council fires, in order to observe the passing scenes, and receive the lessons of wisdom. Their rich, and vivid imagery was drawn from the sublime scenery of nature, and their ideas were obtained from the laborious operations of their own minds, and from the experience and wisdom of their august sages. The most remarkable difference existed between the confederates and the surrounding nations, with respect to eloquence. You may search in vain in the records and writings of the past, or in the events of the present times, for a single model of eloquence among the Algonkins, the Abenaquis, the Delawares, the Shawnees, or any other nation except the Iroquois. The few scintillations of intellectual light, the faint glimmerings of genius which are sometimes found in their speeches, are evidently derived and borrowed from the confederates. Considering the interpreters who have undertaken to give the meaning of Indian speeches, it is not a little surprising that some of them should approach so near perfection. The major part of the interpreters were illiterate persons. * * I except from these remarks the speech of the Onondaga chief Garangula, to M. De La Barre, delivered on the occasion which I have before mentioned ; this was interpreted by Monsieur Le Moine, a French Jesuit, and recorded on the spot by Baron La Hontan, men of enlightened and cultivated minds, from whom it has been borrowed by Colden, Smith, Herriott, Trumball, and Williams. I believe it to be impossible to find in all the effusions of ancient or modern oratory, a speech more appropriate and more convincing ; under the veil of respectful profession, it conveys the most biting irony, and while it abounds with rich and splendid imagery, it contains the most solid reasoning; I place it in the same rank with the speech of Logan. On the 4th of February, 1690, as we are informed by the tradition of the inhabitants, (although history has fixed it on the 8th,) the town of Schenectady which then consisted of a church and forty-three houses, was surprised by a party of French and Indians from Canada ; a dreadful scene of conflagration and massacre ensued ; the greatest part of the inhabitants were killed or made prisoners ; those who escaped, fled naked towards Albany in a deep snow which fell that very night, and providentially met sleighs from that place, which returned immediately with them. This proceeding struck terror into the inhabitants of Albany, who were about to abandon the country in despair and consternation ; on this occasion several of the Mohawk chiefs went to Albany to make the customary speech of condolence, and to animate to honorable exertion. Their speech is preserved in the first volume of Colden's history of the

'Five Nations,' and even at this period it is impossible to read it without sensibility, without respecting its affectionate sympathy, and admiring its magnanimous spirit, and without ranking it among the most respectable models of eloquence which history affords." I have copied this extended extract from Mr. Clinton's address, because it embodies a greater amount of authentic information in regard to the history of the nation of the Iroquois, of which nation, the Senecas, our immediate predecessors, constituted an integral part, and also, because I wish to preserve the record of such a distinguished mind, and cultivated intellect, of the high appreciation in which he held the character of this most remarkable people; there can be no higher, juster, truer, or more honorable tribute paid to their memory. Father La Moine, a Jesuit Missionary of learning and talent, visited the confederates in 1654, as an embassador of the French government in Canada; the following is an extract from his journal: The council was held at Onondaga, and all the Five Nations were represented.

"On the 10th day of August the deputies of the three neighboring nations having arrived, after the usual summons of the chiefs that all should assemble in Ondissonks cabin, I opened the proceedings (says the Father, continuing his journal) by public prayer, on my knees, and in a loud voice, all in the Huron tongue. I invoked the great maker of Heaven, and of earth, to inspire us with what should be for His glory, and our good; I cursed all the demons of hell, who are the spirts of division; I prayed the tutelar angels of the whole country, to touch the hearts of those who heard me, when my words should strike their ear; I greatly astonished them, when they heard me naming all, by nations, by tribes, by families, and each particular individual of any note, and all by aid of my manuscript, which was as wonderful, as it was new. I told them I was the bearer of nineteen words to them.

"The first, that it was Onnonthio, M. De Lauzon, Governor of New France that spoke to them by my mouth, and then the Hurons and Algonkins, as well as the French, for all these three nations had Onnonthio for their great chief.

"A large belt of wampum, one hundred little tubes or pipes of red glass, the diamonds of the country, and a caribou's hide, being passed, these three presents made but one word.

"My second word was, to cut the bonds of the eight Seneca prisoners taken by our allies and brought to Montreal, as already stated.

"The third was to break the bonds of those of the Woolf tribe also captured about the same time.

"The fourth, to thank those of Ontonagu for having brought our prisoner back.

"The fifth present, was to thank the Senecas for having saved him from the scaffold.

"The sixth, for the Cayuga Iroquois, for having also contributed.

"The seventh, for the Oneidas, for having broken the bonds, which kept him a prisoner.

"The eighth, ninth, tenth, and eleventh presents to be given to the four Iroquois nations, a hatchet each, for the new war they were waging against the Cat Nation.

"The twelfth present, was to heal the lost head of the Seneca Interpreter by the Cat Nation.

"The thirteenth, to strengthen his palisades, to wit:

that he might be in a state of defence against the enemy.

" The fourteenth, to ornament his face, for it is the custom of warriors here, never to go to battle, unless with the face painted ; some black, some red, others with various other colors, each having herein, as if particular liveries, to which they cling, even unto death.

" The fifteenth to concentrate all their thoughts ; I made three presents for this occasion, one wampum belt, little glass beads, and an elk hide.

" The sixteenth, I opened Annonchiasse's door to the nations ; that is, they would be welcome among us.

" The seventeenth, I exhorted them to become acquainted with our faith, and made them presents for this object.

" The eighteenth, I asked them not to prepare hence forward, any ambushes for the Algonkin, and Huron nations, who would come to visit us in our French settlement. I made them presents for this purpose.

" Finally, by the nineteenth present, I wiped away the tears of all the young warriors for the death of their great chief Annencraos a short time prisoner with the Cat Nation.

" At each present they heaved a powerful ejaculation from the bottom of the chest, in testimony of their joy.

" I was full two hours making my whole speech, talking like a chief, and walking about like an actor on a stage, as is their custom.

" After they grouped together apart in nations, and tribes, calling to them a Mohawk, who by good luck was there, they consulted together for the space of two hours longer.

" Finally they called me among them, and seated me

in an honorable place. The chief who is the tongue of the country, repeats faithfully as orator, all my words. Then all set to singing in token of their gratification ; I was told to pray to God on my side, which I willingly did. After these songs he spoke to me in the name of his nation:

"First he thanked Onnontio for his good disposition to wards them, and brought forward for this purpose two large belts of wampum.

"Second, in the name of the Mohawks he thanked us for having restored five of the allies of the nation of the Woolf.

"Third, he thanked us in the name of the Seneca Iroquois for having drawn five of their tribe, out of the fire; two more belts ; ejaculations from the whole assembly follow each present. Another captain of the Oneida nation rises; Onnontio said he : speaking of M. Lauzon our Governor, Onnontio, thou art the pillar of the earth, thy spirit is a spirit of péace, and thy words soften the hearts of the most rebellious spirits. After other compliments expressed in a tone animated by love, and respect, he produced four large belts to thank Onnontio for having encouraged them to fight bravely against their new enemies of the Cat Nation, and for having exhorted them never again to war against the French. Thy voice said he, Onnontio is wonderful, to produce in my breast at one time, two effects, entirely dissimilar. Thou animatest me to war, and softenest my heart, by thoughts of peace. Thou art great, both in peace, and war, mild to those whom thou lovest, and terrible to thine enemies. We wish thee to love us, and we will love the French, for thy sake.

"In concluding these thanks, the Onnontagu chief took up the word.

"Listen, Ondessonk, said he to me, five entire nations speak to thee through my mouth. My breast contains the sentiments of the Iroquois nations, and my tongue responds faithfully to my breast. Thou wilt tell Onnontio four things, the sum of all our councils.

"First, we are willing to acknowledge Him of whom thou hast spoken, who is the master of our lives, who is unknown to us.

"Second, our council tree is planted this day at Onontagu—meaning that that, would be henceforth the place of their meetings, and of their negotiations for peace.

"Third, we conjure you to select on the banks of our great lake, an advantageous site for a French settlement; fix yourself in the heart of the country, since you ought to possess our hearts. There we shall go for instruction, and from that point, you will be able to spread yourself abroad in every direction. Be unto us careful as fathers, and we will be unto you, submissive as children.

"Fourth, we are engaged in new wars. Onnontio encouraged us. We shall entertain no other thought towards him than those of peace."

The foregoing extract is valuable in several respects. It furnishes us with a favorable specimen of the Iroquois manner of conducting their public councils, in their primitive state, and of their internal policy and statesmanship, and powers of oratory, uninfluenced by their association with Europeans, or modern civilization. It also enables us to fix, with a good degree of accuracy, not only the substantial truth, of the tradition already related, but the date, of the final overthrow of the Eries, as therein stated at about 1655.

I am not aware of any record of the visit of any European to the country of the Senecas at as early a period as this, and it is not likely their most western villages extended at this time, much beyond the lake which bears their name. It is said the name Iroquois signifies "long house." The confederate tribes or the territory occupied by them was so denominated by themselves. The Mohawks were charged to keep the eastern door, towards the sun's rising, and the Senecas the western, or towards the sun's setting. And it is to be observed, that during all the vicissitudes to which they have been exposed, and the changes through which they have passed, these tribes have virtually occupied the same relative position. In general, their conquests have been pushed from the east, towards the west. The location of the Senecas, is thus briefly alluded to in the French relations under date of 1664–5:

"Towards the termination of the great lake called Ontario is located the most numerous of the five Iroquois nations, named the Senecas, which contains full twelve hundred men in two or three villages, of which it is composed." This is undoubtedly a very imperfect piece of information but we have in the journal of Greenhalgh—probably a dutch Indian trader—a more accurate description of the principal villages of the Senecas, which he visited in 1667. He says: "The Seneques have four towns viz: Canagora, Tiotohatton, Canoenada and Kenthe. Canagora and Tiotohatton lye within thirty miles of ye lake Frontenac and ye other two lye about four or five miles a peace, to ye southward of those.

"They have abundance of corne, none of their towns are stockaded. Canagora lyes on the top of a great hill, and in that, as well as the bignesse, much like Onondago, contayning one hundred and fifty houses, northwestward of Caiougo (Cayuga,) seventy-two miles.

"Tiotohatton, lyes on the brinck or edge of a hill, has not much cleared ground, is near the river Tiotohatton w'ch signifies bending. It lyes westward of Canagora about thirty miles, containing about one hundred and thirty houses, being ye largest of all ye houses wee saw, ye ordinary, being fifty and sixty foot long, with twelve or thirteen fires in one house. They have good store of corne, growing about a mile to the northward of the towne. * * *

"Canoenada lyes about four miles to ye southwest of Canagora contains about thirty houses well furnished with corne. Kent-he lyes aboutt four or five miles to ye southward of Tiotohatton contains about twenty-four houses well furnished with corne. The Seneques are counted to be in all, about one thousand fighting men."

The extirpation of the Erie or Cat Nation, upon the south shore of lake Erie having been accomplished, the Senecas who guarded the western door of the "long house," pushed their enterprises farther west, subduing or driving before them all who opposed their progress. In one of their incursions into the country of the Illinois, a war party of the Senecas, captured, and pillaged, seven canoes, loaded with merchandise, belonging to the French; and actually attacked fort St. Louis, erected by Mons. La Salle on the Illinois river, designing to capture it also, but were defeated in their purpose, by the vigorous defense of the Chevalier De Bangy.

The capture and pillage of these canoes, was made a subject of complaint by the French government in Canada, and a purpose was formed to punish the Senecas, by a military expedition, into their country. With this view an effort was made to negociate a permanent peace with the four eastern nations, of the confederacy, and induce them to remain neutral, while the French visited deserved retribution upon the Senecas.

Preparations were made, and an expedition under Mons. De La Barre was sent into the territory of the Iroquois in 1684, landing upon the shores of Lake Ontario, near Onondaga. But partly from sickness, and partly from want of energy, and perseverance, on the part of the commander, it returned to Quebec, after negociating a treaty of peace with the Onondagas, containing promises of satisfaction for the robbery committed by the Senecas.

The failure of the expedition of Mons. La Barre occasioned dissatisfaction with the French, and in 1685 the Marquis De Nonville was appointed to succeed him in the government of Canada. A new expedition into the Seneca's country, was determined upon, under his command, but was not fully organized until July 1687.

De Nonville's official report of his expedition has been translated by O. H. Marshall, Esq., and published by the New York Historical Society, and in the Colonial Documents. According to this report the French are represented as victorious, but according to the accounts of other and less interested parties, the French were nearly defeated, in a battle which was fought very near the spot where the railroad from Rochester to Canandaigua crosses the turnpike road leading from the village of Victor south, to what is known as "Boughton Hill," in the town of Victor, Ontario county.

The French landed at the mouth of the Irondequoit Bay on Lake Ontario, where they stockaded their boats, and marched across the country, which was mostly what is called "oak openings." The largest village of the Senecas at that time, was upon Boughton Hill, less than a mile south of the railroad crossing spoken of. The Seneca warriors about four or five hundred strong, having notice of the approach of the French through their spies sent out, formed an ambuscade in a thick cedar swamp upon a small stream running through a valley between high hills. The French were entirely unaware of the presence of the enemy, until they rushed out of their concealment with tremendous yells. About two hundred of the Senecas were armed with guns, and all, with tomahawks and scalping knives. The two hundred guns, were fired at the first onset; without waiting to reload, the whole body rushed upon the French, with their accustomed ferocity, and had it not been for the Indian allies, who accompanied the French, their destruction would have been inevitable.

The brief check given to the fierce onslaught of the Senecas, by that portion of the French force accustomed to this mode of warfare, enabled them to recover from what would otherwise have been a total rout. As it was, they were content to encamp for the night upon the field, and when the next day they advanced upon the town, they found it deserted and destroyed.

The account given of this battle by some of the Indians to the English Governor at Albany, differs somewhat from the report of Mons. De Nonville. It is as follows: "When they (the French,) came in sight of the Senecas, the French not seeing them, sat down to rest themselves, and their Indians likewise; the Senecas seeing this, advanced upon the left wing, being Indians, the French seeing them stood to their arms, and gave the first volley, and then the Indians that were on the left wing. Whereupon the Senecas answered them with another, which occasioned so much smoke, that they could scarce see one another, wherefore they immediately ran in, and came to hardy blows, and put the left wing to flight. Some went quite away, and some fled to the rear of the French; when that wing was broke, they (the Senecas,) charged, and fired upon the French, and other Indians. The French retired about one hundred and fifty paces, and stood still.

"The Senecas continued the fight, with their hatchets, but perceiving at last that the French were too numerous, and would not give ground, some of the Senecas began to retreat, whereupon, the French Indians cried out 'the Senecas run,' and the rest hearing that, followed the first party that gave way, and so got off from another, and in their retreat, were followed about half an English mile; and if the enemy had followed them further, the Senecas would have lost abundance of people, because they carried off their wounded men, and were resolved to stick to them, and not leave them. The young Indian that was in the engagement, relates, that after it was over, when the Senecas had got upon a hill, they saw a party of fresh French, come up, the French called to them to stand and fight, but the Senecas replied, 'come out four hundred to our four hundred, and we have but one hundred men, and three hundred boys, and we will fight you hand to fist.' The said boy being asked, if he saw any of the French with any gorges about their necks, it was too hot, they were too numerous.

"There were amongst the four hundred and fifty Senecas, five women, who engaged (fought) as well as the men, and were resolved not to leave their husbands, but to live, or die, with them." Another account says: "The French all acknowledge the Senecas fought very well, and if their number had been greater, it would have gone hard with the French, for the new men were not used to the Seneca's whoop, and hollow, all the officers falling down, close upon the ground, for they jeered one another about it at Mont Royall."

Another account of this battle says: (See Colden's History of the Five Nations, page 80, vol. 1.) "The army marched four leagues the first day (after leaving Irondequoit landing,) without discovering anything. The next day the scouts advanced before the army, as far as the corn, of the villages, without seeing anybody, though they passed within pistol shot of five hundred Senecas, that lay on their bellies and let them pass, and repass, without disturbing them. On the report which they made, the French hastened their march, in hopes to overtake the women, children, and old men, for they no longer doubted of all being fled. But as soon as the French reached the foot of the hill, about a quarter of a league from the village, the Senecas suddenly raised the war shout, with a discharge of their fire arms. This put the regular troops, as well as the militia, into such a fright, as they marched through the woods that the battallions immediately divided and run to the right, and left, and in their confusion, fired upon one another. When the Senecas perceived their disorder, they fell in among them pell-mell, till the French Indians, more used to such way of fighting, gathered together, and repulsed the Senecas.

"There were (according to the French accounts,) a hundred Frenchmen, ten French Indians, and about four score Senecas killed, in the encounter. Mons. De Nonville was so dispirited with the fright that his men had been put to, that his Indians could not persuade him to pursue. He halted the remainder of the day. The next day he marched on with a design to burn the village, but when he came there, he found the Senecas had saved him the trouble, for they had laid all in ashes before they retired. Two old men only were found in the castle who were cut into pieces, and boiled, to make soup for their savage allies."

Gov. Dongan in speaking of the Iroquois says under date of Sept. 8, 1687: "Those Five Nations are very brave, and the awe, and dread, of all the Indians in these parts of America, and are a better defense to us than if they were so many christians." The expedition of Mons. De Nonville contented itself, with visiting three other Seneca villages, in the vicinity, the farthest being only four leagues (twelve miles,) distant. They found them all like the first, deserted and burned. In the neighborhood of all these villages, they found quite extensive fields of corn, not yet ready for the harvest. This they destroyed. They also found old corn of the last year preserved after the Indian mode in "cache," (hid in the ground,) which they also destroyed. The population of these four villages De Nonville estimates, at from fourteen to fifteen thousand, probably an exaggeration.

It is not probable that the Senecas ever returned to reside at Boughton Hill, if indeed at any of the villages destroyed by De Nonville's expedition, and the fact of their residence there, had entirely passed from the memory or knowledge of men. The first settlers in 1785 and for forty years afterwards, although at every annual turning up of the soil by the plough, found great quantities of Indian trinkets, with an occasional relic of civilization, like the part of a gun-lock, and an occasional French metal button, or a copper coin; no knowledge by whom or at what period, these evidences of a former occupation were left, until in 1847, Mr. Marshall with De Nonville's own report in his hand, aided by a map, traced by the hand of an aged chief of the Six Nations, then living, went upon the spot, and with the assistance of intelligent gentlemen living in the vicinity, identified the location of every principal object, minutely described in that report, and brought to light facts, which had faded from memory, or been obscured in darkness for a century. As no mention is made of Kanesadaga, which was for a long period the principal residence of the Senecas near the foot of Seneca lake, it is probable that before the time of De Nonville's expedition, it was not permanently occupied by them, but they may, after that event, have chosen it as their chief town, and remained there up to the time of Sullivan's expedition in 1779—which will be considered in the chronological order of events.

CHAPTER V.

We must now leave the Senecas for the purpose of bringing up the history of other contemporaneous events relating to this particular locality. In the fall of 1679, M. De La Salle with a party of about thirty persons left Quebec, for Mackinaw by way of the lake. The party arrived in the Niagara river late in November. They sailed up as far as the current would permit, made fast their small craft to the shore, and landed. None of the party had ever visited the spot before. They had heard the most extravagant accounts from the natives of the Falls of the " Oneagara" (Niagara.) But so imperfect was their knowledge of the Indian language, that they had formed very imperfect ideas of their magnitude, as well as many other things, concerning them, related by the Indians ; and it is not surprising that in attempting to describe, what no one had ever attempted to do before in writing, that gross errors should have crept into the description. When however, proper allowances are made, for this first attempt at a description of the Falls of Niagara, made under peculiar circumstances, in the middle of winter, with no means at hand of verifying any statements, by actual measurements, it will be admitted the description is graphic, and conveys to the mind a truer, and juster, idea of their real magnitude and grandeur, than can be obtained from many, more modern descriptions, written under the most favorable circumstances. It is to be observed, that the description which we copy, was originally written in French, and translated into the old quaint English, of nearly two hundred years ago. The translation was published in London in 1698.

"Betwixt the Lake Ontario and Erie there is vast and prodigious cadence of water, which falls down after a surprising and astonishing manner, insomuch that the universe does not afford its parallel.

"It is true, Italy and Swedeland, boast of some such things, but we may well say, they are but sorry patterns, when compared to this, of which we now speak.

"At the foot of this horrible precipice, we meet with the river Niagara, which is not above half a quarter of a league broad, but is wonderfully deep in some places. It is so rapid above the descent, that it violently hurries down the wild beasts, while endeavoring to pass it, to feed on the other side, they not being able to withstand the force of its current, which inevitably casts them down headlong above six hundred foot.*

"This wonderful downfall is composed of two great cross streams of water, and two falls, with an Isle sloping along the middle of it. The waters which fall from this vast height do foam, and boil, after the most hideous manner imaginable, making an outrageous noise, more terrible than that of thunder, for when the wind blows from the south, their dismal roaring may be heard above fifteen leauges off.

---

*Probably meaning the fall and rapids both above and below.

"The river Niagara having thrown itself down this incredible precipice, continues its impetuous course, for two leagues together, to the great rock, above mentioned, with an inexpressible rapidity, but having passed that, its impetuosity relents, gliding along more gently, for two leagues, till it arrives at the lake Ontario, or Frontenac; any barque or vessel may pass from the fort, to the foot of the large rock, above mentioned.

"This rock, lies to the westward, and is cut off from the land by the river Niagarà, about two leagues further down than the great fall, for which two leagues, the people are obliged to carry their goods overland; but the way is very good, and the trees are but few, and they chiefly firrs, and oaks. From the great fall unto this rock, which is to the west of the river, (on the west side,) the two brinks of it, are so prodigious high, that it would make one tremble, to look steadily upon the water, rolling along with a rapidity not to be imagined. Were it not for this vast cataract, which interrupts navigation, they might sail with barque, or greater vessels, above four hundred and fifty leagues further, cross the lake of Huron, and up to the further end of the lake Illinois, (Michigan) which two lakes, we may well say, are two little seas of fresh water."

The following is Father Hennepin's description of a voyage across lake Ontario, to the Niagara river in 1678:

"The very same year, on the 18th of November, I took leave of our monks at Fort Frontenac, and after mutual embraces, and expressions of brotherly and christian charity, I embarked in a brigantine of about ten tons. The winds and the cold of autumn were then very violent, insomuch that our crew were afraid to go, in so little a vessel. This obliged us, and the Seur De La Motte, our commander, to keep our course on the north side of the lake, to shelter ourselves under the coast, against the north west wind, which would have otherwise, forced us upon the southern coast of the lake. This voyage proved very difficult, and dangerous, because of the unseasonable time of the year, winter being near at hand.

"On the 26th we were in great danger, about two large leagues off the land, where we were obliged to lie at anchor, all that night, at sixty fathoms of water, and above, but at length the wind coming at the north east, we sailed on, and arrived safely at the other end of the lake Ontario, called by the Iroquois, Skannandario.

"We came pretty near one of their villages, called Tajajagon, lying about seventy leagues from Fort Frontenac, or Catarokouy, (Kingston.)

"We bartered some indian corn with the Iroquois, who could not sufficiently admire us, and came frequently to see us, in our brigantine, which for our greater security, we had brought to an anchor into a river, though before we could get in, we ran aground three times, which obliged us to put fourteen men into canoes, and cast the ballast of our ship overboard, to get her off again. That river falls into the lake, but for fear of being frozen up therein, we were forced to cut the ice, with axes, and other instruments. The wind turning then contrary, we were obliged to tarry there, till the 5th of December, 1678, when we sailed from the northern, to the southern side, where the river Niagara runs into the lake, but could not reach it that day, though it is but fifteen or sixteen leagues distant, and therefore cast anchor within five leagues of the shore, where we had very bad weather all the night long. On the 6th being St. Nicholas day, we got into the fine river Niagara, into which never any such ship as ours entered before.

"We sang there the Te-Deum, and other prayers, to return our thanks to God Almighty, for our prosperous voyage. The Iroquois Tsonnontouans (Senecas) inhabiting the little village, situated at the mouth of the river, took above three hundred whitings, (white fish) which are bigger than carps, and the best relished, as well as the wholsomest fish in the world ; which they presented all to us, imputing their good luck, to our arrival.

"They were much surprised at our ship, which they called the great wooden canoe.

"On the 7th we went in a canoe, two leagues up the river, to look for a convenient place for building, but not being able to get the canoe further up, because the current was too rapid for us to master, we went over-land about three leagues higher, though we found no land fit for culture.

"We lay that night near a river that runs from the westward, (Chippewa) within a league above the fall of the Niagara, which as we have already said is the greatest in the world.

"The snow was then a foot deep, and we were obliged to dig it up to make room for our fire. The next day, we returned the same way we went, and saw great numbers of wild goats, (deer) and turkey cocks, (wild turkeys) and on the 11th we said the first mass, that was ever said in that country. The carpenters and the rest of the crew were set to work, but Monseur De La Motto who had the direction of them, being not able to endure the fatigues of so laborious a life, gave over his design and returned to Canada, having about two hundred leagues to travel.

"The 12th, 13th and 14th the wind was not favorable enough to sail up the river, as far as the rapid current above mentioned, where we had resolved to build some houses.

"Whosoever considers our map, will easily see that this new enterprise of building a fort, and some houses on the river Niagara, besides the fort of Frontenac (Kingston) was like to give jealousy to the Iroquois, and even to the English, who live in this neighborhood (at Albany) and have a great commerce with them.

"Therefore, to prevent the ill consequences of it, it was thought fit to send an Embassie to the Iroquois, as it will be mentioned in the next chapter. The 15th I was desired to sit at the helm of our brigantine, while three of our men hauled the same from the shore with a rop,e and at last we brought her up, and moored her to the shore with a hawser near a rock of prodigious height, lying upon the rapid currents we have already mentioned.

"The 17th, 18th and 19th we were busy making a cabin, with palisadoes to serve for a magazine ; but the ground was so frozen, that we were forced several times, to throw boiling water upon it, to facilitate the beating in, and driving down, the stakes.

"The 20th, 21st, 22d and 23d, our ship was in great danger to be dashed to pieces, by the vast pieces of ice, that were hurled down the river, to prevent which, our carpenter made a capstane, to haul her ashore, but our great cable broke in three pieces, whereupon one of the carpenters surrounded the vessel with a cable, and tied it to several ropes, whereby we got her ashore, though with much difficulty, and saved her from the danger of being broke to pieces, or carried away by the ice, which came down with an extreme violence, from the great fall of Niagara."

After giving a detailed account of the embassy to the principal village of the Iroquois Tsonnontouans (Senecas) which was situated at about thirty leagues in a south easterly direction, and is at the same place, where De Nonville found them in 1687, nine years after, Father Hennepin proceeds to give an account of the building of the first vessel that ever floated on lake Erie.

"On the 14th of January, 1679, we arrived at our habitation of Niagara very weary of the fatigue of our voyage, (to the Seneca village.) We had no other food but Indian corn, but by good luck for us, the fishery of the whitings, I have already spoken of, was then in season, and made our indian corn more relishing. We made use of the water in which the fish was boiled, instead of broth of meat, for when it grows cold in the pot, it congeals itself like some real broth.

"On the 20th, arrived Mons. De La Salle, from Fort Frontenac, from which he was sent with a great barque to supply us with provisions, rigging, and tackling for the ship, we designed to build at the mouth of the lake Erie. But that barque, had been cast away on the southern coast of lake Ontario, by the fault of two pilots, who could not agree about the course they were to steer, though they were then only within two leagues of Niagara. The seamen, have called this place the mad cape.

"The anchors and cables were saved, but several canoes made of barks of trees, loaded with goods, and commodities, were lost. These disappointments were such, as would have dissuaded from any further enterprise, all other persons, but such who had formed the generous design of making new discovery in the country.

"M. De La Salle told us that before he lost the barque he had been with the Iroquis Tsonnontouans, and had so dexterously gained their affection that they had talked to him of an embassy with applause, and had given him their consent to the execution of our undertaking. This good intelligence, lasted but a little while, for certain persons who made it their business to cross our design, inspired the Iroquois, with many suspicions about the fort, we were building at Niagara, which was in great forwardness, and these suspicions grew so high, that we were obliged to give over our building for sometime, contenting ourselves, with a habitation, built with palisadoes.

"On the 22d of the said month, we went two leagues above the great fall of Niagara, where we made a dock, for building the ship, we wanted for our voyage.

"This was the most convenient place we could pitch upon, being upon a river, which falls into the streight between lake Erie and the great fall of Niagara.

"The 26th, the keel of the ship, and some other pieces being ready, M. De La Salle sent the master carpenter, to desire me to drive the first pin. But my profession obliging me, to decline that honor, he did it himself, and promised ten louisd'ors to encourage the carpenters, and further the work. The winter not being half so hard in that country as in Canada, we employed one of the two savages of the nation called the Woolf, whom we kept for hunting, in building some cabins made of the rind of trees, and I had one made on purpose to perform Divine service therein on Sundays, and other occasions. M. De La Salle having some urgent business of his own, returned to fort Frontenac, leaving for our commander one Tonti, an Italian by birth, who had been forced to retire into France after the revolution of Naples, in which his father was concerned.

"I conducted M. De La Salle as far as the lake Ontario, at the mouth of the river Niagara, where he ordered a house to be built for the (black) smith we had promised to the Iroquois, but this was only to amuse them, and therefore I cannot but own that the savages are not to be blamed for not having believed every thing they were told by M. La Motte, in his embassy already related.

"He undertook his journey a foot, over the snow, having no other provisions but a little sack of indian corn roasted, which failed him two days before he came to the fort, which is above four score leagues distant from the place where he left us. However, he got in safely, with two men and a dog, who dragged his baggage over the ice, or frozen snow. When I returned to our dock, I understood that most of the Iroquois were gone to wage a war with a nation on the other side of the lake Erie. In the mean time, our men continued with great application to build our ship, for the Iroquois, who were left behind, being but a small number, were not so insolent as before, though they came now and then, to our dock, and expressed some discontent at what we were doing.

"One of them in particular, feigning himself drunk, attempted to kill our smith, but was vigorously repulsed by him, with a red-hot iron bar, which, together with the reprimand he received from me, obliged him to begone. Some few days after, a savage woman gave us notice that the Tsonnontouans had resolved to burn our ship on the dock, and had certainly done it, had we not been always upon our guard.

"These frequent alarms from the natives, together with

the fears we were in, of wanting provisions, having lost the great barque from fort Frontenac, which should have relieved us, and the Tsonnontouans, at the same time, refusing to give us of their corn for money, were a great discouragement to our carpenters, whom on the other hand, a villain amongst us endeavored to seduce.

"That pitiful fellow, had several times attempted to run away from us into New York, and would have been likely to pervert our carpenters, had I not confirmed them in their good resolutions, by the exhortations I used to make every Holy day, after Divine service, in which I represented to them, that the glory of God, was concerned in our undertaking, besides the good, and advantage of our christian colonies, and therefore exhorted them to redouble their dilligence, in order to free ourselves from all those inconveniences, and apprehensions, we then lay under.

"The two savages we had taken into our service, were all this while hunting, and supplied us with wild goats, and other beasts, for our subsistence, which encouraged our workmen to go on with their work, more briskly than before, insomuch, that in a short time, our ship was in readiness to be launched, which we did after having blessed the same, after the use of the Roman Church. We made all the haste we could, to get it afloat, though not altogether finished, to prevent the designs of the natives, who had resolved to burn it.

"The ship was called the Griffin, alluding to the arms of Count Frontenac, which have two griffins for supporters, and besides, M. La Salle used to say of this ship, while yet upon the stocks, that he would make the Griffin fly above the Raven.

"We fired three guns, and sung Te Deum, which was attended with loud acclamations of joy, of which those of the Iroquois who were present, were partakers, for we gave them some brandy to drink, as well as to our men, who immediately quitted their cabins of rinds of trees, and hanged their hammocks under the deck of the ship, there to lie, with more security than ashore. We did the like, insomuch that the very same day, we were all on board, and thereby out of the reach of the insults of the savages.

"The Iroquois being returned from hunting beavers, were mightily surprised to see our ship afloat, and called us 'Otkon,' that is in their language, 'most penetrating wits,' for they could not apprehend how, in so short a time, we had been able to build so great a ship, though it was but sixty tons. It might indeed have been called a moving fortress, for all the savages inhabiting the banks of those lakes and rivers I have mentioned, for five hundred leagues together, were filled with fear, as well as admiration, when they saw it.

"The best designs are often crossed by some unexpected accidents, which God permits to happen, to try men's constancy, as I experienced at that time. One of our crew gave me notice, that the Seur De Tonti, our commander, entertained some jealousie towards me, because I kept a journal of all the considerable things that were transacted, and that he, designed to take the same from me. This advise, obliged me to stand upon my guard, and take all other precautions to secure my observations, and remove the jealousie that gentleman had of me. For I had no other design than to keep our men to their duty, and to exercises of piety, and devotion, for preventing disorders, and for the furtherance of our common undertaking.

"In the meantime, our enemies spread very disadvantageous reports of us in Canada, where we were represented as rash and inconsiderate persons, for venturing upon so dangerous a voyage, from which, in their opinion, none of us would ever return.

"This, together with the difficulties we labored under for transporting the rigging of our ship, and the other inconveniences, necessarily attending a voyage through an unknown country, lakes, and rivers, where no European had travelled before, and the opposition from the Iroquois, wrought in me an unparalleled vexation. But these reports, were more prejudicial to M. La Salle, whose creditors, without inquiring into the truth of the matter, or expecting his return from fort Frontenac, seized all his effects in Canada, though that very fort alone, the property whereof belonged to him, was worth twice more than all he owed.

"However, it being impossible to stop the mouth of our enemies, who had no other design than to oblige us to give over our enterprise, notwithstanding the great charge we had been at for our preparations, we resolved to wait with patience the opportunities Divine Providence would present us with, and to pursue with vigor, and constancy our design.

"Being thus prepared against all discouragements, I went up in a canoe with one of our savages, to the mouth of the lake Erie, notwithstanding the strong current, which I mastered with great difficulty. I sounded the mouth of the lake, and found, contrary to the relations that had been made unto me, that a ship with a brisk gale, might sail up to the lake, and surmount the rapidity of the current; and that therefore, with a strong north or northeast wind, we might bring our ship into lake Erie.

"I took also a view of the banks of the streight, and found, that in case of need, we might put some of our men ashore, to haul the ship, if the wind was not strong enough." * * Before we could go on with our intended discovery, I was obliged to return to fort Frontenac, to bring along with me two monks, of my own order, to help me, in the function of my ministry. I left our ship riding upon two anchors, within a league and a half of the lake Erie—in the streight between the said lake and the great fall of Niagara." The party returned to the ship, the beginning of August, 1679, and we resume our quotations from the journal of Father Hennepin.

"We endeavored several times to sail up the lake, but the wind being not strong enough, we were forced to wait for it. In the meantime M. La Salle caused our men to grub up some land, and sow several sorts of pot herbs and pulse, for the conveniency of those who should settle themselves there, to maintain our correspondence with fort Frontenac. We found there a great quantity of wild cherries, and 'rocambol,' a sort of garlic, which grow naturally on that ground. We left Father Melithon, with some workmen at our habitation above the Falls of Niagara, and most of our men, went ashore to lighten our ship, the better to sail up the lake.

"The wind veering to the north east, and the ship being well provided, we made all the sail we could, and with the help of twelve men who hauled from the shore, overcame the rapidity of the current, and got up into the lake. The stream is so violent that our pilot himself despaired of success.

"When it was done, we sang Te-Deum, and discharged our cannon and other fire-arms, in presence of a great many Iroquois, who came from a warlike expedition against the savages of Tintomha, that is to say the nation of the meadows, who live above four hundred leagues from that place.

"The Iroquois and their prisoners, were much surprised to see us in the lake, and did not think before, that we should be able to overcome the rapidity of the current. They cried several times 'gannoron,' to show their admiration. Some of the Iroquois had taken the measure of our ship, and immediately went for New York to give notice to the English and Dutch of our sailing into the lake. For those nations affording their commodities cheaper than the French, are also more beloved by the natives.

"On the 7th of August 1679 we went on board being in all four and thirty men including two Recollets who came to us, and sailed from the mouth of the lake Erie, steering our course west, southwest, with a favorable wind.

"And though the enemies of our discovery had given out on purpose to deter us from our enterprise, that the lake Erie was full of rocks and sands, which rendered the navigation impracticable, we run above twenty leagues during the night, though we sounded all the while. The next day the wind being more favorable, we made above five and forty leagues, keeping at an equal distance from the banks of the lake, and doubled a cape to the westward, which we called, cape Francis. The next day, we doubled two other capes, and met with no manner of rocks or sands." They made the "mouth of the streight which runs from the lake Huron into the lake Erie," on the morning of the 10th, so that the first trip through lake Erie was made in less than three days.

They continued their voyage through the streight "the current which is very violent, but not half so much as that of Niagara, and therefore we sailed up with a brisk gale, and got into the streight between the lake Huron, and tho lake St Clair ; this last is very shallow, especially at its mouth." * * * "We sailed up that canal, but were forced to drop our anchors near the mouth of the lake, for the extraordinary quantity of waters which came down from the upper lake and that of Illinois, because of a strong north-west wind had so much augmented the rapidity of the current of this streight, that it was as violent as that of Niagara." After some little delay and trouble they entered lake Huron the 23d of August.

"We sung Te Deum a seeond time to return our thanks to the Almighty for our happy navigation."

On the 24th they continued their voyage, but shaping their course N. N. east, they soon found themselves near the land and changed to N. N. west, crossed a bay which they estimated to be thirty leagues in width, and becoming becalmed among some Islands they sought for good anchorage in vain. "The wind turning then westerly, we bore to the north to avoid the coast till the day appeared." * * *

"The 25th we lay becalmed till noon ; but then run north-west with a brisk southerly gale. The wind turning south-west, we bore to the north, to double a cape, but then the wind grew so violent that we were forced to lie by all night.

"The 26th the storm continuing, we brought down our

main yard and topmast, and let the ship drive at the mercy of the wind, knowing no place to run into to shelter ourselves. M. La Salle, notwithstanding he was a courageous man began to fear, and told us we were undone, and therefore everybody fell upon his knees to say his prayers and prepare himself for death, except our pilot, whom we could never oblige to pray, and he did nothing all that while but curse and swear against M. La Salle who as he said had brought him thither to make him perish in a nasty lake, and lose the glory he had acquired by his long and happy navigations on the ocean."

The storm however abated, and they were able to resume their voyage, having sustained little or no damage, and on the 27th they arrived at Missilimakinak, and anchored in a bay, "at six fathoms water, upon a slimy white bottom." This being the ultimate destination of the ship, we shall follow the journal of the Father no further.

The construction and equipment of the "Griffin," the pioneer vessel of lake Erie, and indeed of these inland seas, exhibits a degree of enterprise and perseverance under difficulties, never surpassed, and seldom equaled. When it is considered that all the material for the rigging and equipment of such a craft had to be transported round the falls, up the steep mountain, and a distance of about nine miles, on the backs of men, four of whom were required, it is said, to lift a single anchor, of which they had two, it will be admitted that these men were the fitting representatives of a class of enterprising men who have, following the example set, built up a commerce upon these lakes that has been the admiration, and astonishment of the world.

So far as Mons. La Salle himself, was concerned, this expedition, of which we have given the history somewhat in detail, appears to have been of a twofold character. He had, at great expense the year before, fitted out a large party of traders, with goods to trade with the Indians for furs. This party had been sent to Mackinaw by way of the Ottawa river, and lake Huron, which was thon the usual route from Quebec. He designed the vessel to take on board a return cargo of furs, the principal of which at that period, was beaver, for the purpose of discharging the debts he had incurred, both for goods furnished his traders, and the expense incurred in building his vessel ; after accomplishing this part of his enterprise, he designed to devote himself to the accomplishment of the second object in view, to prosecute his discoveries on the great river Mississippi.

Nothwithstanding the perfidy on the part of some of his traders who had been sent forward, the season before, who had deserted his service, and squandered the goods intrusted to them, he was able to procure a valuable cargo of furs and skins, and on the 18th of September, the vessel sailed with a fair wind on her return voyage. Her crew consisted of the old pilot, and five men ; she was never heard from afterwards.

There were vague reports having their origin with the natives, that she was lost in a gale which occurred very soon after she sailed. Some attempts have been made to prove that she was lost on lake Erie, and not many miles from this city ; but this is rendered improbable from the fact that M. La Sallo decided himself to go to Quebec, in the middle of the winter of 1679–80 ; "because, (says M. De Tonti in his memoir,) he had heard nothing of the boat which he had sent to Niagara."

"He gave me the comman d of this place (Fort Creavecouer on the Illinois river,) and left us the 22d of March, with five men ; on his road he met with two men whom he had sent in the autumn to Michilimackinac, to obtain news of his boat. They assured him that it had not come down, and he therefore determined to continue his journey." It is most probable, therefore, that the Griffin was lost soon after she started on her return voyage, as reported by the Indians, who saw her at anchor to the north of the lake Illinois, (Michigan.) * * * "But the ship was hardly a league from the coast, when it was tossed up by a violent storm in such a manner that our men were never heard of since." Had she passed down through the streights and river, into lake Erie, she would have been seen by some of the numerous tribes who inhabited the shores of those streights and rivers. But diligent inquiry, never brought any further information.

CHAPTER VI.

It will be readily perceived by what has been related, that the history of the Senecas, and indeed, of the Five Nations, now becomes involved with that of the two great European powers, who were contending for the supremacy over the aboriginal tribes who inhabited this continent. History relates, pretty fully, the transactions that occurred about this period, between the English government at New York, and the French government at Quebec, in Canada, which ultimately led to a war between those two nations.

Perhaps no better idea of the true position of affairs between the parties, in which the whole Six Nations became deeply involved, can be given, than by copying two letters, written about this time, being part of a very wordy correspondence between M. De Nonville, the Governor of Canada, and Gov. Dongan, the Governor of New York:

M. DE NONVILLE TO GOV. DONGAN.

August 22, 1687.

SIR: The respect I entertain for the King, your master, and the orders I have from the King to live in harmony with his Britannic Majesty's subjects, induce me sir, to address you this letter, on the present state of affairs, so as to have nothing to reproach myself with. On seeing the letter you were at the trouble to write to me, on my arrival in this government, I persuaded myself by your discourse, that we should live in the greatest harmony, and best understanding in the world, but the event has well proved that your intentions did not at all accord with your fine words.

You recollect, sir, that you positively asked me in that same letter, to refer the difference about our boundaries, to the decision of our masters. Letters more recently received from you, fully convinced me that you received that which I wrote in reply to your first, to show you that I willingly left that decision to our masters.

Nevertheless, sir, whilst you were expressing these civilities to me, you were giving orders, and sending passes to despatch canoes to trade at Missilimaquina, where an Englishman had never set foot, and where we, the French, had been established more than sixty years.

I shall say nothing of the tricks and intrigues resorted to by your people, and by your orders, to induce all the savage tribes domiciled with the French, to revolt against us. I tell you nothing, either, of all your intrigues to engage the Iroquois to declare war against us.

Your traders at Orange (Albany,) have made noise enough about it, and your presents of munitions of war, made with this view last year, and this, are convictions sufficiently conclusive, not to entertain a doubt of it, even were there not proofs at hand of your wicked designs against the subjects of the King, whose bread you have eaten long enough, and by whom you have been sufficiently well entertained, to cause you to have more regard to his Majesty, though you had not all the orders from his Britannic Majesty, that you have to live well with all the subjects of the King, his ancient friend.

What have you not done, sir, to prevent the Senecas surrendering to me the Outowas, and Huron prisoners of Missilimaquina, whom they treacherously captured last year, and how many goings and comings have there not been to the Senecas on your part, and that of your traders, who do nothing but by your orders, to permit the restitution of the said prisoners, by the said Senecas, who were solicited at the village of the Ontonagues, (Onondagas,) to give me satisfaction. I avow to you, sir, that I should never have expected such proceedings on your part, which, without doubt, will not please the King, your master, who will never approve your strenuously opposing, by threats of chastisement, the Iroquois, coming to me when I invited them to visit me, to arrange with them the causes of discontent that I had, on account of their violences.

Three years ago, sir, you made use of them to wage war against the French, and their allies. You took great pains for that purpose to give them more lead, powder and arms than they asked. You did more sir, for you promised them reinforcements of men to sustain them against the King's subjects. Quite recently, sir, you would again have pushed your ill-will, by sending two parties, by misscarrying your orders to Missilimaquina, and expel us from there, and put you into possession, contrary to the word you have given, not to undertake anything before the arrangement of our Majesties, our masters.

You have sir, still surpassed all that; for after the pains you had taken to prevent the Iroquois assembling at Cataroqui, (Kingston,) where I expected to meet them to settle all our difficulties, and receive from them the satisfaction they should have afforded me, as well in regard to the Huron and Outowa prisoners they would have given up to me, had you not opposed it, as well as for the pillagings, and robberies, that they have committed on us, and all the insults they daily offer our missionaries, as well those they may have actually among them, as those they have expelled, after an infinite amount of ill-treatment, during twenty years they lived in their villages. After you sir, having I say, so little regard for the interest of the King's subjects, and the good of religion, whose progress you thus prevent, you have, sir, quite recently contravened the last treaty entered into between our masters: a copy of which you have received, with orders to obey it; a copy of which you also sent me.

Read it well sir, if you please, and you will then remark how strongly their Majesties have it at heart to preserve their subjects in good harmony and understanding, so that their Majesties understand that the enemies of one are the enemies of the other. If the avarice of your merchants, influence you less than the desire to execute the orders of the King, your master, doubtless sir, I should already had proofs of your good disposition, to execute the said treaty, according to which, you ought not to afford either refuge or protection to the savage enemies to the French colony, much less assist them with ammunition to wage war against it. Nevertheless, I assert positively, that you have, since the publication of said treaty of neutrality, contravened it in this particular, since nothing is done in your government, save by your orders. After that, judge sir, what just grounds I have to complain of, and be on my guard against you.

On my return from the campaign I just made against the Senecas, I received the letter that you took the trouble to write me, sir, on the 11th (20th,) June of this year. You send me copy of the treaty of neutrality, entered into between our masters, of which I also transmitted you a copy, as I had received it from the King, and it was published in this country. Nothing more is required therein, sir, than to have it fully and literally fulfilled on your part, as well as mine. To do that, you must discontinue protecting the enemies of the colony, and cease to receive them among you, and to furnish them with munitions as you have done. You must also observe the promise you gave me, at the time of my arrival, that you would leave the decision of the limits to our masters. You must likewise not undertake any expedition against us, in any of our establishments, the greatest portions of which were before Orange (Albany,) was what it is, or any of Manate (New York,) were acquainted with the Iroquois, and the Ouatouas.

When you arrived in your present government, did you not find sir, in the whole five Iroquois villages, all our missionaries sent by the King, almost the entire of whom the heretic merchants have caused to be expelled, even in your time, which is not honorable to your government. It is only three years since the greater number have been forced to leave. The Father Lamberville alone bore up under the insults and ill-treatment they received, through the solicitations of your traders. Is it not true sir, that you panted only to induce them to abandon their mission? You recollect sir, that you took the trouble to send, under a guise of duty, so late as last year, to solicit them by urgent discourse, to retire, under the pretext that I wished to declare war against the village of the Onontagues. (Onondagas.) What certainty had you of it, sir, if it were not your charge and prohibitions you had given them, against giving up the prisoners I demanded of them, and they surrendered to me?

You foresaw the war I would make, because you wished me to make it against them, and because you obliged me to wage that against the Senecas. In this way, sir, it is very easy to foresee what occurs.

I admire, sir, the passage of your last letter of the 11th of June, of this year, in which you state that the King of England, your master, has juster title than the King to the posts we occupy, and the foundation of your reasoning is, that they are situate to the south of you, just on the border of one portion of your dominion. (domination.) In refutation of your sorry reasonings, sir, it is only necessary to tell you, that you are very badly acquainted with the map of the country, and know less of the points of the compass, where those posts are relative to the situation of Manate. (New York.)

It is only necessary to ask you again, what length of time we [have] occupied those posts, and who discovered them, you or we? Again, who is in possession of them? After that, read the fifth article of the treaty of neutrality, and you will see if you are justified in giving orders to establish your trade by force of arms, at Missilimaquina.

As I send you a copy of your letter, with the answer to each article, I need not repeat here what is embraced in that answer. Suffice it to say this in conclusion, that I retain your officer, McGregory, here, and all your orders for your pretended expedition, who were taken within the posts occupied by the King. My first design was to send them back to you, but as I know that you entertain, and give aid and comfort to the Iroquois savages, contrary to the treaty of neutrality, of November 16th, 1686, agreed to by our masters, causing them to be supplied with all munitions necessary to enable them to wage war against us, I have determined, in spite of myself, to retain all your people, until you have complied with the intentions of the King, your master, and executed said treaty, being obliged to regard you as the King's enemy, whilst you entertain his enemies, and contravene the treaties, entered into between the King of England, and the King, my master.

All that I can tell you for certain is, that your conduct will be the rule of mine, and that it will remain with yourself, that the said treaty be thoroughly executed. I must obey my master, and I have much respect and veneration for one of the greatest Kings in the world, the protector of the Church.

You pretend that the Iroquois are under your dominion. To this I in no wise agree, but it is a question on which our masters will determine. But whether they be or not, from the moment they are our enemies, you ought to be opposed to them, and be their enemies, and if you comfort them directly or indirectly, I must regard you as an enemy of the colony, and I shall be justified in subjecting the prisoners I have, belonging to your government, to the same treatment that the enemies of the colony will observe towards us. Hereupon, sir, I will expect news from you, as well as the fitting assurances you will give me, that I may be certain you do not employ the Iroquois to wage war on us, by giving them protection.

Rely on me, sir. Let us attach ourselves closely to the execution of our master's intentions. Let us seek after their example to promote religion and serve it. Let us live in good understanding, according to their desires. I repeat, and protest sir, it remains only with you. But do not imagine that I am a man to suffer others to play tricks.

I send you back Antonio Leispinard, bearer of your passport and letter. I shall await your final resolution, on the restitution of your prisoners, whom I wish much to give up to you, on condition that you execute the treaty of neutrality in all its extent, and that you furnish me with proper guarantees therefor.

Your very Humble and
Very Obedient Servant,
THE M. DE NONVILLE.

GOV. DONGAN TO M. DE NONVILLE.

8th September, 1687.

SIR: Yours of the 21st August last, I have received, and am sorry that Mons. De Nonville has so soon forgotten the orders he had received from his master, to live well with the subjects of the King of England.

But I find the air of Canada has strange effects on all the Governor's boddyes, for I no sooner came into this province, than Mons. De La Barre desired my assistance to warr against the Sinnekes, upon which I went to Albany, and sent for the Five Nations to come to me, and when they came, was very angry with them for offering to do anything to the French, that might disturb them hunting or otherwise. On which they answered me that they had not done anything to the French, but what

Mons. de la Barre orderd them, which was, that if they met with any French, hunting without his pass, to take what they had from them, notwithstanding if any of their people which were abroad, had done any injury they knew not of, they assured me they would give satisfaction.

I send him word of all this, and assured him satisfaction, but notwithstanding, he comes in a hostile manner on this side of the lake, to a place called Kayonhaga, and there, by the means of the Onnondages, made a peace with the Sinnekes, so if they have committed any fault before that, it was all concluded there. But I appeal to any rational man whatever, whether it was fit for any Governor of Canada, to treat or make any peace with his Majesty's subjects, without the advice and knowledge of the Governor of the province they lived under. But I find the design to ruin these Five Nations, (since you cannot, with bribes or other means, gain them to be of your party,) is of a longer date than three or four years. Since Mons. De Nonville follows the same steps his predecessors trod in, th'o he proposed to himself so fair a beginning.

I am sure he will not make so good an end. For no sooner was Mons. De Nonville in possession of his government, but he begun to build a great many boats and canoes, and put a great deal of provisions and stores in the Cataraque (Kingston,) at which our Indians on this side of the lake, were much alarmed, and came to me to know the meaning of it; upon which, I sent to you by way of Mons. Lamberville to know what you intended by all these preparations; your answer was, as Mons. De Nonville may remember, that the winters being long, and you resolving to have a good number of men at Cataraque you accordingly made provision for them ; and if I had not really believed what you writ to be true, I might have been in as much readiness to have gone on the other side of the lake, as Mons. De Nonville was to come on this. Now, sir I will not answer your hasty way of expressions in your own style, but will plainly let you know the matter of fact as it is. If sir, you will please to peruse those letters, I from time to time sent you, you will find that I still coveted nothing more than to preserve the friendship that is between our masters, and ought to be between their subjects here, and as you well remark, is according to their commands, and I pray sir, which is it of us both, that hath taken the way to untie that knot of friendship. Mons. De Nonville invading the King of England's territories, in a hostile manner, (though his reception has not been according to his expectation,) is so plain a matter of fact, that it is undeniable whether you did it designedly to make a misunderstanding or no. I cannot tell. If you did, I hope it will take no effect; but that our masters at home, notwithstanding all your trained soldiers and great officers come from Europe, will suffer us poor planters and farmers, his Majesty's subjects in these parts of America to do ourselves justice on you, for the injuries and spoil you have committed on them, and I assure you, sir, that if my master gives leave, I will be as soon at Quebec, as you shall be at Albany ; as for Major McGregororie and those others you took prisoners, they had no pass from me to go to Missilimaquine, but a pass to go to the Ottawawas, where I thought it might be as free for us to trade as for you ; and as for giving them any commission or instructions to disturb your people, I assure you do me wrong, and if you please to read his instructions, you will find there, I gave express orders to the contrary; and for your pretention to sixty years possession, 'tis impossible; for they and the Indians who wear pipes through their noses, traded with Albany long before the French settled at Montreal; but in case it were as you alledge, which I have not the least reason to believe, you could only have prohibited their trading in that place, and let them go to some other nation. It is very true, I offered to leave the decision to our masters at home, in case of any difference, and pray, sir, let me know in what I have in the least acted to the contrary. You tell me, I hindered the Five Nations on this side the lake, who, have subjected themselves, their countries and conquests, under the King of England, to go to you at Cataraque. It is very true, I did so, and thought it very unjust in you to desire their coming to you. For the King of England did not send me here to suffer you to give laws to his subjects of this government. You also alledge that I have given orders to those Indians to pillage and war upon your people. Sure sir, you forget what you desired of me. If you will please to reflect on one of your own letters, in which you acquainted me that many of your people ran away into this government, and desired that I would take and send back, any that should be found upon this side of the lake, without your pass; upon which, I ordered those of Albany, and also, the Indians to seize and secure all persons whatever, as well French as English, they should find on this side of the lake, without your pass or mine. Truly, sir, I ought to be rebuked for this, it having been the hindrance of many thousands of beavers coming to Albany. Further you blame me for hindering the Sinakees delivering up the

Ottawawa prisoners to you. This I did with good reason. For what pretense could you have to make your applications to them, and not to me. Nevertheless, I ordered Major McGregory to carry them to the Ottawawa, and if your claim be only to Missilimaquina, what cause had you to hinder McGregory to go to the Ottawawa?

What you allege concerning my assisting the Sinakees, with arms and amunition, to war against you, was never given by me until the 6th of August last, when understanding of your unjust proceedings in invading the King my master's territories, in a hostile manner, I then gave them powder, lead and arms, and united the Five Nations together, to defend that part of our King's dominion, from your injurious invasion. And, as for offering them men, in that you do me wrong; our men being busy all at their harvest, and I leave it to your judgment, whether there was any occasion, when only four hundred of them engaged with your whole army. You tell me in case I assist the Indians, you will esteem me an enemy to your colony. Sir, give me leave to let you know you are a far greater enemy to your colony than I am; it having always been my endeavor to keep those Indians from warring with you, who in your protecting their enemies that have killed and robbed them in their hunting and otherwise, and that not once, but several times, have given them great provocations. But you have taken a way to spill a great deal of christian blood, without gaining the point you aim at, and for you, who have taken the King's subjects prisoners in time of peace, and taken their goods from them without any just grounds for so doing, how can I expect but that you will use them as you threaten. You also say, in your letter that the King of England has no right to the Five Nations on this side the lake. I would willingly know if so, whose subjects they are in your opinion ; you tell me your having missionaries among them. It is a very charitable act, but I suppose, and am very well assured that gives no just title to the government of the country. Father Briarie writes to a gent' there, that the King of China never goes anywhere without two jesuits with him ; I wonder why you make not like pretense to that kingdom. You also say you had many missionaries among them, at my coming to this government. In that you have been misinformed, for I never heard of any but the two Lambervilles who were at Onondagoes, and were protected by me from the insolency of the Indians, as they desired of me and as by letters, in which they gave me thanks, appears; but when they understood your intentions, they thought fit to go without taking leave. But their sending them was for some other end than propagating the christian Religion, as was apparent by some letters of theirs directed to Canada, which happened to come to my hands.

Now you have missed of your pretentions, you are willing to refer all things to our masters. I will endeavor to protect his majesty's subjects here, from your unjust insinuations, until I hear from the King, my master, who is the greatest and most glorious Monarch that ever sit on a throne, and would do as much to propagate the christian faith, as any Prince that lives, and is as tender of wronging the subjects of any potentate whatever, as he is of suffering his own to be injured. It is very true that I have eat a great deal of bread of France, and have in requital, complied with my obligations in doing what I ought, and would prefer the service of the French King before any, except my own, and have a great deal of respect for all the people of quality of your nation, which engages me to advise Mons. De Nonville to send home all the christians and Indian prisoners, the King of England's subjects, you unjustly do detain.

This I thought fit to answer to your reflecting and provoking letter."

CHAPTER VII.

The next year July, 1688, an expedition favored by the English Governor of New York, consisting of twelve hundred warriors of the Six Nations, made a sudden descent, upon the French settlements on the Island of Montreal.

They landed on the south side of the Island, at La Chine, on the 26th of July, where they burned, and sacked all the plantations, and made a terrible massacre, of men, women, and children.

There were above a thousand of the French killed at this time, and twenty-six, carried away captives. The greatest part of which, were burnt alive. The Five Nations only lost three men, in this expedition, that got drunk and were left behind. This however did not satiate their thirst for blood, for in the following October they destroyed likewise, all the lower part of the Island, and carried away many prisoners.*

The French became so weakened, and alarmed, at these reverses, that they were compelled to abandon their posts at Niagara, and Fort Cataraqui (Kingston.) The match which had been placed to blow up the magazine in Fort

*See Colden's History of the Five Nations.

Cataraqui, failing to ignite, the Iroquois on taking possession of the fort, found a large quantity of military stores, provisions, &c., among which, were twenty-eight barrels of powder. This success of the Five Nations, over the French, created great consternation, extending to the western nations of Indians, many of whom, had sought the protection of the French, against the Iroquois, who were the dread of all the surrounding nations. Many of them now sought to form alliances of peace, and friendship, with the Five Nations. The French interests in Canada, received a terrible blow, a large proportion of the able bodied men, had for some time, been employed in the expedition against the Five Nations ; and in trading with the Indians of the far west. Agriculture had been almost entirely neglected. They had lost a large number of inhabitants by the continual incursions of small parties of their savage foes, until it became unsafe to live, outside of fortified towns. At last, the whole settled portion of the country, being laid waste, famine began to threaten the entire destruction of the colony. Had the Indians understood the method of attacking forts, at this time, (says Colden,) nothing could have saved the French from entire destruction ; showing that notwithstanding the intrigues of the French, to divide, and weaken, the influence and power of the Five Nations, and their partial success, in accomplishing their object, by leaving the Senecas, to meet almost single handed, the whole military power of the French, hurled against them, under De Nonville, we see them, within a year, again united, invading the territory of their enemy, and with he resistless fury of a tornado, sweeping them to destruction, almost without resistance.

The French government becoming aware of the desperate state of affairs in Canada, recalled the Mons. De Nonville, the next year, (1688,) and the Count De Frontenac, reinstated, as governor. He brought back from France, thirteen Iroquois prisoners, who had been sent over at the request of the King, to be employed in his galleys.

These prisoners, (one of them a sachem) were to be restored, and it was hoped through that means, and the influence and popularity of the Count Frontenac, to appease the hostility of the Iroquois. "He had formerly been Governor of the country, was perfectly acquainted with its interests; of a temper of mind, fitted to such desperate times, of undaunted courage, and indefatigable, though in the sixty-eighth year of his age."* The French were the more desirous of peace, as they knew, that now "they would certainly have the English Colonies likewise upon them."*

"Four Indians of less note who were brought back with the sachem Towerahet, were immediately dispatched in the Sachem's name, to the Five Nations, to inform them of his return, and of the kind usage they had received, from the Count De Frontenac, and to press them to send some to visit their old friend, who had been so kind to them, when he was formerly governor of Canada; who, still retained an affection to the Five Nations, as appeared by the kindness Towerahet and they had received. This was the only method left, to the French, of making proposals of peace, which it was their interest, by all means, to procure."

*Colden.

Immediately on the arrival of this deputation, word was sent to Albany, by the Six Nations, of the fact, and that a council of the Sachems, was appointed to meet at Onondaga, inviting the Mayor of Albany, (Peter Schuyler) and some others, to be present, to advise with them, in an affair of such great importance, as they, (the Indians) were resolved to do nothing without their knowledge, and consent. Notwithstanding this request, it does not appear that any person of note, or influence, with the Indians, was sent. On the 4th of January, 1690, at the solicitation of one of the principal Sachems of the Mohawks, the magistrates of Albany sent the public interpreter, and another person, to assist at the general meeting, with written instructions. When they arrived at Onondaga, they had a private interview, with one of the returned prisoners, "and found that he had no love for the French;"* but complained of the ill-usage, they had received, at the hands of the French. He related all the circumstances of their captivity, of the grandeur exhibited by the French Court, and the power displayed, in the military exhibitions, which they had witnessed.

The council was opened on the 22d of January, 1690, and was conducted with great formality. A sachem of the Onondagas (as was the custom, that being the place of the council of the Six Nations,) was the first to speak. His address, was a mere opening of the council. He was followed, by Adarakta, the chief Sachem of the French deputation, who delivered the message of "Yonondio," the Governor of Canada. Next, the Mohawk messenger, sent from Albany, delivered his message, word for word,

---

*Colden.

as it had been given him, the interpreter, having a written copy, before him, lest anything should be forgotten. After this, Cannehoot, a Seneca Sachem, stood up, and delivered the message of his people.

After some preliminary remarks of a general character he went on to give a particular account of the treaty made the last year, between the Senecas, and several of the western nations, who had voluntarily, come to treat for peace, and friendship ; and that their bretheren in New York, (the English) were to be included in that treaty. After the ceremonies were all over, Sadekanahtie, an Onondaga Sachem stood up, and said :

"Brethren we must stick to our brother Quider, (Peter Schuyler) and look on Yonondio (the Governor of Canada) as our enemy, for he is a cheat."

The interpreter from Albany, was then desired to inform the council, what he had to say, from their brethren at Albany.

He told them, that a new Governor had arrived in New York, with a great many soldiers from England ; that the King of England had declared war, against the French, and that the people of New England, were fitting out ships, against Canada. He advised them, not to harken to the French, for said he, when they talk of peace, war is in their heart; and advised them to enter into no treaty, except it were made at Albany, for said he, "the French will observe no agreement, made anywhere else."

After consultation, the following answer was given the messenger from Albany :

"Brethron, our firc burns at Albany, we will not send Dekanasora to Cadaraqui, (Kingston.) We adhere to our old chain, with Corlear, (Governor of New York.)

We will prosecute the war, with Yonondio, (the Gov. of Canada) and will follow your advice, in drawing off our men from Cadaraqui, (meaning some of their people, who had been induced to settle there, through the influence of the jesuit missionaries.)

"Brethren, we are glad to hear the news you tell us; you tell us no lies."

"Brother Kinshon,* we hear you design to send sol diers, to the eastward, against the Indians there; but we advise you, now so many are united against the French to fall on them immediately; strike at the root, when the trunk falls, the branches fall of course. Corlear and Kinshon, courage! courage! In the spring to Quebec, take that place, and you have your foot on the necks of the French, and all their friends in America."

The council also prepared a message to be returned to the Governor of Canada, animadverting, in the strongest terms, upon the bad faith of the French; the cruel deceptions they had practiced, particularly toward the Senecas; that they were glad to hear, that the thirteen prisoners taken to France, were returned, that it would be time enough, to talk about peace, when their prisoners were restored; that, in the meantime, they should retain all the prisoners in their hands, till that time. As soon as the council broke up, their resolutions were published to all the several Nations, by the return of the Sachems, who attended the council. A deputation was sent Albany, to assure the brethren, that the Six Nations, were resolved, to prosecute the war, against the French, in token whereof, a belt in which, three axes were represented, was presented to Quider.

---

*Meaning the Gov. of New York.

The Count de Frontenac, to arouse the drooping spirits of the French in Canada, and stimulate them to exertion, planned three expeditons against the English Colonies. He engaged in this desperate measure, as he saw no hope of regaining the ascendancy over the Six Nations, by negotiation.

War had been declared between France and England, and no time was to be lost. These three expeditions were directed against New York, Connecticut, and the last against New England. The party sent against New York, was commanded by Mons. De Herville, and was ordered to attempt the surprise of Schenectady, the nearest settlement to the Mohawks ; by this, the Count De Frontenac, hoped to lessen the confidence of the Six Natians in the English, and the assistance they expected from them. The expedition consisted of one hundred and fifty French "bush-lopers" or Indian traders, and of as many Indians, most of them French converts from the Mohawks, commonly called "praying Indians," settled at a place near Montreal called Cahunaga, (Caughnawaga.) They were well acquainted with the country, round Schenectady, and came in sight of the place, the 8th of February, 1690. The terrible massacre of the inhabitants of Schenectady, which ensued, is a matter of history, and its horrid details need not be repeated here. The effect of it, upon the minds of the inhabitants, in, and about Albany, was such, that many resolved to desert the place, and retire to New York. It was at this juncture that a deputation of Mohawk sachems, came to Albany, to condole with their brethren, according to the custom of the Six Nations, when any misfortune befals their friends. It was on the occasion of this visit, that the address, so much praised by Gov. Clinton, was delivered. It is worthy of preservation, and we shall make no apology for inserting it here. It is dated the 25th of November, 1690.

"BRETHREN :—The murder of our brethren at Schenectady, by the French, grieves us as much, as if it had been done to ourselves ; for we are in the same chain, and no doubt our brethren of New England, will be likewise sadly affected, with this cruel action of the French.

The French on this occasion, have not acted like brave men, but like thieves, and robbers. Be not therefore discouraged ; we give this belt, to wipe away your tears.

Brethren, we lament the death of so many of our brethren, whose blood has been shed at Schenectady. We don't think that what the French have done, can be called a victory. It is only a further proof of their cruel deceit.

The Gov. of Canada sends to Onondaga, and talks to us of peace with our whole house, but war was in his heart as you now see, by woful experience.

He did the same formerly, at Cadaraqui and in the Senacas country. This is the third time he has acted so deceitfully. He has broken open our house at both ends, formerly, in the Senecas country, and now, here. We hope however, to be revenged of them. One hundred of our bravest young men, are in pursuit of them, they are brisk fellows, and they will follow the French, to their own doors. We will beset them, so closely, that not a man in Canada, shall dare to step out of doors to cut a stick of wood. But now we gather up our dead, to bury them, by this second belt.

Brethren, we came from our castles with tears in our

eyes, to bemoan the blood shed at Schenectady, by the perfidious French. While we bury our dead, murdered at Schenectady, we know not, what may have befallen our own people, that are in pursuit of the enemy. They may be dead. What has befallen you, may happen to us, and therefore we come to bury our brethren at Schenectady, with this belt.

Great, and sudden, is the mischief, as if it had fallen from Heaven, upon us. Our forefathers taught us to go, with all speed, to bemoan, and lament, with our brethren when any disaster, or misfortunes happen to any in our chain. Take this belt of vigilance, that you may be more watchful, for the future.

We give our brethren, eye-water, to make them sharp sighted; giving a fourth belt.

We are come now, to the house where we usually renew the chain, but alas! we find the house polluted with blood.

All the Five Nations, have heard of this, and we are come to wipe away the blood, and clean the house.

We come, to invite Corlear, and every one of you, and Quider, (calling to every one of the principal men present, by their names,) to be revenged on the enemy, by this belt.

Brethren, be not discouraged; we are strong enough; this is the beginning of your war, and the whole house have their eyes fixed on you, at this time, to observe your behavior.

They wait your motion, and are ready to join you, in any resolute measures.

Our chain is a strong chain; it is a silver chain. It can neither rust, or be broken.

We, as to our part, are resolute to continue the war. We will never desist, so long as a man of us remains; take heart, do not pack up, and go away; this will give heart to a dastardly enemy. We are of the race of the bear, and a bear, you know, never yields, while one drop of blood is left; we must all be bears; giving a sixth belt.

Brethren, be patient. This disaster is a great affliction, which has fallen from Heaven upon us; the sun which hath been cloudy, and sent this disaster, will shine again, with its pleasant beams; take courage, said he, courage, (repeating the word several times) as they gave a seventh belt.

There was a special address also to the English residents of Albany, at the same time; full of sympathy and encouragement, but notwithstanding this wise counsel and profers of assistance and support, many of the English residents, were so alarmed, and disheartened, that they packed up, and returned to New York.

The Five Nations fulfilled all, and even more, than they promised. The one hundred young warriors, they sent out to pursue the French in their retreat, back to Canada, fell upon their rear, and killed, and captured, twenty-five of them, without loss to themselves; they organized bands, to invade the territory, and harass the French settlements, in Canada, and literally accomplished what they threatened, making it dangerous for them, to go abroad, to procure food or fuel. Under these circumstances, the Count De Frontenac, acted with his accustomed energy, and skill. He sent a small party, under Capt. Louriqui, to relieve the garrison at Mashilimackinak, and prevent a treaty of peace, which was on the point of being concluded, between the Five Nations and the Indians in that quarter. Before they had got far on their journey, about one hundred and twenty miles above Montreal on the St. Lawrence river, they were attacked by a party of the Five Nations, with such vigor, that they were compelled to land, and give battle, in which several were killed on both sides, according to the French account. The French took two of the Indians prisoners, one was taken on to Mackinac, to confirm what the French claimed as a victory ; the other was carried to Montreal by a return party of French, which accompanied the expedition up the river, as an escort or guard.

"To revenge this loss, the Five Nations sent a party against Montreal, attacked a party of regular troops, killed the commanding officer, and twelve of his men." These frequent incursions kept the whole country upon the river in constant alarm.

The Five Nations, were disappointed in their expectation of aid from the English. The revolution in England which dethroned King James, and placed William and Mary on the throne, caused a change of Governors in New York. Gov. Dongan himself, a catholic, although he had conducted the government with energy, and discretion, was recalled, and Col. Slaughter appointed in his place.

The Five Nations felt the effect of these changes, and the delays consequent thereon, and although on their part the war had been prosecuted with perseverance and energy, and even with a good degree of success, yet the disappointment they experienced, in the promised aid, and co-operation of the English, destroyed their confidence in them, particularly on the part of the Mohawks who lived nearest the English. It was not very surprising that under these circumstances they should be ready to listen to proposals of peace, which the Count De Frontenac lost no opportunity to proffer, through the small settlement of their countrymen, the praying Indians, who still remained true to the interests of the French.

It was at this time, (1691,) and under these circumstances, that the Mohawks, sent one of their sachems to their brethren, the praying Indians, who introduced him to the Count De Frontenac, who made him welcome, treated him in the kindest manner, and gave him assurances of his desire for peace, and gave him a belt, with proposals of peace to his nation.

Col. Slaughter then Gov. of New York, being informed of the condition of affairs, appointed a meeting with the Five Nations. Only four, of the Five Nations, were represented in this council. The Mohawks did not attend, to join in the answer. The Oneidas, Onondagas, Cayugas, and Senecas, all answered the Governor, that they were resolved to prosecute the war against the French; they did not approve of entertaining any overtures for peace.

On the fourth day, the Mohawks spoke to the Governor in presence of all the other nations. They admitted having received overtures of peace, through their brethren, the praying Indians; they desired advice, as to what answer they should return to the Governor of Canada. The Four Nations replied to this request, as follows:

"Mohawks, our Brethren, in answer to your proposals from the Governor of Canada, we must put you in mind of his deceit and treachery.

"We need only give one recent instance, how he lately sent to the Senecas to treat of peace, and at the same time fell upon Schenectady, and cut that place off.

"We tell you, that the belt sent by the French Governor, is poison, we spew it out of our mouths, we absolutely reject it, and are resolved to prosecute the war, as long as we live." Then they left the belt lying on the ground.

The Five Nations continued their incursions all winter (1690-1,) in Canada. Forty of the Mohawks, attacked Fort Vercheres, and carried off twenty of the inhabitants.

The Count De Frontenac being informed that a large party of Senecas were hunting beaver, on the peninsular between lake Ontario and lake Erie, sent three hundred men, under the command of Mons. Bellacour, to surprise and capture them ; some of the "praying Indians" were of the party. After encountering incredible hardships, traveling on snow shoes, carrying their provisions on their backs, they surprised the hunting party numbering about eighty persons of both sexes, who, says the narator, "did not run before they had lost most of their men, dead on the spot. Three women were made prisoners, with whom the French immediately returned back to Montreal."

So vigilant, and active, were the Five Nations, that all communication between Montreal and Mackinac was entirely cut off, and several attempts were made in the spring and summer of 1692, to open it, but were in every instance frustrated by the vigilance of the Five Nations.

A considerable party of the Five Nations under the command of a famous war-chief named Black Kettle continued a long time on the St. Lawrence river, in hopes of meeting with other French parties, on their passage towards Mackinac, but finding no further attempts that way, made an irruption into the country round Montreal, over-running the whole country, burning and ravaging wherever they went; some accounts say, Black Kettle had six hundred men with him, others place the number at only two hundred.

M. De Vaudrieul at the head of four hundred men, finally surprised this party, and after a desperate encounter, they broke through the French, and made their escape with the loss of twenty killed. The French lost four officers, and many men. They took five men, nine women, and five children prisoners. The Five Nations in a few days after, attacked a party of French soldiers returning from guarding some vessels from Montreal to Quebec, killing the Captain, and dispersing the whole party. During all the summer of 1692 the French were obliged to act entirely on the defensive, keeping within their fortifications.

These continued incursions of the Five Nations which the French seemed to have no power to prevent, or punish, exasperated the Count De Frontenac to such a degree, that he was left to perpetrate a piece of savage barbarity, which will forever stamp his administration with disgrace; it was no less than condemning two prisoners of the Five Nations, to be publicly burnt alive. Although the influence of the missionaries, was interposed to prevent the execution of this terrible sentence, and even the entreaties of his wife, nothing would divert him from his purpose. He insisted that it was necessary to make an example. That his clemency hitherto had encouraged them in their boldness. Not that these men had been guilty of any particular act of atrocity, but, the Five

Nations, he said had burnt so many French, justified this mode of retaliation, one of the two prisoners dispatched himself in prison, before the execution ; the other was taken to the place of execution by the " christian Indians of the Lorrette," to which he walked with the utmost firmness and indifference. While they were torturing him, he continued singing, that he was a warrior, brave, and without fear ; that the most cruel death, should not shake his courage, that the most cruel torment, should not draw from him, one complaint ; that his comrade, was a coward, a scandal to the Five Nations, who had killed himself for fear of pain ; that it was a comfort to him, to remember, that he had made many French to suffer, as he did now. He fully verified his words, for the greatest torment they could inflict, could not force the least complaint from him, although his executioners exerted their utmost skill, to do it. They first broiled his feet between hot stones ; then they put his fingers into red hot pipes, and though he had his arms at liberty he would not pull his fingers out. They cut his joints, and taking hold of the sinews, twisted them round small bars of hot iron. All this while, he kept singing, and recounting his own brave actions, against the French. At last, they flayed his scalp from his skull, and poured scalding hot sand, upon his head ; at which point, says the witness, the Intendant's Lady, obtained leave of the Governor, to have an end put to the scene, by having him dispatched at once, " to the relief of all who saw, as well as all who read this dreadful act of barbarity."

The death of Gov. Slaughter, very soon after his arrival in the country, was very prejudicial, to the interests of New York. Capt. Ingoldsby, being the military com-

7

mander of one of the companies of foot soldiers, took upon himself the government of the province, without authority. He had little experience in statesmanship, and was obnoxious, to a considerable portion of the people, and was powerless for good. He met the Five Nations at Albany the 6th of June, 1692, which resulted in little else, than a renewal of promises on the part of the English, to prosecute the war with vigor, calling upon the Five Nations to do the same.

Notwithstanding the severe measures pursued by the Count de Frontenac against the Five Nations, he still hoped to negotiate a peace with them. This he hoped to be able to do, through the influence of his agents, the Jesuit missionaries, who resided among them, and the praying Indians, who were Mohawks, and still adhered in their allegiance, to the French. But these efforts proving ineffectual, the Governor of Canada found it necessary to adopt other means, in order to pacify the French people, who were growing despondent. In this emergency, the Count de Frontenac resorted to his old method, of projecting some bold enterprise, that should encourage his own people, and at the same time, show the Five Nations that they had to contend with an enemy, still able to act on the offensive.

An expedition, in the middle of the winter of 1692–3, was determined upon, against the Mohawks. It consisted of about six or seven hundred men, a part regular soldiers, militia of the country, and Indians, commanded by three captains of the regular troops, and thirty subalterns. They were well supplied with everything necessary for the expedition, even to snow shoes, and sleds drawn by dogs, upon the snow. They left Laprarie on the 15th of January, 1693, and after encountering what might be considered obstacles almost insurmountable, reached the first Mohawk castle, in the valley of the Mohawk river, above Schenectady, on the 8th February at night. The Five Nations, not having the least suspicion, of an enemy, were reposing in perfect security, only five men and some women and children, were found there. The next castle not far from it, was in like manner surprised, and taken, without opposition. These castles, being in the vicinity of the English settlement, at Schenectady, most of the Indians were there.

The French went to the next fort, which was the largest, and coming to that in the night, heard some noise, and suspected they were discovered. They approached cautiously, and found the noise, occasioned by a war dance, and entered before they were discovered, but met a bloody reception, having lost thirty men, before the Indians submitted. They took three hundred prisoners, of whom one hundred were fighting men.

When the news reached Albany, Peter Schuyler, a major of militia, offered to head a force, to go to the relief of the Mohawks, about two hundred men were collected, he left Schenectady on the 12th, in pursuit of the enemy. On the 15th, he was joined by about two hundred and ninety Indians, men, and boys. He came up with the enemy on the 17th, but after some ineffectual skirmishing, gave over the pursuit on the 20th, having lost eight killed, and fourteen wounded; and recovered, between forty, and fifty prisoners. Several gentlemen of Albany, went out under Maj. Schuyler, as volunteers, particularly Mr. Van Renselear a gen't of large estate there.

The Count de Frontenac anticipating that this disaster to the Mohawks, would so cripple the Five Nations, that they would have no farther trouble in opening a passage to Mackinac, to enable the French to bring down a great quantity of furs, they had accumulated there. He sent a lieutenant with eighteen Canadians, and twenty praying Indians, to open the passage; but this party, fell in with a party of the Five Nations, who entirely routed them, so that few escaped. At length two hundred canoes, loaded with furs, arrived at Montreal from Missilimakinak, to the great joy of the French.

Early in 1693 the Five Nations, were informed, through the friends of the French, that the Governor of Canada had received from France, large reinforcements of troops, and ample supplies of military stores, provisions, &c. This, taken in connection with their recent severe losses, and the little assistance they had received from the English, influenced the Oneidas to listen to the solicitations of the Jesuit missionary Milet, to send a message to the Governor of Canada for peace. Col. Fletcher, who was now Governor of New York, being informed of this movement called a council of the Five Nations at Albany, in July of that year; after informing them of what he had heard, he told them plainly, that they had been influenced in their action, by the Jesuit Milet, who they had suffered to live too long among them, and advised them, to expel him from among them. He made them a present of ninety guns, eight hundred pounds of powder, eight hundred bars of lead, one thousand flints, eighty-seven hatchets, four gross of knives, besides a quantity of clothing, and provisions. This present he told them, was from their King and Queen, to renew the covenant for all the English colonies. The Five Nations answered in a long, but rather evasive address, thanking the King and Queen for the "large present," and for the ammunition in particular. The reply of the Five Nations on this occasion would do credit to the diplomacy of more civilized nations. It was exceedingly adroit and plausible. Col. Fletcher not being satisfied with their answer, in regard to the removal of the Jesuit Milet, he urged his removal in stronger terms, but the force of his reasons was resisted mildly, with promises of compliance at a future time, under certain contingencies. This did not prevent the preparation, of an answer, to be sent to the Governor of Canada, but through the influence of the Mohawks, who lived nearest the English, the answer was agreed first to be submitted to the English, and their advice obtained thereon; for which purpose, a deputation of several sachems was sent to Albany on the 2d February, 1694. Decanesora, for many years the principal speaker of the Five Nations, now quite an old man, was at the head of this deputation. In person he was tall, and of fine features, he had great fluency of speech, and a graceful elocution, his style of oratory, it is said, "would have been pleasing in any nation." His address was made to (Quider,) Major Schuyler, and the magistrates of Albany, as the representatives of the Governor, who they called Cayenguirago; after which, a copy of the answer proposed to be sent to the Governor of Canada, was submitted. Major Schuyler in his reply, told them, that no consent could be given, to a treaty with the French; and proposed to them, to meet the Governor of New York, at Albany in "seventy days." They agreed to meet the Governor at that time, "but, as for myself, (said Decanesora,) I cannot promise; I am now the representative of the general council, and cannot dispose of myself, except by their directions. If they order me, I shall willingly return." Major Schuyler again asked, whether they promised to stop all correspondence with the French, either by the Jesuit, or otherwise, for seventy days, and, until they should have the Governor's answer. To which Decanesora answered: "I have no authority to answer this question. I shall lay the belt (which had been given them,) down in every one of the castles, and tell them, that by it, all correspondence with the French is desired to be stopped; but I cannot promise that this will be complied with."

Early in the spring of 1694, Decanesora, with other deputies, went to Canada, and in May another delegation met Gov. Fletcher at Albany; but not being able to give the Five Nations any assurance of a vigorous assistance, he called the principal sachems to a private conference, and asked them whether they had made peace with the Governor of Canada. They answered that it only wanted his approbation; and added that they were unable, any longer, to carry on the war, without assistance. "We submit the whole matter to your prudence." He then gave his consent, provided they kept inviolate, their chain, with the English; but told them, that he could make no peace with the French.

Upon submitting the proposals of the Governor of Canada to a full council of the Five Nations at Onondaga, there was a division of opinion among themselves, a large majority objected to the re-building, of the fort at Cadarackui. (Kingston.) The party most in favor of peace, proposed to send a deputation, to procure a modification of the terms of the treaty, which was granted, and to make themselves more acceptable to the French, took thirteen prisoners with them, to deliver up. Among these was the Jesuit Milet, who had been with the Oneidas since 1689, and Mons. Jonscaire, who had been long a prisoner among the Senecas. He had been adopted by a family of the Senecas. He obtained such a reputation among them, that the nation advanced him to the rank of a sachem. He preserved their esteem to the day of his death; and was very useful to the French, in all their negotiations with the Five Nations, after the general peace.

The embassy however, resulted in nothing, as the French Governor insisted upon re-building fort Cadarakui, and including his allies, (the western Indians,) in the peace. He therefore, dismissed them, with presents, promising them further benefits, if they chose to comply with his proposals, but threatened them with destruction, in case they refused.

The Five Nations refusing to comply with the terms proposed by the Governor of Canada, he resolved to force them to a compliance. He sent a party of three hundred men to examine the old French fort at Cadarakui, and to the neck of land between lake Ontario and lake Erie, the usual hunting ground of the Five Nations. This party, met with three or four men whom they attacked, but could not compel to surrender; they defended themselves with such obstinacy, that they were all killed, on the spot. They surprised a cabin, where they took some men and women prisoners, four of the men were publicly burned alive, at Montreal. The fort at Cadarackui was found in better condition than was expected; and in the summer of 1695, the Count de Frontenac, sent a party consisting of both French and Indians, to repair the fortifications, and to protect those engaged at work. The Five Nations immediately gave notice to the English at Albany, that the French again occupied fort Cadarackui, and demanded the assistance promised by Gov. Fletcher, to dislodge them. He met them at Albany in September, complained of their allowing the French to possess themselves of the fort. He advised them to invest the place, and cut off their supplies, as it would be impossible to transport cannon from Albany, which would be indispensible to attack the fort. He gave them one thousand pounds of powder, two thousand pounds of lead, fifty-seven guns, one hundred hatchets, three hundred and forty knives, and two thousand flints, besides clothing, &c.

The Count de Frontenac having secured, and repaired, fort Cadarackui, (it was afterwards called by his name, fort Frontenac,) he resolved to make the Five Nations, feel the weight of his displeasure, at their refusal of the terms of peace offered them. For this purpose he determined to use all the military force, that could be made available in Canada. His forces were assembled at Montreal in June, 1696, but did not leave until July. They reached Cadarackui in twelve days, they crossed the lake to Onondaga river, (Oswego,) passed up the river in canoes, with scouts on each side the river, until they reached the little lake. (Onondaga.) As soon as they had landed they erected a stockade, or breast work, for their protection. A Seneca, who had been some time a prisoner, was sent out as a spy. He gave intelligence to the Onondagas, who he found waiting to receive the French, determined to defend their castle to the last, for which purpose they had sent away their women and children. But upon learning the number of the enemy, that they were armed with cannon, they decided to burn their town, and retire. The French marched in battle array in two columns, the artillery in the rear. The Count de Frontenac, an old man, seventy-three years of age, was carried in a chair, directly in rear of the artillery. In this formidable manner, the aged General marched up to the ashes of the deserted village, and his army, expended the fury of their assault, upon the thick ranks of their standing corn, which was all that was left for them to capture, or to conquer. One old sachem, whose age marked a hundred winters, disdaining to fly, defied the torments of the savage allies of the French, and withstood them with surprising resolution, preserving to the last, his coolness, and courage, taunting his tormentors, with his last breath.

The difficulty of supporting so large an army, in such a country, compelled the Count de Frontenac, to make a speedy return. The Onondagas hung upon their rear in their retreat, cutting off every canoe that became detached from the main body. This compelled them to hasten their march, so that they returned to Montreal the 10th of August, 1696. The French suffered more in this expedition than the Five Nations. The absence of so large a portion of the male population, so long a time, caused agriculture to be neglected, and a famine ensued. This was the last considerable expedition of the French, against the Five Nations. In the ensuing winter an attempt was made upon the English settlements near Albany, but the party was met and entirely routed by some Mohawks and Scahkook Indians.

The war was kept up, in a predatory manner, until the peace of Reswick in 1697. Soon after the news of peace was received in New York, an express was dispatched to Canada, to inform the Governor of Canada that hostilities might cease.

The Five Nations having early news of the peace, took advantage of it, to renew the beaver hunting, in the neighborhood of fort Cadarackui. The Governor of Canada being informed of it, dispatched a considerable body of Adirondacks to attack and surprise them, which they did, killing several, among whom was a distinguished war chief, who after being mortally wounded, most piteously lamented his fate. That after all his great exploits in war, he should ignobly lose his life, at the hands of the despised Adirondacks, who were looked upon by the Five Nations as children. A dispute arose about this time, between the Government of New York and that of Canada, respecting certain French prisoners in the hands of the Five Nations. The Earl of Bellomont, who had been appointed Governor of New York, insisted that the French should receive them from him, at Albany; whereas, the Governor of Canada, refused to recognise the sovreignty of the English government, over the Five Nations, and threatened to continue the war against them, unless they brought their prisoners to Montreal, to deliver them up there, and that all the allies of the French, should be included in the peace. Upon being informed that these terms would not be submitted to, by the Five Nations, the Count de Frontenac threatened to renew the war, and began preparations for attacking the Five Nations, with the whole force of Canada. The firmness of the Earl of Bellomont however, averted the threatened storm, and the matter was referred to their respective governments at home, to be determined by commissioners appointed under the treaty of Reswick. The Count de Frontenac dying before these disputes were settled, by his successor Mons. de Callieres stipulating to make the exchange of prisoners at Onondaga. These commissioners on the part of the French, were three, one of whom was M. Jonciare, who had so long resided among the Senecas, and by whom he had been adopted, and made a sachem. They entered the castle at Onondaga, with great pomp and ceremony, displaying the French flag, under which they marched in procession. They were met with equal ceremony, by the representatives of the Five Nations, without the gate, headed by their great orator, Decanesora, with an address, accompanied with the usual compliments, and assurances of welcome, enforcing his words by the presentation of a belt of wampum, at the close of each part of his speech. When they entered the fort or castle, they were saluted with a salvo of all the fire arms, conducted to the largest cabin, and there entertained with a feast.

The next day the general council of the Five Nations was addressed in reply by the French deputation, accompanied with the usual compliment of giving a belt, at the close of every sentence, or head of the speech.

The French commissioners had full liberty to take home their prisoners, in the hands of the Five Nations, but few of them could be persuaded to return, preferring to remain where they had experienced more real liberty, than among their own people. Several of the sachems of the Five Nations returned with the French commissioners to Montreal, and were received, and treated, with every demonstration of respect, and consideration. The English, had nearly as much difficulty to persuade their prisoners in the hands of the French Indians to leave the Indian manner of life, and in many cases no arguments, no entreaties, or even the tears of near relatives, could induce them to leave their new friends, and their mode of life, to return to the society of their friends and relatives, and the habits of civilization. And in cases where they have been persuaded to return, they soon grew weary of the restraint, and embraced the first opportunity to return to savage life, to spend their days. The children of the natives, taken in childhood, and educated with all the care and assiduity bestowed upon the children of most favored parents in civilized life, invariably choose, when left to their own choice, to return to the Indian mode of life.

CHAPTER VIII.

We have now brought the history of the Senecas (or rather the Five Nations of which they were admitted to be the most numerous and powerful) down to the close of the seventeenth century, a little less than one hundred years after the first settlement of Europeans in their vicinity. Had they left no other record than what is now before us, they would be entitled to a name, and a place in the great history of nations. That a people laboring under all the disadvantages which they did, should have been able to accomplish so much, is truly surprising, and shows that they must have possessed natural endowments that under more favorable circumstances would have made them eminent in all that we admire and respect, in the character of men ; and shows that all that has been said in eulogy of them by Governor Clinton and others, is true, and no more than what they are justly entitled to.

We have dwelt too long, perhaps, upon the detail of events in their early history ; but this seemed necessary, in order to illustrate the character awarded them, and to counteract in some measure, impressions of a different kind, which their subsequent history, decline, and final downfall, have created in the minds of those not conversant with the facts which we have been at some pains to group together, in the order of their occurrence.

The efforts of the French to alienate the Five Nations from the English, and attach them to the government of Canada, did not cease with the termination of the war. For we find that early in 1700, the Earl of Bellomont, who was then Governor of New York, sent a commission (of which Peter Livingston was the head,) to visit Onondaga to meet the Five Nations, then in council, in regard to some communication they had received from the French government in Canada, and to ascertain the feelings of the Five Nations towards the English. In their report to the Earl Bellomont, the commissioners represent that the French are more active than ever, to acquire influence and control over the Indians. That their intrigues are carried on through the influence of the "praying Indians" settled in Canada, and through the jesuit missionaries, who had gained considerable influence over the Oneidas and Mohawks, in particular. They say, that the English ought to furnish the Five Nations with ministers or missionaries, not only to instruct them in the christian faith, but to "put a stop to the diabolical practice of poisoning, by which means those attached to the English, are despatched out of the way."

Early in 1701 the Earl of Bellomont died. This circumstance operated unfavorably upon the negotiations going on to get the Five Nations into a more settled and secure state, and gave the French a great advantage in affording them an opportunity to press their plans and purposes, the more successfully. And in June, 1701, the French sent an embassy to the Five Nations, at Onondaga, which was received with every demonstration of respect, but care had been taken by the government of New York, then under Lieut. Gov. John Nasan, to be represented at this interview, and to influence the Five Nations to peremptorily decline the offer of a missionary to reside among them, and the Five Nations soon after met the Lieutenant Governor of New York, in council at Albany.

Lord Cornbury was appointed to fill the place of the Earl Bellomont, as Governor of New York. It was in this year that the Five Nations by a formal deed, conveyed to the government of New York, their "beaver hunting grounds," bounded by the lakes on the north and west, and the high lands upon the south, to hold for the use and benefit of the Five Nations, which was afterwards confirmed on the part of the Senecas, by their sachems, in a separate instrument. The question of jurisdiction or sovereignty between the French and English, remained for many years unsettled, and was still a subject of controversy in 1720, when the French began to erect more permanent structures at Niagara. The English also began to assert their right of sovreignty in 1721, by sending out from Albany, a party under command of Peter Schuyler, Jr., to establish themselves at the mouth of the Irondequoit, on lake Ontario, and at some point on the Niagara river, above the Falls, or upon lake Erie, in the "Sennekes country."

This was done for the purpose of diverting the trade with the western Indians from Montreal to Albany, and appears to have met with a degree of success, according to a report made by Gov. Burnett, then Governor of New York, to the Board of Trade in London, in that year. The question as to the right of the French to possess the post of Niagara, became one of more serious consequence, and led to a protracted and sharp correspondence, first between the Governor of New York and the Governor of Canada, and afterwards between the two governments at home. In 1726, Gov. Burnett held a council with the now Six Nations, (by the incorporation into the confederacy of the Tuscaroras,) at which the subject of the occupancy of Niagara was fully discussed. The French had claimed that they had obtained consent to the occupancy from the Six Nations. But it appeared that the Senecas, who claimed the land upon the shore of the river, as well as the lake, had never given their consent. The consent claimed by the French, appeared to have been only that of the Onondaga sachems, obtained in rather a surreptitious manner, through the agency of the French missionary resident among them, and had never been confirmed or assented to, by the Senecas, or any of the other Four Nations, but had been objected to by the Senecas especially. Indeed, the Five Nations, from the beginning of the controversy about jurisdiction, claimed not only the territory on the south side of the lakes Erie and Ontario, but upon the north side also. They not only claimed by possession, but by right of conquest, and it is certain that at a very early period of the controversy, they had settlements or villages upon the north side of lake Ontario. In their correspondence with the English government at Albany, they make it a subject of complaint repeatedly, that the French had been permitted to build a fort at Cadarakui (Kingston,) upon their lands, and when, by their energy and perseverance the French had been obliged to abandon that fort, and all the country around it, the Five Nations took possession of, and held it until after the return of the Count de Frontenac, the successor of Mons. De Nonville as Governor of Canada. The Five Nations had also extended their conquests after the extirpation of the Eries, almost indefinitely west, and north-west, as far as the Island of Michilimackinak, and the French had great difficulty in holding that post against their incursions.

Their conquests had been extended to the south also, and at the period of which we now speak, they had settlements on the upper branches of the Susquehanna river, within the present bounds of Pennsylvania. Although the government of the Five Nations was general over the whole confederacy, yet each had a recognized, exclusive title to the territory they occupied. The limits of territory occupied by the Senecas, was less distinctly defined, than that of either of the other nations, and was generally denominated the "Sinnekes country." It included all the present state of New York west of the Cayuga's lands, extending indefinitely west, to the Mississippi river, and in the several conveyances executed by them to the Dutch, and afterwards to the English government at New York and Albany, they denominate the country extending to the lake of the Illinois, (lake Michigan,) as their "hunting grounds."

The wars in which the Five Nations had so long been engaged, particularly that with the French, which they had been obliged to prosecute at a great disadvantage, for many years, necessarily weakened their power, and greatly reduced their numbers. In 1677, a careful enumeration showed that the Senecas alone could bring one thousand fighting men into the field; in 1736, the whole Six Nations could furnish but little more than that number. It is not likely the principal town or village of the Senecas had been removed since the abandonment and destruction of Canagora, at the time of De Nonville's expedition (at Boughton Hill,) into their country, in 1687. They never returned to that locality to reside, (that being their uniform custom,) but removed further interior, probably to Kanesedaga, at the foot of Kanesedaga lake, where they remained until Sullivan's expedition into the Seneca's country in 1779.

This lake had previously borne the name of the Kanesadaga lake, and when the Tsonnontouons (Senecas,) made their principal residence there, they called their town Kanesadaga, and the lake received the name of Seneca, from the fact of the Sennekas (as they were called by the English,) residing there. The same may be said in regard to the origin of the names of the other lakes, Cayuga, Oneida, Onondaga, &c., and the Mohawk river.

The names by which the several nations were called by the French, were entirely different from those of the English, having little similarity either in sound or signification, and there is a very great diversity in the mode of spelling all these names, both in the English and French authors, and documents. Sometimes this discrepancy is so great, that an ordinary reader would not recognize their identity.

As has been observed, the question of jurisdiction over the Indian territory, was soon transferred from the Six Nations to the French and English. The French determined to occupy Niagara, where La Salle, fifty years before, had taken possession in the name of the French government. In order to have some color of authority for this proceeding, they dispatched M. de Jonciare on an embassy to the Senecas, to procure their consent to erect a permanent trading house, in fact to build a stone fort. It will be remembered that M. de Jonciare had been given up to the French, after a long residence with the Senecas, as already related. Charlevoix, who visited Niagara in 1721, relates as follows: "M. de Jonciare received his orders for the execution of the project of a settlement at Niagara. He went to the Tsonnonthouans, (Senecas,) and assembled the chiefs, and after having assured them that he had no greater pleasure in the world, than to live among his brethren; he added also, that he would visit them much oftener, if he had a cabin among them, where he might retire when he wanted his liberty. They replied that they had never ceased to look upon him as one of their children. That he might live in any place, and that he might choose the place that he judged the most convenient. He required no more, he came directly here, fixed upon a spot beside of the river, that terminates the canton of the Tsonnonthouans, and built a cabin upon it. The news was soon carried to New York, and caused there so much the more jealousy, as the English had never been able to obtain, in any one of the Iroquois cantons, what was now granted to Seur Jonciare."

He adds that "although they used every means to dislodge M. Jonciare from Niagara, they never could accomplish it. 'It is (said they,) of no consequence that M. de Jonciare dwells there, he is a child of the nation, he enjoys his right, and we have no right to deprive him of it.'"

It would be interesting to know more of the personal history of this man, than can be gathered from the mere allusions which are made to him, in the public documents relating to the transactions in which he was engaged.

Chabert Jonciare (or Jean Coeur, as it was sometimes written by the English) literally John Hart, appears to have been a young French soldier, captured by the Senecas, in some of their forays against the French in Canada some time prior to 1700. As was their custom when young persons of either sex fell into their hands, he was adopted by the Senecas, and relishing their mode of life, he took a Seneca wife, and raised a family of children. After many years residence, having acquired their language, and being elevated to the dignity of sachem, he seems to have acquired great influence, particularly with the Senecas, which he exerted in favor of the French. He appears to have had two sons at the time he was liberated, and probably took his family with him to Montreal.

He was immediately employed by the government, and given a subordinate military commission in 1700, and continued in active service during the remainder of his life, sometimes in one capacity, and sometimes in another, but generally to advance the French interest and influence among the Six Nations, through his brethren, the Senecas. He was bold, active, and unscrupulous. In 1721 he was charged by the English with the murder of Mons. Montour, a French gentleman who like himself, had taken a native wife, of whom we shall have occasion to speak. He was however, vindicated in the act, by M. Vadrieul then Governor of Canada, who said :

"It was by my orders he killed the Frenchman, named Montour, who would have been hanged, had it been possible to take him alive and bring him to this colony."

In 1730 Jonciare appeared in the " Sinakees country, with several French soldiers with him. He told the Senecas that having disobliged his governor, he had been ducked and whipped, and banished; and had come to them for protection; as when he was a prisoner with them, they had saved his life, and adopted him as a brother; he wanted to build a house at a place called Tiderondequat (Irondequot) at the side of the Kaderach-qui (Ontario) lake, about ten leagues from the Senecas castle, and about midway between Oswego and Yagere (Niagara.)

The following message of the Governor of Canada to the Senecas, in 1741, shows the position held by Chabert Jonciare, at this period, and that the Senecas were in good correspondence with the French:

"CHILDREN:—Your son Jonciare has sent me your message by the blacksmith, and reported your situation to me. Children, I sympathize with you on account of the famine you have suffered, which prevented your coming down this year. The spring has been so unfavorable that it has been impossible to send to Niagara, provisions enough for your supply.

I will adopt such precautions in future as shall obviate the recurrence of this misfortune; you know what the commandant told you from me on that occasion, and that he divided a piece of bread with you.

Your son Jonciare wrote me that you would always be my true friends, and would not discontinue to co-operate in good affairs. I on my part, shall not cease to be your true and good father.

Children, In regard to Cask-on-chagon (Genessee river) you ought to reccollect that you asked me to allow your son Jonciare to settle there, that he may live more comfortably, and that I refused your request on account of the English, who would feel at liberty to ask permissio to form another establishment."

It is to Jonciare belongs the credit of early noticing the Oil Springs which are now attracting so much attention. In 1721 he informed Charlevoix who was then on his journey to the west, of which he has left a journal "of the existence at a place called Ganos, at the portage between the Genesee and the Belle (Ohio) river, a fountain the water of which, is like Oil, and a little further on there is another exactly like it.

"The Indians use it to allay all kinds of pain." He had been sent there to locate the Shawnees on the Ohio river, and was a very active agent of the French government, up to the time of his death at Niagara, in 1740. The Senecas applied to the French for his son to come and reside with them, on the death of the father, which was readily granted. The son was called a " French Indian" by the English. He spoke the language fluently, as well as the French ; and soon became as active and useful to the French, as ever his father had been. In 1741 he asked to be released from his agency in the Senecas country, on account of ill health, and his younger brother, Clauzonne Jonciare, was appointed in his place. He Chabert appears however, to have still remained in the employ of the French government, for his name is signed with that of his brother, to the capitulation of Fort Niagara to Sir William Johnson, in 1759. The brother which succeeded him among the Senecas, must have been quite young at the time of the liberation of the father, as we find in 1742 he was sent by the Marquis Beauharnois, who was then Gov. of Canada, "to the Senecas, to learn their language."

In the French account of the surrender of Fort Niagara, is the following notice of Chabert Jonciare, Jr :

" The other Indian was an Iroquois that Mr. Chabert

Jonciare had sent with a letter, announcing that he would come next day. He had removed to the river Chenondac (Chippewa) all the property he could, twenty horses which belonged to him, and some oxen he had brought down on his own account from Detroit. He burned the fort of the carrying place (Schlosser,) as it was not tenable. His brother, Jonciare (Clauzonne) had arrived on the previous evening, having been brought down by the Iroquois, the bearer of the letter. M. Pouchot made him (the messenger) a present."

In a Note it is said: "M. Chabert Jonciare held a contract for transporting stores across the portage, and possessed much greater influence over the Indians of western New York, that Sir William Johnson."

The following notice of the brothers Jonciare, is taken from the Maryland Gazette of August 30, 1759, and is dated at Albany.

"There are ten other officers, one of which is the famous Monsieur Jonciare, a very noted man among the Seneca Indians; and whose father was the first that hoisted French colors in that country. His brother, also a prisoner, is now here, and has been very humane to many Englishmen; having purchased several of them from the Senecas.

CHAPTER IX.

The frequent change of Governors of the colony of New York, and the high party spirit which characterized this period of its history, left little time for those in power, to pay proper attention to their Indian relations. They were for the most part, left in the hands of the traders, and others who desired to possess their lands.

But the French were by no means idle. The Mohawks, by reason of their proximity to the English settlements, had been kept in partial correspondence with them, but the other nations had been left almost entirely under French influence. The French had kept possession of all the important trading posts upon the lakes, and had extended a line of posts, from Quebec to New Orleans. Every important carrying place, between the lakes, and the Ohio river, was in their possession; and for nearly forty years very little was done by the English, to assert jurisdiction over the territory claimed under the treaty of Utrecht.

The Senecas, who were remote from the settlements of the English, were more accessible to the French. The principal town or castle, (Kanedasaga) being only ten leagues from Tierondequatt (Irondequot,) a convenient landing-place upon the south shore of the lake Frontenac and only thirty leagues from Niagara, where was a French trading post, and fort, and had it not been for the indissoluble union of the Five Nations, which nothing could sever, the Senecas would have been entirely alienated from the English, and through the influence of M. de Jonciare, and other French emissaries, have been entirely drawn away, to the French interest.

The question of jurisdiction, between the French, and the English, having been transferred to their respective home governments, it ceased in a great measure, to occupy public attention in the colonies; and a good degree of apathy seemed to prevail, on the part of the English. Not so however on the part of the French. Their emissaries were more active among the Six Nations, than ever. Speaking of this period, Mr. Campbell in his "annals of Tryon county," says:

"From the commencement of this century, down to 1750, the French Missionaries and agents were very successful. That body of men, the French jesuits, who by their zeal, put to shame many men engaged in a better cause, entered upon this field of labor, with great ardor. At one time they doffed the clerical habit, and putting on the Indian garb, accompanied the warriors on distant and hazardous expeditions, and at other times, astonished their savage audience, with the splendid, and imposing rites, and ceremonies, of the Romish church. They spoke in glowing terms, of the recourses, and magnificence, of 'le grand Monarque,' as they termed the King of France. They obtained permission for the French to build forts in their territory, and in short, when the last French war broke out in 1754, the four western tribes went over to the French and took up the hatchet against the English."

There is no doubt that the Senecas and some of the other Five Nations were in regular and intimate correspondence with the French at this period; for in July, 1742, we have in the "Paris documents" a full account of a conference, held by the Marquis Beauharnois, then Governor of Canada, with a deputation of Senecas, and Onondagas, who visited him. The destruction of the fortifications built by the English at Chouaghen (Oswego,) began to be threatened, about this period, by the French; and upon the news of a declaration of war, in 1744, there was a general stampede of English and Dutch traders, from that post, where a pretty lucrative trade had grown up, with the western Indians, who had been induced to come, with their canoes laden with furs, to that place, instead of stopping at Niagara, where the French had a trading house, as the Indians gave a preference to English goods, over the French. As long as the trade at Oswego, was successful, the English at Albany and New York were satisfied; but this sudden interruption, was considered a great public calamity, and the Governor of New York in a communication to the Assembly in August, 1744, says:

"The Province has suffered considerable damage, this summer, by the precipitate retreat of our Indian traders, from Oswego. Upon notice of the French war, most of them left the place, immediately upon the alarm, sold what they could, of their goods, to those few of their brethren, that had sense, courage, and resolution, to stay behind, and brought the remainder back with them. You will judge, what a baulk, and discouragement, this instance of pusillanimity, has occasioned, to those number of Indians of the far nations, who have rarely come to trade with us, but perhaps, finding the French had no goods to supply them at Niagara, resolved to proceed to Oswego, whence some of them found the place was basely deserted, by most of the people, and no goods to exchange for their furs ; upon information whereof, many other Indian canoes were turned back, before they reached the place. How mean an opinion, must these savages entertain of us, when they find our people so easily frightened as it were, with a shadow, and that the great gains which are constantly reaped by this advantageous trafic, are not sufficient, to excite a resolution in our traders to stand to the defense of this fortress, the loss of which, would determine that trade, and it is to be feared the Indians too, in favor of our natural enemies, the French. How fatal such an event would prove to this colony in particular, and the British interest upon the continent in general, may be easily forseen."

The war between France and England, embarassed the French operations among the Indians by cutting off the regular supply of goods for the trading posts. The following extract from a communication of M. de Beauharnois, Governor of Canada to Count de Maurepas, shows the condition of the French interests at this time (1745,) among the Five Nations :

M. DE BEAUHARNOIS TO COUNT DE MAUREPAS.

"I have already acquainted you, my lord, with the disposition of the Five Nations as respects Choueguen (Oswego.) The advantages we have gained in the interior of the colony might possibly have created alarm, had we been in a condition to follow them up by being supplied with goods and effects necessary to fit out new parties, and to meet the wants of the trade of the posts. The circumstances in which we are placed by the want of these supplies, must make us desire more than ever, that the Five Nations should observe the neutrality they promised. Nevertheless, I shall neglect no means possible, to induce them to co-operate in what his majesty appears to require of me in this regard. Sieur de Jonciare is already notified to give that matter all his attention ; his activity and vigilance may be relied on, if there be any prospect of success. M. de Longueil might have suited for that negotiation, but that officer is very corpulent, and illy adapted to make these sort of journeys. Those nations who adopted his oldest son, in the council I held with them last summer, appear always much attached to the family. I expect to send him to assist Seur de Jonciare, should circumstances become more favorable."

The English government was no less embarassed, by the want of harmony, between the different Governors, and the colonial Assembly, which characterized its proceedings, for many years at this period of its history. The refusal to grant appropriations of money, by the Assembly, was the principal.

We have now arrived at a point in our history, which makes it proper to take some notice of one who was prominent in all the public affairs of this period, but particularly so, in relation to the affairs of the Six Nations.

Hitherto there seemed to be, no one representing the interests of the English government, that could exert an influence over the Indians equal to the French.

Wm. Johnson afterwards Sir Wm. Johnson, was born in Ireland, about the year 1714. He came to this country in 1734 as the agent of his uncle, Sir Peter Warren, to superintend a large estate, purchased by him, on, and near, the Mohawk river. To fulfill the duties of his appointment, Mr. Johnson located himself upon the estate of his uncle, what was afterwards called "Mount Johnson" (now Johnstown,) about midway between Schenectady and the carrying place (now Rome) the then termi nus of boat navigation on the Mohawk river. Here, he of course became extensively acquainted with the Indians. He studied their character, and acquired their language. He first became known to them as a trader; he established a trading house at Johnstown, where he kept a large depot, of Indian goods, which he imported from England. He dispatched traders in all directions to the Indian settlements, to buy furs, and to induce the Indians to come to Mount Johnson to trade. In this he was very successful. Being a young man of good education and superior talents, by a course of sagacious, wise measures, he gradually became very popular, both with the Indians, and whites. His house soon became the resort of all classes, particularly of the Six Nations, and he ultimately obtained a greater influence over them, it is said, than was ever attained by any white man.

"His constitution (says Mr. Campbell) was unusually firm, his mind hardy, coarse, and vigorous, unsusceptible of those delicate feelings, by which minds of a softer mould are in a great measure governed, destitute of those refined attachments, which are derived from a correspondence with elegant society, and unconfined by those moral restraints which bridle men of tender consciences, he here saw the path open to wealth, and distinction, he determined to make the most of his opportunity. He occupied the house he built at Johnstown; he also built a house upon the bank of the river, but that was occupied by his son, John. A daughter of his, married Col. Guy Johnson, a nephew, and another Col. Claus. Joseph Brant, the celebrated Mohawk chief, of whom we shall have occasion to speak hereafter, was sent to the "Moors Charity School," at Lebanon, Connecticut, established by the Rev. Doct. Wheelock, with several other Indian boys, where they received an English education at Col. Johnson's expense.

Brant, was a particular favorite, and was employed by Col. Johnson in the public business, after he returned from school, particularly in that relating to the Indians. After the death of Lady Johnson, who was of Dutch or German descent, a sister of Brant was received into the family of Col. Johnson, and was treated with the respect, and occupied the position of a wife, without the legal preliminaries necessary to constitute that relation.*

The encroachments of the French, both upon the trade and territory, of the English, had now become such, as to attract the attention of all the colonies; and one object of the "plan of union," was to unite the force of all the colonies, to resist it. Col. Johnson had received the appointment of Colonel of the warriors of the Six Nations, in 1745. The following extract of a reply of the Indians to a speech made to them by the Governor of New York, shows the estimate in which Col. Johnson was held:

"BROTHER:—As to your desiring us to listen to our good friend, Col. Johnson, we are very much obliged to you for it, and in answer thereto must tell you, that for

*It is said he was married to Molly Brant, a short time before his death, according to the rites of the Protestant Episcopal Church, in order to legitimatize his children by her.

these twelve months past, and better, we have minded nor listened to nobody else, neither do we intend it; and Brother, you may depend upon it, that whatever news we have among us, shall be immediately brought to him; and in return, we expect you to do the same that you have done this year past, and then the world shall be convinced that we are one body, and inseparable."

The capture of the posts occupied by the French, upon territory claimed by the English, was among the first things proposed by Gen. Braddock. And the assistance of the Six Nations, and their allies, being considered of the highest importance, Col. Johnson was recommended as "a proper person to command, in chief, the said service." He received accordingly, a commission as Major General, and immediately entered upon the organization of a force, to attack Crown Point; and to engage the warriors of the Six Nations, in the enterprise, and as a necessary preliminary to provide for their security, by promising them forts, or castles, in their several towns, or territory. Col. Johnson set upon the performance of the responsible duties devolving upon him in his new appointment with great vigor, in which he was seconded by the Governors of all the different colonies, and also by Gen. Braddock, who was then in Virginia. He was reappointed sole superintendent of the Six Nations, an office he had resigned sometime previous.

In August, 1755, with a force of about two thousand eight hundred men of all arms, he commenced his march for Crown Point, and arrived at the "great carrying place" on the 14th. There was already some dissatisfaction exhibited by some of the provincial troops, requiring great care, and discretion, on the part of the General in command, who of course was a stranger to most of them. A general council of war was held at this place, attended by all the principal officers, at which Gen. Johnson submitted some questions as to the disposition of the forces, particularly in regard to the reserves, which had been promised, and provided, by several of the colonies, in addition to the force then present. The decision was, that these reserves, should be sent to join the army, with all possible dispatch. A little acquaintance with their chief, seemed to inspire the men with new confidence, and the army having received some reinforcements of warriors from the Six Nations, proceeded on to lake St. Sacrament, which he named "lake George, in honor of his Majesty, the King." His effective force, was now increased to over three thousand men. He proceeded to erect a fortification at this place, "where no house was ever built, or a rod of land cleared." Before this work was completed, some Indian scouts brought intelligence of the advance of a large party of French, upon the camp they had left at the great carrying place. About two hundred and fifty New Hampshire troops, had been left at this place, and five companies of a New York regiment. On receiving this intelligence, Gen. Johnson sent off an express, with orders to Col. Blanchard in command, to withdraw all the troops within the fortifications there, and defend themselves as best they could, until relieved by reinforcements, which he would send. One thousand men, under command of Col. Williams, of one of the Boston regiments, with about two hundred Indians, were detached for the relief of Col. Blanchard. Before this detachment had reached the point of its destination, it was met by an overwhelming force, and after a brave resistance, in which they suffered heavy loss, and were near being surrounded, they were compelled to retreat. Another party of about three hundred, were detached from the fort, to cover their retreat, the whole falling back, under cover of a breast work of trees, which had been erected around the fort. The French advanced in regular order, along the road, opened by the English, directly upon the centre of the works, and halted, at the distance of about one hundred and fifty yards; their regulars in the centre, their Indians and Canadian militia, on each flank. The French commenced the attack, by their regulars, firing by platoons, without doing much execution, being at too great a distance. During all this time not a gun had been fired by the English, within the fortification, but their artillery, with which they were well supplied, had been placed in the most advantageous position for defense, under the direction of Capt. Eyre, and opened with tremendous effect. Although the French regulars stood their ground manfully, but the battle becoming general, the fire from the artillery of the English, served with grape and cannister, and of the infantry, protected by the breastwork of trees, became too hot for them, and they were thrown into disorder, but soon rallied, and moved to the right, of the fortification, where the assault was maintained for more than an hour, with great resolution. This attack failing, and the fire from the English artillery being kept up, with deadly effect, the fire of the French grew weaker, which being perceived by the English, the Indians leaped over the breastwork, and rushed upon the flying columns of the French, killing and capturing great numbers, turning what was already a defeat, into a perfect rout.

Among the wounded and prisoners, was the Baron Dieskeau, the aged French General, commanding the expedition, lately arrived from France. He was brought into the tent of Gen. Johnson, and treated with all the consideration and care, that his high position, and unfortunate condition required; being shot through the legs, and both his hips. In his own brief report of the battle, he says: "I know not at present my fate. From Mr. de Johnson, the General of the English army, I am receiving all the attention possible to be expected from a brave man, full of honor, and feeling." His wounds were considered mortal, but he recovered, but never regained his lost reputation.

Gen. Johnson received a severe wound from a musket ball, lodged in his thigh, which was never extracted. For his valuable services rendered the English cause, and his good conduct on this occasion, he was created a Baronet, by the King, and the House of Commons voted him a gratuity of five thousand pounds sterling, besides his salary as general superintendent of Indian affairs. Baron Dieskeau attributed his defeat to the refusal of his Canada Iroquois to fight their brethren, in his report to his government.

The Indians suffered severely on this occasion, particularly the two hundred that accompanied Col. Williams in the morning to relieve the camp at the "great carrying place;" several of their principal sachems were killed; among them the celebrated Mohawk chief, Hendrick. Mounted on one of Col. Johnson's horses, he led the assault by the Indians, himself firing the first shot. His horse was killed under him. Hendrick becoming entangled, being unwieldy, and somewhat disabled by age, could not extricate himself, to escape, and was killed by a bayonet.

They were indulged in their own mode of warfare, so far as to permit them to take the scalps of the slain enemy. In his official report of this battle, Gen. Johnson says "old Hendrick, the great Mohawk sachem, we fear is killed." We have the following notice of this celebrated chief, in a note to the appendix of the annals of Tryon county :

"Old King Hendrick, (or as he was sometimes called, the great Hendrick,) lived in the town of Minden, in Herkimer county, and near the upper Mohawk castle. The site of his house, says Dr. Dwight, is a handsome elevation, commanding a considerable prospect of the neighboring country. It will be sufficient to observe here, that for capacity, bravery, vigor of mind, and immovable integrity, united, he excelled all the aboriginal inhabitants of the United States, of whom any knowledge has come down to the present time. A gentleman of very respectable character, who was present at a council held with the Six Nations by the Governor of New York, and several agents of distinction from New England, informed me, that his figure, and countenance, were singularly impressive, and commanding. That his eloquence, was of the same superior character, and that he appeared as if born to control other men, and possessed an air of majesty unrivaled within his knowledge."

"In all the wars with the French, he led forth his Mohawk warriors, and fought side by side with Sir William Johnson. Through all the intrigues of the French, he remained faithful to his alliance.

"He was also highly esteemed by the white inhabitants.

During some of the negotiations with the Indians of Pennsylvania, and the inhabitants of that state, Hendrick was present at Philadelphia. His likeness was taken, and a wax figure afterward made, which was a very good imitation. After the death of Hendrick, an old friend, a white man, visited Philadelphia, and among other things, was shown this wax figure. It occupied a niche, and was not observed by him, until he had approached within a few feet. The friendship of former days, came fresh over his memory, and forgetting for the moment, Hendrick's death, he rushed forward and clasped in his arms the frail icy image of the old chieftain."

The following anecdote is related as a well authenticated fact:

" Hendrick was at the house of Sir William Johnson, when he received two or three suits of rich military clothes. The old King a short time afterwards came to Sir William and said, 'I dream. Well, what did you dream ? I dream you give me one suit of clothes. Well, I suppose you must have it,' and accordingly he gave him one. Some time after, Sir William met Hendrick, and said 'I dreamed last night. Did you ? What you dream ? I dreamed you gave me a tract of land,' describing it. After a pause, 'I suppose you must have it, but and he raised his finger significantly, you must not dream again.' "

This tract of land, extended from the east to the west of Canada Creek, in the now county of Herkimer, and was about twelve miles square. The title was afterward confirmed by the King of England, and it was justly called the "royal grant."*

---

*See Annals of Tryon County.

Although the capture of Crown Point was not the immediate result of the expedition under Gen. Johnson, yet the defeat of Baron Dieskeau, ultimately produced its evacuation by the French, and although the result of the campaign was not entirely satisfactory to the Colonists, yet the goverment at home looked upon it, not only as in the highest degree creditable to the good judgment, skill, and bravery, of Gen. Johnson and his army, but as greatly beneficial to the interest of the King. The following complimentary letter was addressed to him, by his majesty's order :

Nov. 11th, 1755.

"Sir :—Your printed circular, containing an account of the success of his majesty's arms, in the action near lake George, on the 8th of September, and of the gallant behavior of the troops under your command, has been laid before the King ; and I have his majesty's command to take this early opportnnity, of expressing to you the sense his majesty has, of the great and eminent service, you have performed, in the defense of his just rights, and in your country's cause. The prudent spirit, and resolution, which do so great honor to your conduct, on this important occasion, meets his majesty's highest approbation, and the King is pleased to order, that you do signify to the officers, and private men, who have so eminently distinguished themselves, that their resolute, and undaunted behavior, has given his majesty the greatest satisfaction. The prudent judgment and precaution, which you showed in sending to the New England governments, before the action, for reinforcements, must likewise have its share of praise, which is so justly due, to your whole conduct. The alacrity, and dispatch, with which the reinforcements were raised, is greatly to be commended, and there is reason to hope, that this will enable you to pursue the advantages you have already gained.

The colonies which have so readily and vigorously exerted themselves on this great occasion, will always find favor and protection, from his majesty.

And, I have particular satisfaction, of having it in charge, to acquaint you, that the King has been graciously pleased to confer upon you, as a distinguishing mark of his royal favor, and approbation of your conduct, the dignity of a Baron of Great Britain, and the Patent will be transmitted to you, by the first convenient opportunity." Sir, etc.,

T. ROBINSON.

It is not likely that few, if any of the warriors of the Six Nations, except the Mohawks, were present, or participated in the engagement at lake George. The Mohawks the day after the battle, took formal leave of the General, and returned home ; alleging, as a reason, that they had sustained a great loss in the death of a large number of their principal sachems, and as was their custom, they wished to return home, to condole with their people for the loss.

They also expressed fears, that during their absence, their own homes were exposed to be attacked, and destroyed, by the enemy, and none to defend their wives and children, but their old feeble men.

Early in 1756, the French organized an expedition against Oswego, with a view to reduce the fort built there by the English. The expedition was under the command of the Marquis de Montcalm, and consisted of about three thousand men. He invested the place on the 11th of August, and after a brief seige, captured the fort on the 14th, taking most of the garrison prisoners of war, among whom (says the French account) were one hundred and twenty women. The English fleet of six vessels was also captured, with but little fighting, either on land, or water. The French found a large quantity of military stores and provisions, which were destroyed, and did not restrain their savage allies, from many cruel acts of barbarity. Col. Mercer, who commanded the English forces, was killed early in the engagement, the command devolved on Lieut. Col. Littlehales, who got little credit, for either courage, or military skill.

It does not appear that any of the Six Nations engaged in the defense of Oswego. The French did not expect their assistance, but expected them to remain neutral, which expectation seems to have been realized. This apathy on the part of the Six Nations, may be attributed at least in part, to the iufluence of M. de Jonciare, who visited the Senecas, and in succession, all the other Five Nations, prior to the attack of the French upon Oswego. He was accompanied by Mons. Longueville.

Mons. Durant who met them at the mouth of the Choueguan (Oswego) river, on their return, asked Jonciare what he had accomplished in their journey. He replied: "I have beat the bush; Mons. Longueville will take the birds; our voyage will do him honor at the court of France."

CHAPTER X.

When all the circumstances are taken into consideration, it is not surprising that the Six Nations, particularly the Senecas, were at a great loss how to act. The want of harmonious action in the English colonial government, which had characterized its proceedings for many years, to the almost entire neglect of their relations with the Six Nations; the land grants in Pennsylvania and Maryland, by which they claimed they had been defrauded of their hunting grounds by the English, and the unrestrained rapacity of the English traders, by which the price of goods sold to the Indians, had been greatly increased; while that of beaver had been greatly diminished, while their morals had been greatly corrupted, by the unrestrained introduction of rum among them; while on the other hand, the French had made the most of their opportunity, by sending their emissaries among them, particularly the Senecas, furnishing them with goods at all their trading posts, extending from Quebec to Mackinaw in the northwest, through the lakes to the Ohio and Mississippi rivers. Through the influence of these missionaries, and agents, who in many cases became closely allied to the Indians, adopting their mode of life, frequent embassies or visits of large delegations of their leading men, were made to the Governor of Canada at Montreal, receiving marked attention, and loaded with valuable presents, affording opportunities through interpreters, for a free interchange of views and feelings, and in every way cementing a stronger alliance every year. There was another respect, in which the policy of the French, served to give them an advantage over the English. In all their negotiations with them, they never proposed to buy their lands.

This circumstance was used with great power, and success, by the agents of the French; and was indeed, in striking contrast, with the policy and practice of the English. And although the Indians had the same irrepressible thirst for the brandy of the French, that they had for the rum of the English, it should be recorded to the credit of the French missionaries, that they uniformly, and often successfully, resisted the introduction and use, of spiritous liquors among the Indians. Sir William Johnson, in his communications with the English government, often refers to these two evils, as the greatest obstacles in the way of obtaining influence, or control, over the Indians, and urges that the Ohio and Pennsylvania land grants and patents, be abrogated, and the sale of spiritous liquors restrained by law. Col. Johnson, in one of his communications to the government, says: "The Indians ought to be redressed, or satisfied, in all their reasonable and well founded complaints, of enormous, and unrighteously obtained patents for lands. * * * Missionaries of approved character, abilities and zeal, with due encouragement, would be of unspeakable advantage, to promote our interests amongst them ; and subvert the French, whose industry in this article, has been of infinite service to them."

The loss of Oswego, and other disasters which immediately followed, darkened the prospects of the English cause, and discouraged all efforts at conciliating the Indians to the English interest. The tardiness of the English, in performing what they had promised, created distrust in the minds of the Indians, of their ability to resist, much less to expel, the French, from the territory claimed by the English. Sir William Johnson was however, indefatigable in his efforts, and held frequent consultations with the Six Nations. The feelings of the Senecas at this time, may be better understood by the following extract of a speech, delivered at one of these councils in 1756, by Skanonyade, or the half king of the Senecas. "We were told (said he,) last year, that large canoes were to be built to keep provisions from being carried to supply the French at Niagara. We see the vessels have been built a long time, and yet we see provisions, &c., daily come to Niagara, without any more interruption, than when you had no canoes." At another council the same year, Kagswoughtaneyonde, a great sachem and warrior, of the Senecas, alias Belt, stood up and addressed himself to the whole body of Indians, in the following speech:

"BRETHREN HERE PRESENT: I have seriously considered all that our brother Warraghiyagey (Sir William Johnson,) said to us two days ago, and for my part, I am clear in it, that what he proposes is right, whereupon I am determined to comply with it, and shall as soon as I get home, let all my nation know what our brother said, and my opinion and resolution, in which if they should differ with me, I am determined to leave the country, and live with my brothers, the English."

In November, 1757, a descent was made by a party of French and Indians, upon the settlement at German Flatts, on the Mohawk river, entirely destroying the settlement, taking about one hundred and fifty men, women and children prisoners, destroying a large amount of stock, and other valuable property, besides carrying away a considerable amount of plunder. In regard to this affair, much complaint was made of the conduct of some of the Oneida nation, living in the vicinity. That although they were apprised of the approach of the French, they gave no information to the inhabitants, in time to enable them to escape, and that some of the Oneidas, aided the French, in their murderous enterprise. This however, was denied by Canaghquieson, the chief Oneida sachem, who said:

"BROTHER: (addressing Mr. Croghan,) I can't help telling you, that we are very much surprised, to hear that our brethren the English, suspect and charge us, with not giving them timely notice of the designs of the French; as it is well known that we have not neglected to give them every piece of intelligence that came to our knowledge. Brother, about fifteen days before the affair happened, we sent the Germans word, that some Swegatchie (Oswegachie,) Indians told us, the French were determined to destroy the German Flatts, and desired them to be on their guard. About six days after that, we had a further account from Swegatchie, that the French were preparing to march. I came down to the German Flatts, and in a meeting with the Germans, told them what we had heard, and desired them to collect themselves in a body at their fort, and secure their women, children and effects, and make the best defense they could; and told them at the same time, to write to brother Warraghiyagey, (Sir William Johnson,) but they paid not the least regard to what I told them, and laughed at me, slapping their hands on their buttocks, saying, they did not value the enemy. Upon which, I returned home, and sent one of our people to the lake, (meaning the Oneida lake,) to find out whether the enemy were coming or not. After he had staid there two days, the enemy arrived at the carrying place, and sent word to the castle at the lake, that they were there, and told them what they were going to do; but charged them not to let us at the upper castle know anything of their design. As soon as the man sent there, heard this, he came on to us with the account that night, and as soon as we received it, we sent a belt of wampum to confirm the truth thereof, to the Flatts, which came here the day before the enemy made their attack. But the people would not give credit to the account, even then. This is the truth, and those Germans here present know it to be so. The aforesaid Germans, did acknowledge it to be so, and that they heard such intelligence."

It was during this year, 1756, that Sir William Johnson, by direction of the English colonial government, had erected forts, or castles, in all the principal towns of the Six Nations. The following are extracts from the Johnson manuscripts, records some interesting particulars:

"Kendaruntie, the great Seneca warrior, with eight more men of his nation, came down to guard the men hither, whom Sir William Johnson had sent up to build their fort." It is also stated under the same date, that six Seneca warriors, who came down with one Abeel, an

Albany trader, to help him down with a parcel of skins, which he fraudulently got, in the Senecas country, told Col. Johnson that they were ill treated by Capt. Willliams, at the carrying place, &c. At 8 o'clock Sir William had a meeting with the Senecas, who came down with John Abeel's skins." This is the first mention made, of the father of the celebrated chief "Abeel" alias "O'Bail," alias "Cornplanter," who subsequently figured so largely in the affairs of the Six Nations, particularly of the Senecas. Under date of June, 1757, we have a list of the following delegates of the Senecas, to visit Sir William Johnson:

SENECAS OLD CASTLE—Tageghsady, Tawistawis, Sachems.

CENOSIO CASTLE—Karonghyanaghqui, Hayadondy, a head warrior, and forty others.

Tudyuscung, a Seneca chief.

A series of continual disasters resulting from folly, and mismanagement, rather than from want of means and military strength, alarmed the British nation, and the King found it necessary to change his counsels. The celebrated William Pitt was placed at the head of the new ministry, and a large appropriation of men, and means, was made, for three separate expeditions against the French, in America, who had possession of a line of posts extending from Quebec to New Orleans. One of these expeditions was against Niagara, which had remained quietly in possession of the French. Early in 1759, Sir William Johnson, in an official communication to his government says: "The Six Nations in general, and the Chenocio (Genessee,) Indians in particular, (who are a brave, and powerful tribe of the Seneca nation, and live near Niagara,) are, as your Lordships will see, by the proceedings I now send you, very desirous of driving the French from Niagara; and equally pressing that we should undertake it. * * * * If an attempt upon Niagara, through lake Ontario, should be made a part of the plan of operations for this year, I am persuaded I could join His Majesty's troops that way, with the main body of the warriors of the Five Nations, together with others of their allies and dependents."

The expedition against Niagara was organized under the command of Gen. Prideaux, consisting of little over two thousand men, and left Oswego for Niagara, on the 1st of September, 1759. It was joined by Sir William Johnson with about six hundred warriors of the Five Nations, and this number was increased to one thousand, when the expedition arrived at Niagara, in the vicinity of the fort. Gen. Prideaux immediately commenced a a seige. Early in the progress of it, he was killed by the premature discharge of one of his own guns (acohorn.) The command devolved on Sir William Johnson. The seige was conducted upon strictly scientific principles, by regular approaches.* During these operations the Indian scouts brought information, of the approach of a body of French and Indians, from the west, to reinforce, or relieve the beseiged fortress. A force was immediately detached to intercept their advance. A considerable portion ot this force, consisted of Indians, the friends, or allies of the Five Nations. A parley between the Indians was held. The western Indians declared they did not come to fight their brothers, the Five Nations, but the English. The result was, they separated themselves, and joined their brethren. The French were attacked, defeated, and all killed, wounded, taken prisoners, or put to flight. Upon learning the fate of his reinforcements, the French Commandant surrendered the fort and all his forces prisoners of war.

On this occasion a tragical event occurred. Cadet Moncourt of the Colonials, had formed an attachment with an Indian, to whom he became bound in friendship. This Indian, who belonged to the English army, seeing his friend a prisoner, expressed a great deal of sorrow at his situation, and said to him: "Brother, I am in despair at seeing you dead, but take heart, I'll prevent their torturing you," and killed him with a blow of his tomahawk; thinking thereby, to save him from the tortures to which prisoners among themselves are subjected.

The capture of Niagara which had long been, and still was, considered the key to the "Senecas country," although it gave the English possession of the fort, and consequently of the "carrying place," it did not immediately transfer the allegiance of the Senecas from the French to the English. The Jonciares, father and sons, who were thoroughly in the interests of the French, had for nearly fifty years, exerted that influence, not in vain; and it was soon discovered by the English, that they not only had an enemy in the Senecas, but that their influence with the other nations of the confederacy and their allies, the Delawares, the Shawnees, &c., was working secret mischief, and soon culminated in open hostility, on the part of some of these tribes, residing upon the southern and south-western border of what was admitted to be the territory of the Six Nations. The causes of the difficulties, so far as they appeared on the surface, seemed to be in relation to their lands. This had been a subject of complaint on the part of the Indians, for many years ; but instead of obtaining any redress, or satisfaction, they had been put off with the promise, that their complaints had to be referred to their great father over the water, which required time, and indeed the whole question became so complicated, by the interference of parties interested, that the true merits of the case could not be understood, by the government at home. The controversy involved the Governors of several of the colonies, particularly the "Proprietaries of Pennsylvania." Dr. Franklin, as the accredited agent of the government of Pennsylvania, and the "proprietaries" as they were called, addressed a memorial to the King, setting forth the grounds of these complaints, and difficulties, asking for his interposition, and as stated in the memorial " to take the premises into your royal consideration, and do therein, as to your Majesty in your great wisdom, shall see meet."

This petition with a vast amount of correspondence upon the subject, was referred to "his Majesty's privy council for plantation affairs," who made an elaborate report thereon. The complaint of the Indians was that in some cases, the purchases had been made of parties not authorized to sell. In other cases, large tracts had been taken up, and surveyed, when but a small tract was sold, and conveyed by deed. The report of the council which evinced a desire to protect the Indians, and procure for them justice, admit that the troubles are mainly owing to the neglect of the government, to define the boundaries of their own territory, and to assert the jurisdiction, which the treaty of Utrecht clearly awarded to the English government, in 1701. During this long period of neglect, parties in nearly all the colonies, had instituted independent negotiations with the Indians for the purchase of large tracts of land, or rather to extinguish the Indian title to them. Not knowing, or regarding, the nature of the relations subsisting between the Crown and the Five Nations, in respect to these lands, which were called their "hunting grounds," which the Five Nations had ceded to the Crown, to be held for the benefit of those nations, and their posterity.

Although Sir William Johnson had exerted himself with great diligence and address to the settlement of these difficulties, he found his efforts frequently embarrassed, and sometimes thwarted, by the interference of conflicting interests, influences, and even authority. In 1760, in a communication to the Commissioners of the Board of Trade, he makes this a subject of complaint. "If (says he,) the Indians are admitted to be under a complicate or multifarious influence, or management, especially at this time, it must make any application to them uncertain, the service liable to many inconveniences and render the Indians more difficult to treat with, while the power of acting, seems to be divided, and the plan of directing them, not mutually concerted by me, and those who affect and assume to be supernecessary."

In a letter of a later date than the above, alluding to his trouble in conciliating the Indians, during this period, he says:

"It is not easy for me to describe the variety of business, and trouble, in which I have been involved, since the commencement of the Indian war. But I have the satisfaction to find, that my labors have secured these frontiers, and communications, as well as preserved the fidelity, of five out of the Six Nations, with those of Canada, and many others." He undoubtedly alludes to the Senecas as the one of the Six Nations, which at this time 1763, he considered as in hostility, against the English, notwithstanding peace had been declared between England and France.

It was at this period 1763, that Pontiac, the great Ottoway chief, attempted to unite the western Indians, against the English, and to dispossess them of the country about the lakes, recently conquered from the French, and it is said that he exerted a wider influence than any other man was ever able to do among these nations. The hos tility to the English was undoubtedly excited by the French, who still held possession of Louisiana, and all the entire valley of the Mississippi, with the streams tributary to that river. The Senecas had at this time settled some small villages on the head waters of the Belle river (Ohio,) and considering the influences brought to bear upon them, through the untiring zeal and activity, of the Jonciares, father and two sons, for more than fifty years it is not surprising that they should have been brought to sympathize with this great movement of Pontiac. This feeling exhibited itself in an open attack upon the English at the carrying place upon the Niagara river.

Before the surrender of fort Niagara to the English Chabert Jonciare Jr. (his father being dead) was in command of the carrying place around the Falls of Niagara. This profitable privilege had been granted him, by the French, as a reward for his services, and had been assented to by the Senecas, who shared in the profits, as they considered him one of their children, his mother being a Seneca woman. Jonciare had a considerable amount of property invested in this business, which of course was destroyed by the overthrow of the French ; Jonciare himself being taken prisoner, together with his brother Clauzonne Jonciare, at the surrender of the fort.

The carrying place of course came into the possession of the English, and was put in charge of one John Steadman, an Englishman. This greatly exasperated the Senecas. They considered the carrying place as their own ; it had long been in possession of one of their children. The feelings of the Senecas, in respect to this subject, as well as many others, which had alienated them from the English, were well understood by Sir William Johnson, and the train of wagons from the landing (Lewiston) to little Niagara (Schlosser,) was always furnished with a guard of soldiers. As this was the only practicable route from east to west, at that time, for the English, this and other carrying places were of the utmost importance to them, as they had been to the French.

The necessity of furnishing the different western posts at Detroit, Mackinac, etc., which had been surrendered by the French, made the safety of these carrying places, of great importance to the English, and no pains were spared, not only to secure safety to these supplies, but to insure dispatch in their transit, over this long line of communication. The teams were composed chiefly of oxen ; each team having one driver, the master, or overseer, accompanying the train on horseback. The train on this occasion, must have been large, as it appears that with one officer, and twenty-four soldiers, the party consisted of ninety-six persons. In their progress up the river, the train, with its escort, had arrived opposite what is called the " devil's hole," when owing to the shape of the ground, the road ran near the edge of the precipice. It was at this point the Indians formed an ambush, entirely out of view of their unsuspecting victims, who, as they approached this narrow defile, were fired upon by their concealed foe ; nearly all were killed or wounded, at the first fire ; the Indians rose from their concealment, with a tremendous yell, rushed upon their helpless victims, and the tomahawk and scalping knife soon finished the bloody work. The following account is from the manuscripts of Sir William Johnson, under date of September, 1763 :

"I have this moment received an express, informing me that an officer and twenty-four men who were escorting several wagons and ox-teams, over the carrying place at Niagara, had been attacked and entirely defeated, together with two companies of Col. Wilmot's Regiment, who marched to sustain them ; our loss on this occasion, consists of Lieuts. Campbell, Frazer, and Roscoe, of the Regulars, Capt. Johnson and Lieut. Dayton, of the Provincials, and sixty privates, killed, with about eight or nine wounded.

"The enemy who are supposed to be Senecas, of Chenussio, scalped all the dead, took all their clothes, arms and amunition, and threw several of their bodies down a pr cipice.

"I am greatly apprehensive of the fate of the Detroit, they being in much want I fear, at the garrison; and as all our cattle etc., which were at Niagara, are either killed or taken, it will be impossible to get any necessaries transported over the carrying place for the remainder of the season. I shall immediately send belts to all the friendly nations, and use every effectual measure for preventing the destruction of our settlements from the enemy

Indians, who are but too much encouraged from their repeated successes."

The subjoined account of this transaction, was related to Mr. Maud, an English gentleman, who visited the falls in 1800, by the son of John Steadman named below :

"The portage or carrying place which is now from Queenstown to Chippewa, was previous to 1792 from a place opposite Queenstown (Lewiston) to Fort Schlosser. In 1760 John Steadman was master. In 1763 the Indians attacked the train of wagons and its gaurd, consisting in soldiers and wagoners of ninety-six persons. Of these, ninety-two were killed on the spot, three jumped down the precipice over-hanging the river, and John Steadman putting spurs to his horse, galloped to Fort Schlosser. The three who jumped down the precipice, (considered by them as certain death, which they preferred to the tomahawk of the Indians,) were preserved by shrubs and brushwood breaking their fall. One was a drummer, whose drum falling into the river, gave the first news of this defeat, at Niagara.

"Peace being concluded with the Indians a few months after this massacre, they, of their own free will, gave a grant to John Steadman of all the land he galloped over in his flight. This tract so granted, begins at "bloody bridge" the scene of action, and terminates at Fort Schlosser. Its extent in depth from the river is such as to make the whole amount to about four thousand nine hundred acres. The reason they gave this grant was, they considered his escape, as miraculous, and that this gift was an atonement to him, and the Great Spirit, who protected him, for their guilt in having attempted to kill him. Many of the Indians assured him that they had deliberate and fair shots at him, and that had he been a deer, he could not have escaped their rifles."

The Steadman family with slight exceptions, kept possession of the farm at Fort Schlosser and probably the carrying place, many years ; aided by influential friends, application was made to the Legislature of the State of New York, after the Revolution, for a confirmation of the Indian grant, to at least, what Steadman had enclosed, and improved, being about fifteen hundred acres ; but like a multitude of similar claims in other parts of the State, the Legislature refused to recognize them, and who ever will take the trouble to examine the record of Legislative proceedings, will find frequent mention made of the Steadman farm upon the Niagara river.

The carrying place round the falls was originally upon the Canada or west side of the river, but it had been changed to the eastern or American side, the distance being found to be much shorter, upon the American side. We at this period have very little idea of the amount of transportation over this carrying place. It is probable that the train attacked and plundered by the Senecas, in 1763, consisted of from forty to fifty teams. In 1800 Mr. Maud, from whose journal we have already quoted, in passing down on the Canada side in August of that year, says :

"There is a portage at this place, which employs numerous teams, chiefly of oxen, each cart (wagon) being drawn by two yoke of oxen or two horses. I passed great numbers on the road taking up bales and boxes, and bringing down packs of peltries. Fourteen teams were at the wharf waiting to be loaded." * * "On the opposite side of the river to Queenstown, the government of the United States design to establish a landing, or rather renew the old portage to Fort Schlosser." * *

"Another scheme of the Anglo-Americans is to do away with the necessity of a portage, by substituting a canal in its place; this object, can be best explained by a quotation from Capt. Williamson's account of the Genesee.

"The fall was found to be three hundred and twenty feet from Steadman's Landing (Fort Schlosser) above the falls, to Queenstown Landing below. The distance to be cut for the proposed canal, did not exceed four miles, nearly three of which is on a level with the navigable part of the river, above the falls."

CHAPTER XI.

In April 1764 a treaty of peace was concluded, by Sir William Johnson with the Senecas at Johnson's Hall: in which they agree to stop all hostilities against the English, give up all prisoners, deserters, and negroes among them, cede the carrying place on the Niagara, including all the land from about four miles below Fort Niagara, to the creek above Fort Schlosser, or little Niagara, on both sides of the river, being about fourteen miles long, and four miles wide, and agree never to obstruct the carrying place, or the free use by the English of said tract. The signatures to the treaty are:

Sayenqueraghta, Wanughissue, Taganrondie, Taanjaqua, Tagaanadie, Kaanyes, Chonedagan, Aughnanawis.

The Senecas were to have a full pardon for all past offenses, and to remain in perpetual peace. At this treaty, as appears from subsequent proceedings and the signatures of the chiefs or sachems attached to it, a portion of the Senecas were not represented. Those residing at Chenissio, and upon the head waters of the Belle (Ohio) river had to some extent been drawn to sympathize with, if not to co-operate in the great movement headed by Pontiac. They had attacked and destroyed the train and its escort at the carrying place on the Niagara, and were implicated in some atrocious murders committed on the Susquehanna; and it required all the address of Sir William Johnson in connexion with the wisest chiefs and sachems of the other Five Nations, to bring the Chenissio Senecas back to their allegiance to their brethren, and to peace with the English; and great efforts were made by the chiefs of the Mohawks, the Oneidas, the Onondagas, and Cayugas, to conciliate the "enemy Senecas," as they were called, by the English, and they were finally induced to send delegates to another council, held at Johnson Hall, in August of the same year; first being assured, that they should have an open road to go and retürn, or in other words, that the lives and liberty of their delegates should be guaranteed.

This conference was held with much ceremony, and managed with great caution, and skill, both on the part of Sir William Johnson, and the Indians. Twyarunt, chief speaker of the Onondagas, addressed the following formal speech to the Senacas, and Delawares (who were considered the friends and allies of the Senecas,) in the presence of Sir William Johnson, and all the chiefs and sachems of the Five Nations:

"Brethren of the Senecas and Delawares:—We are here met, to the number of four Nations, in the presence of Sir William Johnson, to the end, that he may see, and be convinced of our undivided endeavors, to bring you to give a direct and just answer, such as may be depended upon, that our wives and children may live in peace, and be no longer involved in numberless distresses. You have been for a long time in a bad road. It is therefore high time, that you return back into that of our ancestors, who always employed themselves in good affairs, and continually told us that they were never the authors of bloodshed and death. For this reason, we are overjoyed, that you are now come, after having been so long called upon.

"You very well know, the promise made by you at Niagara, to Sir William Johnson. Your engagement was then reasonable, and did not require too much of you. You had therefore best to blot out all the past, and act better for the future, than you have hitherto done; and this is most strongly recommended to you, in the name of the Onondagas, Cayugas, Oneidas, and Mohawks." Gave a belt.

Then Gaustrax, the Seneca Chief, stood up and said:

"BRETHREN OF THE FIVE NATIONS:—I have attended to what you have said on this belt to us. You may be assured that we think of nothing but peace, and to that end will deliver up all the English people, as is recommended to us; and we will send messengers to collect them immediately; and as the Delawares have agreed to leave hostages for the performance of their promise, I agree to stay here, as an hostage on behalf of my nation, for the like purpose. But should the messengers not be able to succeed in getting the prisoners, I shall then beg Sir William Johnson's permission, to go myself, accompanied by Mr. Perthias the Interpreter, when I doubt not of obtaining them all."

He returned the belt given him by the four Nations.

Sir William Johnson addressed the Senecas in reply, as follows:

"BRETHREN OF THE SENECAS:—You must be sensible, that the greatest part of your nation, have been our most inveterate enemies, during the late hostilities. I will not now enlarge on that head, as it was the subject of our treaty at Niagara last summer. All I have to say upon it now is, that I expect you will consult your own interest, and happiness, and to that end, carefully avoid a breach with your brethren the Engltsh, for the time to come. On this, all your happiness entirely depends, and if you repent of your late conduct, and are come rightly to your senses, you will find the necessity of strictly abiding by all your engagements.

"Your not bringing down the rest of the prisoners, immediately after the delivery of those last year to me, agreeable to your engagement, has had a very bad appearance, and you cannot excuse yourselves. You have therefore, nothing left to convince the English of your sincerity, but by your future actions; words will not be sufficient; and therefore, I expect, that within forty nights from hence, you will bring down every prisoner yet amongst you, and every deserter, in which you cannot deceive me, for I know their numbers; and until you perform this punctually, I expect you will leave another of your chiefs of Karathyaradaris with Gaustrax, as hostages for the discharge of your engagement."

This engagement was fulfilled on the part of the Senecas and Delawares of the Susquehanna, by delivering up twenty-five persons of both sexes, held as prisoners by them.

In September of this year, in an official letter, Sir William Johnson says:

"Having this moment heard of the death of the Chief of all the Senecas, who was for some years past sincerely attached to our interests, I am apprehensive that the discontent among these jealous and troublesome people, will be considerably augmented ; on which account, but particularly from some information I daily receive, I purpose immediately under a pretense of a tour for health, to visit the Onondaga country, which being the place where the great confederacy meets, I hope to profit something from the discovery I make." * *

The result of this visit was anything but satisfactory to Sir William Johnson, but confirmatory of the fears he had expressed, as appears by the report he made, in which he says:

"The Indians with whom I held a congress, were very desirous to know whether I had received any satisfactory accounts from Court, respecting the intended boundary line, the summary process for justice, the grievances concerning lands, murders, and intrusions of the frontier inhabitants, and other matters, on which they had been promised relief. In answer to which I gave them many assurances that these matters were under consideration, and orders actually sent, to the Governor of the province on the subject of lands.

"They answered that they had no expectation from that quarter, and that the application to his Majesty was founded on a certainty that they could expect no redress elsewhere.

"That on this and every other subject of grievance, they had patiently waited for redress, several years, that they were now quite tired, and began to despair of it, that all the nations were becoming impatient and dissatisfied, and could not restrain their warriors."

The principal causes of the disaffection of the Senecas, which extended more or less to all the Six Nations, with the exception, perhaps of the Mohawks, grew out of the course pursued by the English in regard to their lands. The Indians attached value to them as their "hunting grounds;" of course for this purpose they required an immense territory, and the settlement of a few or even one individual family upon these grounds, would drive the animals from a large territory; and the constant encroachment of the new settlers upon these hunting grounds was as constant a subject of complaint, and as the government afforded them no relief, they often asserted their own rights, by exterminating, or capturing the intruders bodily. The principal sources of these difficulties were upon the head-waters of the Susquehanna, Delaware and Ohio rivers. The Senecas who guarded the "western door" of the confederacy, had at this period pushed their frontier settlements to the banks of these rivers, and were often brought into conflict with the white settlers. The French emissaries were still in the country. They stimulated the Indians (over whom they possessed far greater influence than the English) to acts of hostility, against these settlers; the consequences soon became too apparent, in the wholesale murders, and captures of entire families, and sometimes of settlements, made by the Indians, of those they considered as intruders upon their rights and property. Of course the settlers became greatly exasperated against the Indians, and did not fail to inflict the full measure of their vengeance upon them whenever they had an opportunity to do so.

The following extract of a letter written by Sir William Johnson to the Lords of Trade in 1764, shows the nature of these transactions:

"The late murder committed on the friendly Conestoga Indians residing in, and under the protection of Pennsylvania, by a number of riotous persons, who without any cause, surprised and killed, six of these peaceable people, occasioned Mr. Penn to issue a proclamation, for discovery of the authors thereof, and to place the rest of that people in Lancaster, where they were lodged in the workhouse, for better security. But the rioters, not alarmed at the proclamation, came, in a body, armed, broke open the workhouse, and barbarously murdered fourteen more of these Indians, and even threatened to come down to the city of Philadelphia, and kill a number of peaceable and well disposed Indians, taken into the protection of that city.

In October, 1768, a great treaty was held by Sir William Johnson at Fort Stanwix, with the Six Nations, the Shawnees, Delawares, and Senecas, of Ohio, at which more than two thousand Indians were present. Several weeks were occupied, in completing the business transacted, the principal of which was, the settlement of the question of a boundary line between the whites and the Indians. The Governors of several of the colonies were present at this treaty. Gov. Penn, of Pennsylvania, after waiting several days for the arrival of the delegates from some of the more distant nations, who were slow in coming, was obliged to leave, and placed his affairs in the hands of two commissioners, to represent that colony. After much discussion and negotiation, conducted entirely by Sir William Johnson, on the part of the English, assisted by his two sons-in-law, Col. Guy Johnson, and Col. Claus, the boundary was agreed upon, and the treaty signed by the chiefs of all the Six Nations, and their dependents the Delawares, Shawnees, &c. This line extended from near lake Ontario, at the junction of Canada and Wood creeks, to Owego on the Susquehanna, thence through Pennsylvania, Maryland, &c., to the mouth of the Cherokee or Tennessee river. The settlement of the boundary line question, although it removed an occasion of complaint, did not remove the cause, of the dissatisfaction of the Indians. This lay deeper, and was of more difficult cure. It is more than once alluded to by Sir William Johnson, in his correspondence with the government at this period. It was the alarming increase of the number, and growing power, of the English.

The reason assigned by Sir William Johnson, for not fixing or closing the boundary line to lake Ontario on the north, was, that the property to the north of the present point of termination, belonged to the Oneidas and Mohawks, and could at any time thereafter "be closed at a very moderate expense, should his Majesty require it." One of the stipulations contained in the treaty fixing the boundary line was, that no settlements of the whites should be permitted west of that line. The difficulty of fulfilling, or enforcing this stipulation, seems to have been foreseen by Sir William Johnson, and feared by the Indians. The neglect of their complaints, and failures to fulfill their promises to the Indians by the English, had educated them to expect disappointment, notwithstanding they had unwavering confidence in the integrity, and good intentions, of their friend, Sir William. But upon the frontier, particularly at the southwest, upon the Susquehanna, and the Ohio rivers, a degree of hostility on the part of the settlers, against the Indians, existed, and was strengthened, and made aggressive, by the success of the British arms, and the rapidly augmenting numbers of settlers. And it was soon found that the boundary line, was no restraint upon the rapacity of the land speculators and squatters, and from negotiations between the Indians and the government, there was a sudden transition to a state of hostilities between the Indians and the frontier settlers, many of whom had already pushed their claims beyond the limits of the boundary line.

The following letters of Sir William Johnson to Gen. Gage, written at this time, shows the state of Indian affairs about this period, and the influences that were operating to produce disaffection among them:

SIR WILLIAM JOHNSON TO GEN. GAGE.

April 18th, 1767.

I have had a particular information of the murder of the Delaware Indian at Redstone creek. It appears from the information of several white men, that the quarrel arose through the instigation of Col. Creasap, of Maryland, who trades on that frontier, and (probably from interested motives,) had actually told the deceased that if he met with any traders in the country, or going to it, he should take their liquor from them, and cause the kegs to be staved. This is one of the consequences of suffering the traders to ramble where ever great profits may seduce them, and I consider it as only a prelude of what is to follow, unless they are timely and effectually restrained.

SIR WILLIAM JOHNSON TO GEN. GAGE.

April 24th, 1767.

I am well informed that Chabert Jonciare, is preparing to set out with a cargo of goods for Niagara, and heartily wish he could by some means be prevented; for I am convinced that no good can come of that journey, and that he will be as ready to infuse dangerous sentiments into the minds of the Indians, as they will be to give credit to all he says, from the great esteem in which he is held by them.

July 1st, 1767.

"Since my last of the 12th, Mr. Chabert (Jonciare,) arrived here, together with Lieut. Carleton, nephew to the Governor, with letters very much in favor of the former, representing his quiet and good behavior; the ill-treatment he met with in France, which must prejudice him against that nation; that having now brought a large cargo for the purpose of trade, he and family must be ruined, unless allowed to dispose of it. From all which, and from his repeated entreaties, and assurances, of behaving in such a manner as should render him worthy that indulgence, I was at a loss how to refuse him, and therefore have wrote by him to Brig. Gen. Carleton acquainting him, that I should give you notice thereof. If Mr. Chabert, will act the part of a wise man, and a man of honor, as I am willing to hope, I imagine he will not abuse such indulgence, and therefore, as I cannot take upon myself to make any further objections to him, I must submit the matter entirely to your consideration."

Early in 1769, Sir William Johnson made a visit to the Onondagas, Cayugas, and Senecas, for the purpose of learning the particulars in regard to the outrages committed upon the frontier settlements, in which it was alleged the Six Nations were involved. At Onondaga, he was overturned in his canoe, and the wound in his thigh, received a severe hurt, which nearly rendered him incapable of proceeding, but after a little delay, he pursued his journey to Seneca, (Kanesadaga,) where he had summoned the chiefs of that nation, living near the head of the Ohio river, to meet him. The Indians assembled to the number of more than two thousand. A spirit of general discontent was soon manifested. The Senecas began by a long detail of their grievances, complaining of a general neglect on the part of the English to observe the provisions of the late treaty. That their trading posts were neglected, that frauds upon them were practiced more than ever; that the agents, interpreters, and blacksmiths, which they had been accustomed to have among them, had been withdrawn, and that they were informed that a war between the English, and the Spanish and French, was imminent, and they were invited and encouraged by the emissaries of the French still among them, to engage in it, which, notwithstanding the advice of the chiefs to the contrary, was a great temptation to their warriors. That the French had predicted all these evils, and experience had proved it too true, and "they were full of resentment through disappointment."

In his report to the Earl of Hillsborough, Sir William Johnson says: "On my way home I was overtaken with the news of a murder of a young Seneca lad, who was fired upon on the river Susquehanna, by some of the frontier inhabitants, without the least provocation given; (of which I have since received an account from Pennsylvania,) as the father of this lad, has generally lived within the settlements, and with the whole family demonstrated the most zealous attachment to the English, and were much respected by the Indians, the murder is a very unlucky accident at this time, but it is not alone; several others have been lately committed, by the infatuated and lawless inhabitants on the frontiers of Virginia, &c., who, as they have hitherto acted with impunity, are encouraged to go on. And though the effects of all this, have not been sensibly felt for sometime, they begin at length to make their appearance, particularly about the Illinois, and Ohio, of which your Lordship will doubtless receive information, from the commander in chief; the Indians having killed several people, attacked and plundered several trader's boats, and in short blocked up the communication of the Ohio, so that it is no longer practicable for trading; * * whilst at the same time they are endeavoring to form a more strict alliance (among themselves,) than ever, for purposes that are but too obvious, seeming only to wait the success of their negotiations, for the commencement of hostilities." * * *

In the mean time no provision was made by the colonies for defraying the expenses of the department of Indian affairs. The government of New York voted only one hundred and fifty pounds for that purpose this year. Instances were not unfrequent, when for some act of a single individual, either real or pretended, the Indians were pursued by the inhabitants, and whole families, and sometimes whole villages cut off. Sir William Johnson deplores the state of feeling existing between the frontier settlers and the Indians, and mentions the case of one Callender, a trader, on his way to fort Pitt, with twenty-five horses loaded with Indian goods, who was attacked near Bedford, by thirty white men disguised and painted like Indians, who destroyed and carried away the greatest part of his goods, declaring "they would suffer none to pass on to the Indians." * * The political troubles which began to agitate the public mind, both in Massachusetts and New York, about this period, caused serious embarrassment to the management of Indian affairs. In 1770, a combination against the importation of foreign goods, was formed in New York, and it was with the greatest difficulty that Sir William Johnson was able to get "out of the hands of the committee of non-importers," a cargo of Indian goods which were of the greatest importance to enable him to keep his promises to them. The delay in obtaining the ordinary supplies for the Indian trade, had been used by the French emissaries with great effect against the English, and had shaken the confidence of the Indians in them.

Great dissatisfaction had been given the Shawnees and Senecas residing on the Ohio river, by fixing the boundary line on that river. They claimed the land between that river and the lake, and this dissatisfaction was felt by the Senecas residing at Chenissio (Genesee,) and reports came to Sir William Johnson "that the Six Nations were concerned in exciting the Shawnees, and the Delawares and many others to make war upon the English."

The following circular letter from Lord Hillsborough to the Governors of Quebec, New York, New Jersey, Virginia, North Carolina, Maryland, and Pennsylvania, dated Whitehall, November 15th, 1770, shows the light in which the English government viewed the state of affairs at this time:

"SIR:—The enclosed extract from a letter I have lately received from Sir William Johnson, will fully inform you of the complaints made by the Six Nations of Indians and their allies and confederates, at a congress held in July last, at the German Flatts, of the abuses and violences committed by the traders and frontier inhabitants of several of his majesty's colonies, and the enclosed extract of the conference, will point out to you how earnest the Indians have been in these complaints, and what is likely to happen if they are not redressed.

"After the King had thought fit from regard to the claims and opinions of the colonies, to leave it to them to make such regulations concerning the Indian commerce, as they judged proper, there was good reason to hope that a matter on which their interest and safety do so much depend, would have been an immediate object of their serious deliberation. But contrary to all expectation, nothing effectual appears to have been done, and as the Indians have in the strongest manner, expressed their impatience, under the abuses to which they are constantly exposed, the King has commanded me to signify his pleasure that you should without delay, fall upon some measures of putting Indian affairs under such regulations, as may have the effect to prevent these abuses of the trade, and those violences and encroachments of the frontier inhabitants, which the Indians so justly complain of

I am etc.,

HILLSBOROUGH."

In 1772, Sir William Johnson sent a deputation to the Ohio, for the purpose of ascertaining the true state of the case. Thomas King, a chief of the Mohawks was at the head of the deputation. He is spoken of by Sir William as a man of superior capacity and of unquestioned fidelity to the English. He accomplished his mission, but died on his way back. The report of this embassy made by one of the survivors rather confirmed previous reports, and to some extent implicated the great Seneca chief. Agastarax (or Gastrax) who was recently deceased; another general council had already been appointed at Sciota, at which Sir William Johnson informs Lord Hillsborough he should take care that the Six Nations should be represented by those whose fidelity could be relied on. As his own impaired health would not admit of his taking the journey himself, his deputy would be present to watch the proceedings. In 1773 Sir William Johnson visited England, and it is probably from this fact, there is little or no record of events occurring this year, relating to the Indian affairs, found among his manuscripts.

In a report to Governor Tryon, Oct. 22d, 1773, the Mohawks numbered only four hundred and six souls, the Oneidas, fifteen hundred, the whole Six Nations about two thousand fighting men; making at least ten thousand souls in all. "The Senecas alone are one-half that number."

CHAPTER XII.

It was during this year (1772,) that events occurred on the Ohio, which undoubtedly influenced subsequent transactions, if indeed they did not produce the Indian war, which resulted so disastrously to the Six Nations. In a report to Earl Dartmouth, Sir William Johnson says:

"My negotiations with the Senecas was interrupted by intelligence that a certain Mr. Cressop, an inhabitant of Virginia had murdered forty Indians on the Ohio, for the most part of the Six Nations."

The agent of Sir William Johnson on the Ohio, reported that he "received information from Capt. Crawford and one Mr. Neville from Virginia, that on the way to this place they met a number of inhabitants settled below this (Wheeling) moving off; among whom was a party who had several Indian scalps, and related their having taken them, as follows:

"That a number of Indians having encamped at the mouth of the Yellow Creek, they, with one Greathouse, had collected themselves at the house of one Baker, opposite to the said Indians, and decoyed two Indian men and two women, over to their side of the river, to drink with them; who, upon finding them intoxicated, fell upon them, and knocked them in the head, and scalped them. That soon after, two other Indians came over, to see what detained their friends, and were served in the same manner. After this, the Indians appeared uneasy, and six of their men were coming across the river to look after their people, who approached near the shore, observed them, the said white people, where they were lying in ambush for them, and attempting to return to their camp, were fired upon, and two of them were killed, who dropped into the river; and two others they observed fall dead in the canoe; and the fifth, upon their landing, they could discover, to be very badly wounded, so that he could scarce get up the bank, and that they heard the women and the children at the camp, raise a very melancholy cry.

"Among those who were killed, was an Indian woman, the wife of one of our traders, who had a young child upon her back, which she had bore to him; and after some altercation between those murderers, whether they should put the child to death, they agreed to take it along with them.

"The said Mr. Neville asked the person in whose custody the child was, if he was not near enough to have taken its mother prisoner, without putting her to death in that inhuman manner; he answered, that he was about six feet distant, and that he had shot her in the forehead, and cut the strap, by which the child's cradle hung at her back; and that he intended to have dashed its brains out; but that he was struck with some remorse at seeing the child fall, with its mother. That one of his companions recommended their taking it along with them, that they might have an opportunity of sending it to its father, to take care of it; aud that after they had perpetrated this barbarous murder, they made off with their families; also they further said that by this time, the whole country was deserted, as Michael Cressup, who committed the first mischief, was there likewise, on his way to Red Stone."

Alexander McKee, who was the agent of Sir William Johnson on the Ohio, made a report of the facts as they occurred at this time, which appear to be entirely authentic; of which the preceding, and following, are extracts, and serve to illustrate the true condition of things, to a fuller extent than has hitherto been done:

"On May 1st, 1774, the following alarming intelligence arrived at Fort Pitt, by one Stevens, who had proceeded in a trader's canoe, which was attacked on the 16th, by the Cherokees, in order to have carried her to Sciota, who gave the following particulars, viz:

"That on the 25th upon his way down the river, and near Wheeling Creek, he observed a canoe coming up the river, which suspecting to be Indians, he made to the opposite shore, to avoid them; but upon his approach near the shore was fired upon, and a Shawnese Indian in the canoe with him, was killed; upon a second fire from the shore, a Delaware Indian who was also in the canoe, was killed; said Stevens further says, he could not perceive who it was, fired upon him, as they lay concealed in the weeds, and upon throwing himself into the river, observed the canoe that was coming up to be white people, upon which he made towards them, and found it to be one Michael Cressop, with a party of men who denied knowing anything of what had happened to them, although from circumstances, he the said Stevens, is well convinced that the above murder was done by some of said Cressop's associates. Stevens likewise informed me, that while he was in company with said Cressop, he heard him make use of threatening language against the Indians, saying:

"He would put every Indian to death he met on the river; and that if he could raise men sufficient to cross the river, he would attack a small village of Indians living on Yellow Creek.

"The same evening one Maj. McDaniel of Virginia, who had been down the river as low as Kanhaway, returned to this place, with an account that a skirmish had happened between a party of Virginians and the Indians, near the big Kanhaway, that a number were killed on both sides, which had occasioned the surveyors and land-hunters, from that colony, to return, and that on his way hither, on the 5th inst., he was at Michael Cressop's house, at or near Wheeling, when an account was brought to said Cressop, by one McMahon, that five Indian canoes had stopped at his house, on their way down the river, containing fourteen Indians, who asked him, the said McMahon for some provisions, which he refused to give them, and told them that two of their brethren had been killed by the white people, the day before; the Indians replied that if it was so, they knew nothing of it, and then proceeded down the river. That upon this information, the said Cressop procured fifteen men, pursued them, and overtook them near Grave Creek, where they had stopped and drawn up their canoes, in the mouth of a creek that was hardly perceivable, on account of the bushes; where they had prepared themselves to receive the white people suspecting that they would be followed, after what Mc Mahon had told them; and that upon the said Cressop observing the Indians, he fired upon them, upon which a skirmish ensued between them ; but the Indians retired after losing one man, and one man was killed on the white people's side. Cressop and his party found sixteen kegs of rum, and two old saddles, and some bridles in the deserted canoes." This dastardly transaction was soon followed by another outrage, which though of less magnitude, was not less atrocious in its spirit, while it was even more harrowing to the feelings of the Indians. The event referred to was the murder by a white man, of an aged and inoffensive Delaware chief, named the "Bald Eagle." He had for years associated with the whites more than with his own people, visiting those most frequently, who entertained him and treated him with the greatest kindness. While paddling his canoe alone, on his return from a visit to the fort at the mouth of the Kanhawa, he was shot dead by a man who it was said had suffered at the hands of the Indians, but had never been injured by the object upon whom he wreaked his vengeance; after tearing the scalp from his head, the white savage placed the body in a sitting posture in the canoe, and sent it adrift down the stream. The voyage of the dead chief was observed by many who supposed him living and upon one of his ordinary excursions.*

Equally exasperated, at about this same time were the Shawnees against the whites by the murder of one of their favorite chiefs, "Silver Heels," who had in the kindest manner, undertaken to escort a party of white traders across the woods from the Ohio, to Albany, a distance of nearly five hundred miles.†

*McClung, as cited by Drake.

†Heckewelder.

May 23d, 1774, (at Pittsburgh.)

"I called a meeting (of Indians) with Kayashota the white mingo, and some other Six Nation Chiefs, at Col. Croghan's house; where was present the commanding officer of the militia, (Capt. Connoly) and several other gentlemen, when I informed them (the Indians) of the melancholy murders of their people as before mentioned, which they had not before heard, and assured them at the same time, of its being done by a few inconsiderate white people, and not by the intention, or knowledge, of any of our wise people; that I made no doubt but the Governor of Virginia when he was made acquainted with the unhappy loss they had sustained by his people, would fall upon every measure, to make them ample satisfaction, as it was not done by the intention of government. That in the meantime, I enjoined them, to afford all the assistance in their power in accommodating the unfortunate breach of friendship, that had happened between our people and them, as a general difference could not be attended with anything but the utmost distress on their side." They returned for answer:

"That they had considered what we had said to them, and as the chiefs of the Delawares were expected in to-night, or to-morrow, they would cousult with them and know what reply to make. That we might be assured that they would do everything in their power to keep matters quiet, which they made no doubt might be done, from the general disposition of their own people, provided we would be strong, on our parts in preventing our rash people from committing any further outrages against the Indians."

The following is the answer of the Shawnese to Capt. Connoly and others:

"BRETHREN :—It is you that are frequently passing up and down the Ohio, and making settlements upon it, and as you have informed us that your wise people are met together to consult upon this matter, we desire you to be strong, and consider it well.

"Brethren, you see, you speak to us at the head of your warriors, who you have collected together at sundry places on this river, where we understand they are building forts; and as you have requested us to listen to you, we will do it, but in the same manner that you attend to us. Our people at the lower town, have no chiefs among them, but are all warriors, and are preparing themselves to be in readiness, that they may the better be enabled to hear what you have to say.

"Brethren, you tell us not to take any notice of what your people have done to us; we desire you likewise, not to take any notice of what our young men may now be doing; and as no doubt, you may command your warriors, when you desire them to listen to you, we have reason to expect that ours will take the same advice from us, when we require it, that is to say, when we have received peaceable tidings from Virginia."

March, 1774.

The address of Kayashota or Kayagshota the Seneca chief, to Capt. Connoly, commandant of the militia, at Fort Pitt:

"As I understand you had an appointment to command in this country, I therefore take this opportunity of informing you, that at this time, it will be very detrimental to the public interest, to suffer liquors to be sold, or carried into the Indian towns, for I am sorry to observe that there appears at present, a great deal of confusion, and discontent among many of the Indian tribes, and the addition of rum, will serve greatly to increase their disorderly conduct. I spoke to the traders last fall, on this subject, and desired they would desist for their own sakes, as well as for ours, from taking such quantities of rum, with them, a trading, but I received no answer, from them, and it seems since, they pay no regard to what I recommend to them, but have continued this pernicious practice. This is the reason I would therefore request you to use your influence in preventing them, until things appear more settled. Gave a string of Wampum."

The events upon the frontier of Virginia, which occurred about this time, have additional interest imparted to them by the celebrity which history has given to some of the principal actors in them. Logan, whose name is immortalized in the celebrated address he delivered to Lord Dunmore, Governor of Virginia, was a chief of the Six Nations. His father, Shikelimo, or Shikellimus, or Shickalamy, (the name being spelled in all these various ways,) was a distinguished chief of the Oneida Nation,* (and not of the Cayugas as has been stated,) who lived in 1743 at Shamokin, in Pennsylvania. He was the friend of James Logan, long the Secretary of the Proprietors, as they were called, hence the name of his son. Logan, had with others of his family, removed to the country of the Shawnese, on the Ohio, where he resided in 1773-4, and had become a leading sachem, or chief.

Michael Cresap, at this time, appears to have been an Indian trader, as his cabin or trading house, upon the

---

*Colden. See names of chiefs of the several Nations present at a council at Philadelphia, July, 1742.

bank of the river, near Wheeling, is spoken of in connection with current events. His knowledge of the country, his Indian experience, and military reputation, pointed him out as the most suitable person to command the organized body of settlers, traders, and land jobbers, who combined to make aggressive demonstrations against the Indians, to redress real or pretended grievances, charged against them by the whites. Many murders were undoubtedly committed by this party, under Cresap, but whether he ought to be held responsible for all that was suffered by the Indians, is not so clear; and perhaps history, has laid upon his shoulders a weight of responsibility, which in part, at least, ought to be borne by others. He being chosen the leader, the war which followed, was called "Cresap's war." That the cruelties against the Indians, some of which we have already related, were perpetrated, there is not a shadow of doubt. And the effort to mitigate, or to throw the responsibility of them, upon the Indians themselves, must fail, when the facts, as they are recorded in the correspondence of Sir William Johnson, (now made public,) are viewed in the light of impartial history, and cannot fail to place the responsibility of the cruel scenes enacted on the Ohio, in 1773-4, upon the parties where it rightfully belongs.

It was in one of these massacres (for they can be called nothing else,) that Logan's family relatives were killed. Fired with indignation and revenge, it is not surprising that he, with others of his people, became exasperated to the highest pitch of desperation. Being their acknowledged chief, he soon, and almost as a matter of course, became the recognized leader of his people. And he undoubtedly headed several parties in their murderous attacks upon, and indiscriminate slaughter of the whites. He headed a party of only eight warriors, who made a descent upon a white settlement in the Muskingum, in 1774, with fatal success. But in all these warlike forays, the humanity of Logan was conspicuous. In one instance, he so instructed a prisoner, doomed to almost certain death by running the gauntlet, that he was enabled to escape almost without injury. In another case, he cut with his own hands, the cords which bound a prisoner to the stake, and by his influence, not only saved his life, but procured his adoption into the family of an Indian friend. So persistent was he, in this line of conduct, as to bring upon himself the reproach of some of his own people, who called him "the white man's friend." The war which was begun, and at first carried on in this desultory manner, soon assumed more gigantic proportions, and an army of two or three thousand men, was organized by Lord Dunmore, Governor of Virginia.

This army was divided into two wings. The left wing, composed principally of the chivalry of Virginia, mostly armed with rifles, was entrusted to the command of Col. Andrew Lewis, with instructions to proceed directly to the mouth of the great Kanhawa river, while his Lordship with the right wing, was to cross the Ohio at a higher point, and fall upon the Indian towns, on that side of the river. Col. Lewis arrived at the junction of the Kanhawa with the Ohio, early in October, 1774. In the morning his pickets were fired upon by a body of Indians. Immediately upon the alarm (although it was before sunrise,) he put his forces in order to advance and attack the Indians, but they had scarcely left their encampment, before they were met by from eight to fifteen hundred Indians. The onset was impetuous upon both sides. The Virginians had encamped upon the point of land between the two rivers, giving the Indians the important advantage, of being able to retreat, while they (the Virginians,) could not. The Indians were led by Logan, assisted by other chiefs, among whom were the celebrated Shawnee chief Cornstock, Ellenipsico, (his son,) and Red Eagle. Col. Charles Lewis, who led the right of the Virginians, fell, almost at the first fire; both parties sought every advantage, by fighting from behind trees, but the battle was at the first decidedly in favor of the Indians, and two of the Virginia regiments, after severe loss, especially in officers, were compelled to give way. Col. Flemming, who commanded the left, though severely wounded in the beginning of the action, by two balls through his arm, and another in the breast, bravely kept the field, cheering his men, and urging them not to lose an inch of ground, ordered them to outflank the enemy. But the assault of the Indians, was so vigorous, and their fire so severe, that like the right, the left too, had to yield. Just at this critical moment, Col. Field's regiment was brought to their relief, and the impetuosity of the Indians was checked, but with the loss of the gallant Col. Field, who was killed at the moment his regiment was brought into action. He was succeeded in command, by Capt. Isaac Shelby, afterwards Governor of Kentucky. The Indians were forced to fall back to avail themselves of a rude breastwork, of logs and brush, which they had taken the precaution to construct for the occasion; here they made a valiant stand, defending their position against every endeavor to dislodge them, fighting like men who had not only their soil, their homes, to

12

protect, but deep wrongs to revenge. "The voice of the mighty Cornstock, was often heard during the day, above the din of battle, calling out to his warriors, be strong! be strong! and when by the repeated charge of the Virginians, some of his men began to waver, he is said to have struck his tomahawk into the head of one who was attempting to fly."*

Towards night, finding that each successive attack upon the line of the Indians weakened his own force, without making any sensible impression upon the Indians, a final attempt was made by throwing a body of troops into the rear. Three companies, led by Capt. Shelby, taking advantage of the bed of a small creek, covered by tall weeds and grass upon its banks, enabled them to accomplish the movement, unobserved by the Indians; and falling vigorously upon their rear, compelled them to abandon their rude works, with precipitation. The Indians fled across the Ohio, and continued their retreat to the Scioto.

This battle, considering the numbers engaged, has been ranked one of the most bloody, on record. The loss of the Indians was never known, but must have been severe; it is said that in addition to the killed and wounded, borne away, numbers of the slain were thrown into the river, and thirty-three of their warriors were found dead upon the field, the following day. The loss of the Virginians was also severe. Two of their colonels were killed, four captains, many subordinates, and between fifty and sixty privates, besides a much larger number wounded.† It is said Cornstock was opposed to giving

---

*Drake. Official report.

battle at the mouth of Kanhawa, but being overruled in council, resolved to do his best.

Upon their arrival at Chilicothe, a council of Indians was held to decide what was next to be done. Cornstock addressed the council. He said: "The long knives are upon us, from by two routes. Shall we turn and fight them?" No response being made to the question, he continued: "Shall we kill our squaws and children, and then fight until we are killed ourselves?" As before, all were silent, whereupon Cornstock struck his tomahawk into the war post, standing in the midst of the council, and remarked with emphasis: "Since you are not inclined to fight, I will go and make peace." Saying which, he repaired to the camp of Lord Dunmore, who having crossed the Ohio, was now approaching Scioto. Cornstock was accompanied by several other chiefs, on this mission of peace, but Logan refused to go with them. He was in favor of peace, but scorned to ask it. The chief speaker on this occasion was Cornstock, who did not fail to charge the whites with being the sole cause of the war, enumerating the provocations which the Indians had received, and dwelling with peculiar force upon the murders committed in the family of Logan. A peace was concluded, and so important was it considered by Lord Dunmore to have the name of Logan to the treaty, that he dispatched a special messenger, Col. John Gibson, to the cabin of the great "Mingo Chief." His assent to the treaty was obtained, but with an eloquent rehearsal of his own, and his people's grievances. This conference with Col. Gibson, was alone, in a solitary wood, and at its close Logan uttered the speech or message to Lord Dunmore, which has given his name a place among the greatest orators.

LOGAN'S SPEECH.

"I appeal (says he,) to any white man, to say if he ever entered Logan's cabin hungry, and he gave him not meat. If ever he came cold and naked, and he warmed him not. During the course of the last long bloody war, Logan remained idle in his cabin, an advocate for peace. Such was my love for the whites, that my countrymen pointed as they passed, and said Logan is the friend of the white man. I had thought to live with you, but for the injuries of one man, Col. Cresap, the last spring in cold blood, and unprovoked, murdered all the relatives of Logan ; not even sparing my women, and children. There runs not a drop of my blood in the veins of any living creature. This called on me for revenge ; I have sought it ; I have killed many, I have fully glutted my revenge. For my country, I rejoice at the beams of peace, but do not harbor a thought, that mine is the joy of fear. Logan never felt fear. He will not turn on his heel to save his life. Who is there to mourn for Logan, not one!"

The following is a copy of the pretended speech of "Lonan," by which the attempt is made to invalidate the claim of Logan to its originality.

"Speech pronounced by the savage Lonan, in a general assembly, as it was sent to the Governor of Virginia, Anno, 1754:

"Lonan will no longer oppose making the proposed peace with the white man. You are sensible that he never knew what fear is, that he never turned his back in the day of battle. No one has more love for the white man than I have. The war we have had with them, was long, and bloody, on both sides. Rivers of blood have run on all parts, and yet no good has resulted therefrom to any. I once more repeat it, let us be at peace with these men. I will forget our injuries, the interest of our country demands it. I will forget, but difficult indeed is the task. Yes, I will forget. Major Rogers cruelly and inhumanly murdered in their canoes, my wife, my children, my father, my mother, and all my kindred. This roused me to deeds of vengeance. I was cruel in despite of myself. I will die content if my country is once more at peace. But when Lonan shall be no more, who alas! will not drop a tear for him."*

This is evidently a version of the same transaction, related by the Abbe Robin in 1781—the date, and some other parts of the speech having been altered, either by mistake or design.

Extract of the affidavit of Col. John Gibson, sworn and subscribed before J. Barker, at Pittsburgh, April 4th, 1800:

"This deponent further saith, that in the year 1774, he accompanied Lord Dunmore on the expedition against the Shawnees and other Indians, on the Scioto. That on their arrival within fifteen miles of the towns, they were met by a flag, and a white man by the name of Elliott, who informed Lord Dunmore that the chiefs of the Shawnese, had sent to request him to halt his army, and send in some person who understood their language. That this deponent, at the request of Lord Dunmore, and the whole of the officers with him went in. That on his arrival at the towns, Logan, the Indian, came to where this deponent was sitting, with Cornstock, and the other

*Nouveau Voyage dans L' Amerique, Septentrionale en l'Annee, 1781 et Campagne de' l' Armee de M. le Compte de Rochambeau par M. L'abbe Robin. The Abbe was a Chaplain in the army of our French Auxiliaries.

chiefs of the Shawnese, and asked him to walk out with him. That they went into a copse of wood, where they sat down, when Logan, after abundance of tears, delivered him the speech nearly as related by Mr. Jefferson, in his notes on Virginia.

JOHN GIBSON."

This affidavit, ought to be conclusive in regard to the authenticity of Logan's speech, as given by Mr. Jefferson. Heckewelder, says "there is no doubt that the speech was delivered by Logan, as given by Mr. Jefferson, except, that it had a force and beauty in the original Indian, that cannot be given in a translation."

The attempt that has been made to throw doubt, or suspicion upon the authenticity of Logan's speech, which has been admired wherever read, while it is not creditable to the motives of those who are the authors of it, must as signally fail of its wicked purpose. The treaties, and indeed all the negotiations with the Indians in Virginia and elsewhere, at the period named, have been pretty fully recorded. Had there been any such speech made as that attributed to "Lonan," prior to Logan's day, it is not likely we should have been left to search for it, in some obscure book, of some equally obscure French author.

Logan, like thousands of his race, fell a sacrifice to the "white man's fire water." Does it become the "white man" to reproach the memory, or disparage the character, of the victim of his own crime?

After the peace of Chillicothe, Logan, it is said, sank into a state of deep mental depression, declaring that life was a burden to him. He became in some measure deranged; he went to Detroit, and there yielded to habits of intoxication, and at last became a victim to the same ferocious cruelty, which had already made his heart desolate. He was murdered by a party of whites while returning from Detroit to his own country.*

Other accounts say he was killed by his own nephew, while in a drunken brawl.

---

*Thatcher.

CHAPTER XIII.

In July, 1774, Sir William Johnson held his last council with the Six Nations, at Johnson's Hall. He had summoned the chief sachems of all the Six Nations together with their dependents.

The principal object of the council related to the late troubles on the Ohio. Sir William evidently foreseeing the troubles which portended, had for some time exerted all the means in his power, to induce the Six Nations to withdraw their people from their settlements there, and to bring them together, in their villages within the boundaries of New York. A very strenuous effort was made by the principal chiefs of the Six Nations, to accomplish this ; and had their great friend lived, it might have been accomplished.

" Proceedings at a Congress with all the chiefs and warriors of the Six Nations, at Johnson's Hall, in June and July, 1774.

Present—The Hon. Sir William Johnson, Bar't, Sup't. Guy Johnson, Esq. Sir William's Dep'ty, Ass't., Daniel Claus, Esq., Dep'ty Ag't for Canada.

On the 19th of June, a large party of Onondagas &c., arrived at Johnson's Hall and acquainted Sir William Johnson, that the chiefs, &c., of all the Six Nations were on their way to his house, to hold a conference on the critical state of Indian affairs, and other matters. From the 19th of June to the 8th of July, parties continued to come in, amounting in the whole to near six hundred.

"On the morning of the 8th of July, one of the prisoners, confined in the Jail for the murder of the Frenchman on Lake Ontario, died, and the Indians held a conference with Sir William, earnestly requesting that the other prisoner might be restored to them, as they had been lately so ill-treated at the southward, and as the one had died as they apprehended through the circumstances of a confinement, to which he had not been accustomed, for all which, and as it appeared agreeable to the General from the state of affairs, and as they had brought in all the skins they had been able to collect, as a restitution for the robbery, Sir William agreed to their request; and they thereupon delivered up some packs, and a quantity of loose bear, raccoon, and other skins, which with those delivered up at Ontario, amounted nearly to the real loss sustained by the Canadians, which appeared to have been much exagerated. The Senecas expressed great satisfaction on the occasion, and Sir William told them that he expected they would act a faithful and becoming part, for this instance of lenity, which they owed to their particular solicitations, his Majesty's compassion, and that he expected this would be the last instance of irregularity on their parts.

At a meeting of the Six Nations at Johnson's Hall, the 9th of July, 1774.

Present—Sir William Johnson, Baronet, Superintendent, Guy Johnson, Esq., Daniel Claus, Esq., and several other gentlemen.

"Conaghquieson, an Oneida chief, opened the meeting with the ceremony of condolence with the Indians, on the death of the young Indian prisoner, who died the day before, to which the Indians returned thanks in the usual manner. Giving six strings, and two black strouds.

"Then Serihowane, a Seneca chief, proceeded upon the business they assembled for, and addressed Sir William Johnson as follows:

"BROTHER WARRAGHIYAGEY.—You told us last fall to remember and keep up strictly, to the old engagements, entered into with the English, which was in general, intended for our interest, and welfare, and that you was apprehensive that the sincerity of the Senecas, was not as perfect as you could wish. We can assure you Brother, of the contrary on our side, and shall be happy if the English on their part are as sincere towards us, and we beg you will not give ear, to every report that is made to our prejudice.

"Brother, to convince you that we keep fresh in our memory the engagements entered into with you, we now produce to you the chain belt of alliance, and friendship, you delivered to us at Niagara, in 1764, after the Senecas had got bewildered and acted an unbecoming part towards you.

"We can assure you Brother, ever since, we have endeavored to our utmost to keep that chain bright, and the path of peace unobstructed, notwithstanding which, we have observed with concern that many of our people were still suspected of insincerity, which we cannot think we deserved, from the English. Showed the belt.

"Brother, you likewise recommended to us, to collect all our straggling people, about the Ohio and its branches, and convinced us that it was for the good of the public, that they should be brought under our eyes to prevent them from being led astray by bad people. This, Brother, we have endeavored and are still endeavoring to do. But hitherto, without success, which is in a great measure owing to the conduct of the English, the neglect of the Provinces, and the behavior of the traders. When you convened us at Niagara, and after settling every matter for our mutual welfare, you told us we should enjoy a plentiful trade, and mentioned to us the different marts, where we could have our necessaries, and trade with the English, which we really accordingly enjoyed, and trade was carried on for some years to our mutual satisfaction. But to our sorrow, that regulation by some means or other, did not continue long; and as you informed us soon after, the management of trade was left to the regulation of the respective Provinces. But the Provinces have done nothing, and the trade has been thrown into utter confusion by the traders being left to their own will and pleasure, and pursuit of gain, following our people to their hunting grounds, with goods and liquor, where they not only impose on us at pleasure, but by the means of carrying these articles to our scattered people, obstruct our endeavors to collect them, which we might have easily effected, if the traders had been obliged to bring their goods to Niagara, or other markets, as before.

"Brother, you cannot imagine the many ill consequences this change in the regulation of trade, has occasioned. But we shall still persevere, and hope you will give orders to your resident at fort Pitt, to assist us in removing our people living at Conawago, and elsewhere.

"Brother, we are sorry to observe to you, that your

people are as ungovernable, and rather more so than ours; you must remember that it was most solemnly, and publicly, settled at Fort Stanwix, in 1768, on behalf of the great King of England, our father, and the Governors, and the Commissioners, of the several Provinces, then assembled there, that the line pointed out, and fixed, between the whites and Indians, should forever after be looked upon as a barrier between us; and that the white people, were not to go beyond it.

"It seems Brother, that your people entirely disregard and despise the settlement agreed upon, between their superiors, and us; for we find that they, notwithstanding that settlement, have come up in vast numbers to the Ohio, and gave our people to understand, they would settle where they pleased. If this is the case, we must look upon every engagement you made with us, as void, and of no effect; but we hope it is not so; and that you will restrain your people, over whom you say you have authority; and make them lay aside their ill designs, and encroachments, as it has already occasioned jealousies and ill blood, and may be productive of infinite mischief, and trouble; and we must beg, that if you insist upon your people settling so near ours, they may be subject to some authority, that can keep them in order. We entreat you will make known this our request to his Majesty, and the Governors of these unruly people; until which time, and until the return of Kayaghshota, from his embassy to the nations on the Ohio, we promise ourselves, as well as on behalf of our head women, who have much influence with our young men, to keep them quiet, they being much affected and exasperated at the cruel murders, committed by these lawless people, on their friends and relations. Gave a belt.

"Brother, you recommended to us, the Six Nations, last fall, to consider the distressed situation of the Montauk Indians, who being surrounded by white people of Long Island, were in a fair way of being dispossessed of all their lands by them, on which they requested, that we would afford them a piece of land, in our country, to which they might retire and live peaceably hereafter. We have taken your desire into consideration, and agree to fix them at Canaworaghere.* We are glad of the opportunity of serving them in this respect, and shall with pleasure, take them under our protection, in the same manner that fond parents do their children, and hope they may prove deserving of it. Gave a belt.

"Then a Cayuga war chief arose and addressed Sir William Johnson, saying that he must inform him how disagreeable it was to their Nation, to have traders continually among them, who sell rum, and thereby occasion much mischief, and trouble, and requested they might for the future be prevented to go there, in order to avoid accidents, that might happen to them; that they thought it not so far, if they had any thing to sell, to bring it to the market, on the Mohawk river, and therefore desired that neither the white people, nor the Indians, be allowed to come to Cayuga, or trade for the future. That if they choose to pass through their towns on their way to the Seneca's country, they had no objection, but only desired they would not dispose of any thing to their people. Gave a belt.

"P. M. Sir William Johnson had a conference with the chiefs, wherein he communicated to them, the particulars of the account he had received from the southward,

*Vernon, †Oneida county.

respecting the late murders, with the steps taken by his deputy on the occasion; after which, he enlarged on the many irregularities committed by the Indians, about the branches of the Ohio, and Mississippi, and some late murders charged against them, as the cause of the late ill behavior of Cressup and his associates; and after using many arguments to convince them they should exert more authority over their allies, and keep them in better order, he lastly, gave them a particular account of the different schemes of the Shawnese, and their friends, for several years past, to cast an odium on the Six Nations, with a view that the latter might lose our friendship, and then be induced to join in their evil designs, adding that it was now high time to stop these doings, and that charity for these weak people, induced him to wish, that the Six Nations would save the English the disagreeable trouble, of compelling these troublesome people, to alter their behavior. He likewise fully explained to them the consequences, should the Shawnese, &c., continue to prosecute their revenge on the provinces of Pennsylvania and Virginia, without waiting to obtain regular justice, whenever they appeared to be injured.

"Monday, July 11, 1774, Sir William addressed the Indians as follows:

"Brothers: I have considered your speeches, and am always glad to hear, that you preserve in remembrance, your engagements, which I trust you will be equally careful to fulfill. You now all see, that through my representations, and the tenderness of the English government, you have the prisoner restored to you. I hope you will make good use of this, and every other act of kindness, you receive, and then you need not apprehend that you are in any wise suspected, or fear evil reports, to which I am by no means inclined to give ear.

"Brothers, I am glad you have preserved the great belt I delivered to you at Niagara; and I hope you will keep the contents of it, and all others I have given, in remembrance; for if you do, you cannot neglect endeavoring, to the utmost, to keep your people in good order; and prevent those who live at a distance, from following evil counsels, which draw reflections on your confederacy. Brothers, I told you long since, the reasons why the affairs regarding trade, were left to the direction of the colonies. Who, it was imagined, would best restrain their own people; and I also showed you, the difficulty, and time, it must take, to make regulations, adapted to their respective circumstances, and yours. I am persuaded the colonies have it still at heart, but I cannot think it any material obstruction to the withdrawing your people from about the Ohio. And I apprehend, it is in your power to redress yourselves, in the particular you complain of, without giving offense. For wherever you find traders, obtruding themselves upon you, with liquor, or following your parties to their hunting grounds, you may easily tell them to retire to more convenient places; as you will not allow them to go about in the way you mention. In which case, I have great reason to think, that such traders will withdraw, and give you no trouble.

"Brothers, I am sorry to hear of the encroachments of some of our people, (the English,) of which you so often complained. This you may be assured, is without the consent or knowledge, of the government; and the King will take measures to prevent intrusion. But, it does not so materially affect you, as it affects some of your southern dependents; several of whom, have acted such a part of late, as to encourage some of our ignorant frontier inhabitants, to commit irregularities, of which otherwise, I hardly think they would be guilty. These men will be sought after, and punished.

"It is your business to enquire into the conduct of these your dependents, and to punish those, who by their misconduct, afford encouragement to others. You may easily believe, that in so extensive a country, and among such a number of people, it is a matter of difficulty, to find out, and punish, the authors of mischief; although we have good, and sufficient laws for that purpose.

"But none of our principal men are concerned in these acts, whilst many chiefs of the nations to the southward, are the real authors of the mischiefs done by the Indians. I would therefore advise you, to put a stop to such evils in time; and you may rest assured, that I will lay these matters you complain of, before his majesty, and the governors concerned, that everything shall be done on our part, to restore peace, and afford you satisfaction, where you have a claim to it. At the same time I must greatly approve of the steps of my deputy, on the late unfortunate affair, as well as Kayaghshota, and the Delawares. I expect you will strengthen their hands on this occasion, and that I shall soon receive favorable accounts from that quarter.

"Brothers of the Cayugas, I have heard the complaint you have made of the traders among you, and I apprehend if you pursue the advice I just now gave to the rest of your confederacy, it will have the desired effect. However, I shall willingly do everything in my power, for preventing their giving you any trouble; and I expect you will be satisfied with my endeavors for that purpose."

Almost immediately after delivering this speech, Sir William ordered pipes and tobacco, and some liquor for the Indians, and adjourned with a design to give them time to consider the principal objects of the council. But having been very weak, from his former indisposition, the fatigue brought on him a relapse, which in about two hours threw him into a fit, in which he suddenly expired.

Immediately on the death of Sir William Johnson, the Indians assembled in the greatest apparent concern, and confusion, and proposed sending off their runners, with belts of alarm, to all their nations.

But Col. Guy Johnson, the Deputy of Sir William, prevailed upon them to wait until the next morning, assuring them that Sir William had not been unmindful of their interests, in case of his decease; but had recommended his, (Col. Johnson's) appointment, as superintendent of Indian affairs ; assuring them, that he should early in the morning, give them more particular information, upon which they returned to their encampments.

Tuesday, July 12, 1774.

"On this day, Col. Guy Johnson assembled the chiefs, and addressed them as follows :

"Brothers :—As it is not conformable to your customs, that those who have suffered a great loss, should speak first, I should have declined addressing you, till after the ceremony of condolence, did you not express so strong a desire to send extraordinary messages through the nations, with the news of the late melancholy accident. Upon this occasion I am necessiated to advise you, lest it might occasion too great an alarm, that the worthy Sir William Johnson, agreeable to the desire you have often signified, recommended it to the consideration of the King, that I should be in his stead. His Majesty's answer is not yet arrived ; but there is no doubt, that from his esteem for all good and faithful Indians, of his doing what he should think best; and in the mean time, you may acquaint all the nations, that though I feel myself at present, unequal to the load, when I reflect on the conduct and character, of the great and good man, who left us yesterday ; yet as I have long lived under his direction, and transacted for many years his correspondences respecting you, I trust the Great Spirit will give me strength, and wisdom, to conduct these important matters, in some measure, oorresponding with his great example. It remains for you Brethren, to be strong, and steady, in your engagements, all which, I am well acquainted with, and to show your friendship to the English, and your respect and reverence for the memory of your great and good adviser, by supporting me, under this arduous undertaking, which if you do, you may always be assured of my sincere regard.

"Send these words through the nations; assuring them that the fire still burns, and the road is still open to this place; and let it be told Kayagshota, (who was sent to the Ohio, on a mission of peace) that he may be strong, and continue his good endeavors, for the preservation of peace, and the security of yourselves and your posterity, whose interest I shall be ever desirous to promote." A belt.

After which the Indians returned thanks, promising to forward the belt as directed, and to consider on the ceremony of condolence to be performed after Sir William's interment, requesting likewise, to be permitted to attend his funeral.

The corpse of Sir William Johnson was carried from Johnson Hall, to Johnstown, and deposited in the family vault, in the church which he erected, attended by upwards of two thousand persons, from the neighboring county, with the Indians, who behaved with the greatest decorum, and exhibited the most lively marks of sorrow. The pall was supported by his excellency, the Governor of New Jersey, the Judges of the Supreme Court of New York, and other persons of note, who happened to be at Johnstown at that time; and on their return from the funeral to Johnson Hall, the Indians acquainted Col. Johnson that they would perform the ceremony of condolence the next day.

Thursday, July 14th, 1774.

The chiefs of the Six Nations, assembled early in the morning, to perform the ceremony of condolence for the death of Sir William Johnson.

PRESENT—Guy Johnson, Esq., Dep'ty. Agent, Daniel Claus, Esq., Dep'ty. for Canada, James Duane, Esq., G. W. Bayard, Esq., St. John DeLancy, Esq., Col. Daniel Campbell, Mr. Jessup, Joseph Chew, Esq., and John Duncan, Esq.

Conoghquieson, Chief of Oneida, with three strings cleared the sight, &c.

Then with a double belt, covered the body.

Then with a belt of six rows, covered the grave, and addressed Col. Johnson, as follows, viz:

BROTHER:—It yields us vast pleasure, to find that the fire, which was in danger of being entirely extinguished by the great loss we have sustained, is for the present rendered bright by you. The good words which you have spoken to us yesterday, having revived us, and kept our young men within reasonable bounds, who would otherwise lost their senses ; we rejoice at it, and accordingly with this belt, we cause the fire to burn clear as usual at this place, and at Onondaga ; which are our proper fire places, and we hope the great King will approve and confirm it. A belt of 7 rows.

" Brother, with this belt, we sweep the fire place clean. Remove from it all impure and disagreeable objects, so that we may set round it, and consult together, for the public good as usual. A belt of 7 rows.

" Brother, with this belt, that when our ceremonies are performed, you will apply your attention to our affairs, and continue to give good advice to the young men, as your father did. A bunch of strings.

" Brother, we know that you must be loaded with grief on this melancholy occasion, we therefore cleanse your body, and wash your inside, with clear water, so that you may once more attend to, and proceed upon business.

" Brother, the heavy cloud which hung over you and us, has prevented us from seeing the sun. It is therefore our business with this string, to clear the sky which was overcast, and we likewise with this string, put the sun in its proper course, that it may perform the same as before, so that you may be able to see what is doing, and pursue the good works of peace. A belt of 6 rows.

Then added: " Brother, since it hath pleased the Great Spirit to take from us our great Brother Warraghigegy, who has long desired at our request, to put you in his place, we very much rejoice to find you ready to take this charge upon you, without which we should be in darkness, and great confusion. We are now once more happy, and with this belt we expect you to take care of our affairs, to follow his footsteps, and as you very well know his ways, and transactions with us, that you will continue to imitate them for the public good." A belt of 6 rows.

Then Tyerhansera, chief of the Mohawks, spoke as follows:

"BROTHER:—The business being so far happily set on foot again, we think it necessary to observe to you, that this is a very critical time, and that our Brother having suddenly died at a time when great troubles are begun to the southward, it is incumbent upon you, to be strong, and to follow closely his practices in all things, as you knew them. Our business with our Brother was nearly brought to a conclusion, and his last words to us, concerning the great troubles in Virginia, to withdraw our people, were answered by us in the papers lying before you.

"Brother, we must tell you it is the white people only, who prevent it; for if they did not make a practice of coming in great numbers with rum, into that country, our people would be wise, and come to our fire places; but they are tempted to stay there, and now Brother, we must desire you to be strong, and to use all your endeavors to put a stop to your people, and fulfilling his promise to us, that we may be enabled to bring them away, as you desire. Another thing Brother, we have to say, is to remind you, that at the Fort Stanwix Treaty in 1768, we gave up a great deal of land, which we did not expect would be suddenly overspread with white people; but we now see with concern, that they do not confine themselves within their limits, which must end in troubles. We therefore beg that they may be restrained and brought under some government. These things, Brother, and particularly the murders and robberies that your people commit, have kindled a flame, which is yet small, but unless quenched in time, will overspread the country, so that we can't stop it; we therefore hope for your vigorous endeavors to put it out."

Then Conoghquieson stood up and with a large black belt, said:

"BROTHER:—We now speak in the name of our whole confederacy, and dependents; expressing our thanks, that agreeable to our former request to Sir William Johnson, we now see you taking care of our affairs. We earnestly expect you to take care of them as that great man did, who promised you to us; and we desire, that you will send these our words to the great King, who we hope will regard our desires, and approve you, as the only person that knows us, and our affairs; that business may go on as formerly; otherwise in this alarming time of trouble, without your care and attention, our affairs will fall into great confusion, and all our good works will be destroyed. We beg therefore, that you will accept our good wishes, and that you will continue to take care of the great business in which we are all concerned." A black belt of 9 rows.

And then added that they would retire for the present and wait for Col. Johnson's answer, which he told them they should have in the afternoon.

P. M. Assembled as before:

PRESENT. His Excellency, Gov. Franklin, of New Jersey, Capt. Chapman, Mr. Bayard, Mr. Duane.

Col. Johnson addressed them as follows:

"I am extremely happy, that by your condolence, and our mutual performance of these ceremonies, occasioned by the death of your late worthy superintendent, I am now able to lift up my head, and proceed upon business of public concern; and am particularly glad that you join me, so heartily in making up the fire, which was very nigh being extinguished. Be assured that nothing shall be wanting on my part to preserve it. Brothers, I am very happy to find that my acting for the present, in consequence of your former desires, proves so agreeable to you, and you may be assured, that however unequal I am, to follow the steps of so great and experienced a man, I shall endeavor, so long as I am authorized, to do everything in my power, for the interest of the public and your own. But I expect at the same time, that your good behavior will continue as an encouragement to me, to follow his example." Col. Johnson then answered Tyorhansera as follows:

"Brother, I well remember the wise maxims that governed your late worthy adviser, in the business on which you came here last; and you may be assured, that I shall, to the utmost, strive to put his last words and promises into execution, by a faithful representation of your grievances, to those persons in authority, whose duty it is to correct the abuses of which you complain. But I cannot help thinking, that it is in your power to bring your people from among those tribes, who, by their daily practices, endeavor to bring a general reflection on your confederacy, and I trust that you will join heartily with Kayagshota in this good work, whereby you will pay a kind tribute to the memory of your deceased faithful friend, and show your influence over these your own people.

"Brothers, of the Six Nations dependent, I have heard

your words, and kindly thank you for the regard you express for me, and the desire you show for my conducting your affairs. This matter has already been laid before His Majesty, who regards all faithful Indians, and will act therein as he sees most fitting, with which determination it is your business to acquiesce. I shall, however, comply with your request; at the same time it is my duty to communicate your transactions to the General of the army, who is newly returned to this country, and has long known and regarded you; and whose authority will enable me to do what is necessary at present, and I earnestly desire that you shall act such a part as shall entitle you to the attention of government, by that fast hold of the chain, and giving all your assistance towards restoring peace in the country, and security to yourselves, as the only means of convincing His Majesty of your fidelity; and I desire that these my words, may go to the setting sun." A belt.

"Brothers, the purport of the intelligence that came from the Governor of Pennsylvania, in regard to the ravages committed by the Shawnees and others, in his Province, are of such a nature, that I expect that you will enable me to assure him, that you will immediately discountenance, and put an end to all such cruelties—otherwise, your reputation as a powerful confederacy, will greatly suffer in the eyes of the English, and the resentment of that Province may fall heavy on that deluded people, who have done so much mischief, without waiting for that justice which government was willing to afford to your complaints."

Conoghquieson then rose and said: "Brother, you all know that Kayagshota, with three of our people of the greatest consequence, are at present employed in the good work you recommend. But further to promote it, we have agreed to send this 'belt' forward, through the nations, with a deputation, to consist of two or three chiefs from each of our nations, to enforce it—and we are glad that the Governor of New Jersey is present, to hear what we have said, as he may assist in making our sentiments and grievances known to the neighboring Governors."

To which His Excellency answered: "that the inhabitants of New Jersey had no concern in any of the disputes, but were well disposed towards them, and that the Indians might recollect, that three men were formerly executed under his administration, and that, through his inclination to do them strict justice. But that nevertheless, he would be aiding in promoting peace and harmony between the English and the Indians."

They were then treated with pipes and tobacco, as is usual, after which they adjourned.

Friday, July 15.

Col. Johnson assembled the Indians, and spoke as follows:

"Brothers:—It pleases me much to find you unanimous in your late resolutions, as it is a proof of your sense and fidelity; at the same time, it is so essential to your importance and happiness, that I will not entertain a doubt of your determined intentions, to check the incursions of your dependants, who run about like drunken men, and ought to be disarmed, by those who are sober and peaceable, lest the English should have to raise their powerful arm against them, which might have dreadful consequences. On my part, you may be assured, I shall communicate your grievances respecting the affairs at the Southward, to the Governors interested, who will do their utmost to restore order and tranquility."

The Indians returned thanks for this speech, and shook hands, purposing to return home the day following, and in the afternoon the Colonel had a private interview with Sayenquaraghta,* and some other principal men, to whom he pointed out the danger to which the Ohio Senecas would be exposed, unless the present disturbances were accommodated; and concluded with advising them, by all means, to withdraw their people from the rest, who were endeavoring to alienate them from their own confederacy.

Saturday, July 16.

"Col. Johnson gave a handsome present to the chiefs, and to those who were instrumental in apprehending the murderers, as well as to those who had acted a good part on receiving the news of the late murders on the Ohio, after which, they took their leave, with many expressions of satisfaction, having first presented the chiefs, who were to go to the Southward, and explain the purport of their embassy."

November, 1774.

Literal translation of the message of the Six Nations to the Shawneese, etc.:

"YOUNGER BROTHERS:—We are come running to you from the great fire place. Take notice of what I have to say, as I am the older brother. It happened that you came lately to the middle of the council house to our fire place of peace, for the Six Nation Confederacy. You

---

*Old King, the grand father of Young King, who subsequently resided at Buffalo Creek.

there spoke to us on a subject we did not understand. We would not give ear to, or agree to it, as our fire place is for peace ; and we tell you, we will only listen to affairs of peace there.

"Younger Brothers, we are now here, and we tell you before all the Nations, who observe you, and see all your bad works, we have been twice here to advise you to peace ; but you have not attended, and in compliance with our ancient customs, we are come the third time, to tell you, you must be at peace. This is the third time, and the last, that you shall hear from us, if you do not hearken to us. We charge you to consider the case of your warriors, your women, and your children. And we desire you sachems, to use your authority over your people, that they may mind what we say. Leave the business of war. Repent, and mind peace alone, and then you will be preserved. Quarrelsome people are dangerous ; we advise you for your good, for we pity you, and we know from our superintendent, that the King is inclined to desire that you should be at peace, and has sent orders to Virginia to promote it. Mind our words, they are strong. They are the words of the Six Nations ; who are the heads of the confederacy. All the northern nations have left their belts in our hands, and referred themselves to our government, and determination. They have joined their words to us, who are the head of the whole ; and you now see them all in us, here present ; who are now sent with authority to charge you to follow our advice." A very large belt is then given.

CHAPTER XIV.

The death of Sir William Johnson, was a great calamity to the Indians. They had for nearly forty years looked up to him, as to a father. They had entire confidence, not only in his wisdom, but in his friendship. Hence his unbounded influence over them. They had observed for years, his increasing infirmities, and did not conceal from him their own anxiety in regard to it; and it had been in view of these often expressed fears, of his sudden dissolution, that he had recommended the appointment of his son-in-law, Col. Guy Johnson, to be his successor as general superintendent of Indian affairs. Col. Guy Johnson accordingly succeeded to his office, but not to his influence over the Indians.

Having long been deputy superintendent under his father-in-law, he was entirely familiar with the duties of the office, which he was called to fill; but he does not seem to have possessed that wisdom and discretion, which so eminently characterized his illustrious predecessor.

The political troubles which for some time, had agitated the public mind, among the whites, grew more violent, and soon culminated in open rebellion against the King.

There are other versions of the death of Sir William Johnson, differing somewhat in their details, but lacking the authenticity of that just related. The time, and circumstances of his death, were such as to favor the idea that it was premeditated; and the idea is still prevalent to a considerable extent, among the common people in the vicinity of his former residence, that he preferred death, to meeting the crisis which he saw was inevitable, of deciding between disloyalty to his King, or separation from the people he loved, and by whom he was beloved, and respected. The tradition is (says Stone in his life of Brant) that on the day of his decease he had received dispatches from England which were handed him while sitting in Court, and with which, he immediately left the Court House, and walked to his own house. These dispatches it was afterwards reported, contained instructions to him, to use his influence with the Indians, in behalf of the Crown, in the event of hostilities.

Another version of the tradition is that on the day in question, he had received dispatches from Boston, the complexion of which in his own mind, indicated, that a civil war was near and inevitable. In such an event, he saw that he must either prove recreant to his principles, or take part against the Crown; and to avoid either alternative, it has been extensively believed that he put an end to his own life. But there is no just ground for this uncharitable conclusion. It is true, he had on the evening of the 24th, received dispatches from Massachusetts, the tenor of which, by excitement may have hastened the malady, to which his system was predisposed. It was a busy day at Johnstown; the Circuit Court was in session, at which however, Sir William was not present, being engaged in holding a treaty with some of the Six Nations. In the course of his speech to the Indians on that occasion, he alluded to the dispatches he had received, and stated to them, that troubles were brewing between the Americans and their King, advising them not to abandon the cause of the latter, who had always been benevolent, and kind to them. "Whatever may happen," said the Baronet, "you must not be shaken out of your shoes."

In the afternoon of that day he was taken with a fit: Col. Johnson his son, was absent at the old Fort, distant nine miles; an express was sent for him, and mounting a fleet English blood horse, he rode for the Hall, in all possible haste; his horse fell dead when within three quarters of a mile of the house, having run upwards of eight miles in fifteen minutes. The Colonel hired the horse of some one standing by, and pushed forward to the Hall; on entering the room, he found his father in the arms of a faithful domestic, who attended upon his person. He spoke to his parent, but received no answer, and in a few minutes afterward the Baronet expired, of apoplexy, beyond a doubt. This was early in the evening, while the Judges of the Court were at supper in the village, one mile distant. A young Mohawk Indian entered their apartment, and announced the event.

The history of the private life of Sir William Johnson remains somewhat in obscurity. It has been said that his wife who bore the title of Lady Johnson, was a German Emigrant, who with her family were sold for their passage, (as was customary then, in all the colonies,) she was purchased by Sir William, and became his lawful wife, else his son by her could not have inherited his father's title and estate, which it is admitted he did. After the death of Lady Johnson, Miss Molly Brant (as she was called) was received into his family, as has been already stated. She seems to have borne herself with propriety, and it is said was greatly beloved and respected during the life of Sir William, for her many amiable qualities. She was undoubtedly a woman of superior abilities, as she seems to have exerted a wide influence, particularly over her own people, which was of great service to Sir William. He must have had seven half-breed children; three sons and four daughters, as it appears from the public records that he partitioned the tract of land called "the Royal grant," equally among them.

The rebellion which broke out in Boston, soon began to show itself in the valley of the Mohawk. The celebrated "Boston Port Bill" had gone into operation only a month before Sir William Johnson's death; very soon after, a public meeting was held in the Palatine District, at which strong resolutions were passed, seconding the proposition for a general Congress, for mutual consultation in regard to the existing state of political affairs in all the colonies.

The Congress met in September, 1774, and adopted a declaration of rights, and agreed upon an address to the King. The papers put forth by that assembly, were characterised by marked ability, and had a powerful effect upon the public mind. The Provincial Assembly of New York, was the only legislature in the colonies that withheld its approbation from the proceedings of the congress. The Johnsons, and their adherents in the valley of the Mohawk, were particularly active in counteracting the revolutionary spirit, which began to manifest itself. At this juncture, the influential loyalists of Tryon county, made a demonstration against the proceedings of the congress of the preceding autumn. A declaration in opposition to those proceedings, probably drawn up by the Johnsons, received the signature of a majority of the grand jurors, and a great portion of the magistrates of the county. This created great excitement among the whigs, who were in attendance at the court in Johnstown, and led to public meetings, and the appointment of committees, in almost every district of the county. One of these meetings was interrupted by the Johnsons, Col. Claus, Col. John Butler, and a large number of their retainers, armed with swords and pistols. Guy Johnson mounted a high stoop, and harangued the people at length, and with great vehemence; at length, becoming so abusive that he was interrupted in his speech, by a whig of the name of Sammons, who pronounced him a liar. Johnson seized Sammons by the throat, a scuffle ensued, in which others became engaged, and clubs, whips, swords, and pistols were used, but no one seriously hurt.

This proceeding on the part of the Johnsons, greatly exasperated the whigs of Tryon county, and a meeting was held at Cherry Valley, and strong counter declarations were passed, condemning the proceedings of the loyalists at Johnstown, and approving in the most unequivocal terms, of the proceedings of the congress.

Strong suspicions began to be entertained that the Johnsons, Butlers, (father and son,) and Col. Claus, were endeavoring to alienate the Indians from the colonists, and prepare their minds in the event of open hostilities, to take up the hatchet against them. This led to the necessity, on the part of the colonists, to use corresponding measures to counteract these influences, and cultivate a friendly interest among the Indians of the Six Nations; or at least to secure their neutrality. To this end a correspondence was opened with them through the Rev. Mr. Kirkland, a Missionary among them, by the provincial congress of Massachusetts. An address was forwarded to the Six Nations, to be presented to the Chief Sachem of the Mohawks, and by him communicated to all the rest of the Six Nations. The congress was not mistaken in addressing the patriotism of Mr. Kirkland, who, although one of the most amiable, and spiritual minded of men, had, it would seem, already incurred the displeasure, or at least excited the suspicion of Col. Johnson; as the following letter, which he wrote "to the committee of Albany," will disclose:

"Cherry Valley, Jan. 9, 1775.

GENTLEMEN :—

I am much embarrassed at present. You have doubtless heard that Col. Johnson has orders from government to remove the dissenting missionaries from the Six Nations, till the difficulties between Great Britain and the colonies are settled. In consequence of which, he has forbidden my return to my people at Oneida. He has since given encouragement that I may re-visit them after the congress is closed, but to be plain, I have no dependence at all on his promises of this kind. He appears unreasonably jealous of me, and has forbidden my speaking a word to the Indians, and threatened me with confinement, if I transgress. All he has against me, I suppose to be, a suspicion that I have interpreted, to the Indians, the doings of the continental congress, which has undeceived them, and too much opened their eyes, for Col. Johnson's purpose. I confess to you, gentlemen, that I have been guilty of this, if it be a transgression.

The Indians found out that I had received the abstracts of said congress, and insisted upon knowing the contents. I could not deny them, notwithstanding my cloth, though in all other respects I have been extremely cautious not to meddle in matters of a political nature. I apprehend that my interpreting the doings of the congress to a number of their Sachems, has done more real good to the cause of the country, or to the cause of truth and justice, than five hundred pounds in presents would have effected."

Mr. Kirkland undoubtedly spoke the honest truth in this letter. His influence, particularly among the Oneidas, was great, and deservedly so. "Had he (says Col. Stone,) undertaken the task, he might, beyond all doubt, and easily, have persuaded the Indians to espouse the cause of the Colonies. But he did no such thing; or at least he avoided the exertion of his influence any further than to persuade them to the adoption of a mutual course of policy. This determination was an act of their own volition, after listening to the interpretation of the proceedings of the Congress."

The following notice of this eminent man is from a note by the editor of the Colonial Documentary History. A copy of his manuscript journal, of his first visit to the Senecas in 1764–5, has been preserved, and is deposited with the Buffalo Historical Society, and exhibits a degree of self-sacrificing devotion to the work he had undertaken, very rare in one so young, and which his whole life was a most striking illustration. This journal is interesting on several accounts, and serves not only to exhibit the character of the missionary, but it also exhibits the Indian character, and the social and political condition of the Senecas, at the time he first visited them.

"Rev. Samuel Kirkland, a distinguished missionary among the New York Indians, was born at Norwich, Connecticut, in 1742; was sent to the Mohawk Indians to learn their language. He entered Princeton College in 1762. In 1764 he returned to the Mohawk country to teach school, and perfect himself in that language, and received his collegiate degree in 1765. He was employed among the Senecas in 1765 and 1766. On the 19th of June of the latter year, he was ordained at Lebanon, as a missionary to the Indians, and in July following, took up his residence at Oneida castle. He continued to labor among that tribe for forty years. During the revolutionary war, he was in the pay of the United States, and in 1779, was brigade chaplain in Gen. Sullivan's campaign against the Indians of western New York. After the peace, he remained among the Oneidas, and in 1788, assisted at the great Indian council for the extinction of their title to the Genesee country. So sensible was the State government of the value of his services, that in the year 1789, it granted him a tract of land two miles square, in the present town of Kirkland, whither he immediately removed. In 1792, he made a liberal endowment of land, for the purpose of founding a school, which was originally called the 'Hamilton Oneida Academy,' and has since been incorporated under the name of 'Hamilton College.' After a life of much public usefulness, he died on the 28th of February, 1808. His remains were carried to the church, in Clinton, Oneida county, and interred near his house. A noble man, the friend of his race, both red and white; a long line of good deeds proclaim his zeal and liberality, in promoting the interests of religion and learning."

1764. JOURNAL OF REV. SAMUEL KIRKLAND.

Nov. 16th. Arrived at Johnson Hall; kindly and politely received by Sir William, who expressed his approbation of my design, and wished me success; when I returned from Onohaghkwage, would have me come to his house and make it my home, till I proceeded to the westward.

24th. Set out from Johnson Hall, accompanied by Joseph Woolley, whom I was to introduce to Onohaghkwage, in the capacity of a school master, to instruct their children, and learn their language. The second night, lodged at Cherry Valley; treated very kindly by Capt. Wells. The next day engaged Col. Harper, who had considerable knowledge (as I was informed,) of the Indian language, to go with me as a pilot and interpreter.

27th. Reached a small village a few miles on this side Onohaghkwage, the residence of Good Peter, (commonly so called from his religious character;) were obliged to wait for nearly an hour on the banks of the river, and late in the evening, before we could make the Indians hear and come with a canoe to carry us over the river.

28th. My arrival was welcomed by Good Peter, with great cordiality, and they were glad I had brought a person to teach their children, and learn their language, acquiring the knowledge of which, would render him of great service to their nation, and they would adopt him into their tribe. They promised to take the best care of him they could. Joseph Woolley expressed his thanks to them. Good Peter then made some remarks upon my mission to the Senecas. He apprehended it was too soon, that their minds were not yet calmed after the tumults and troubles of the late war. However, he knew some very influential characters among them, who were great friends to Sir William, and had always been friendly to the Americans. He then mentioned the names of a number, and further observed that notwithstanding there were some friendly Indians among them, he considered it a very bold, if not a hazardous enterprise, but if my heart was bent upon it, God was Almighty, and everywhere present; he could preserve me there as well as anywhere else, and from his very heart he wished God the Father, and his son Jesus Christ, to be with me and protect me, as I was professedly going to publish the good news of His gospel. We tarried here one day to rest and refresh ourselves, and the next morning took an affectionate leave. Poor Joseph Woolley could not refrain shedding a tear at my departure; I tried to console him, so also did Good Peter. Returned to Sir William Johnson's, after stopping a short time at Cherry Valley, and making some consideration to my pilot and interpreter, who had been very kind to me. I tarried at Sir William Johnson's until the 17th of January, 1765, for want of convoy. There was a Seneca Indian, for part of the time, at Sir William's, but he did not choose to venture me with him alone I occasionally visited a Mr. Wemple, at Caghwage, (about five miles from Johnson Hall, as he had considerable knowledge of the Seneca language, though rather a bad pronunciation. I found I could pick up a little from him, and I wished to improve every opportunity to progress in the Seneca language. At length arrived a company of Senecas, two of which were distinguished for their humanity, and obliging dispositions. Sir William told me he would trust me in the care of these two Indians, and in a few days he would make the necessary preparations, if I chose it, and would venture to set out in such severe weather, with such a body of snow upon the ground. I returned my thanks to him, for his extraordinary attentions to me, and told him I chose to undertake the journey at all hazards, as I trusted I was in a good cause, and hoped I was sincere in undertaking it. He advised me at the same time, to cultivate an acquaintance with these two Indians, whom he had chosen for my convoy.

I derived great advantage, both for my journey and mission, while at Johnson Hall, from the description Sir William gave me of their situation, their manners and customs, their orderly and decent behavior in their public councils, and the general character of almost every chief man in the Six Nations; their talents, and prevailing dispositions. He gave me a very good account of Sagwayeangwlaghton, with whom he expected I should take up my residence; also, the venerable old chief of Onondaga, called by the white people "Bunt," in Indian Tsinryoyota, i. e. the sinew. Sir William considered him as one of the first sachems in the Six Nations, for good sense, humanity, and integrity; and he had a grave and dignified appearance; a very large and well built man, inclining to be very gross, and corpulent. He was treated with very great respect, and veneration, by all the Five Nations, a few Senecas excepted. Sir William likewise told me that if I was cordially received by the Senecas, I should, in a week or two, be adopted into some one of their principal families, and that I must pay particular attention to my new relations, and it would give me the liberty of applying to them for anything I wanted. Probably I might receive this adoption into the head sachem's family. It is usually performed with some ceremony, a short speech made on the occasion. He further advises me not to ridicule any of the traditions of their fathers, till I was master of their language, and then I might take them up gently and on national grounds.

Jan'y 16. He called these two Indians into the sitting room, and delivered to them a speech, of considerable length; and then handed them a large belt of wampum, in confirmation of what he had spoken on the occasion, and told them to deliver it to the Seneca chiefs in full council, and the purport of his speech which they had heard from his own mouth. They replied that he might keep his mind quiet, they should be faithful to their trust, and they believed he never knew them otherwise, although there are many bad Indians in their nation; and if any evil should befall this young white brother by the way, they would share with him, or both fall by his side. But they apprehended no danger from any quarter. He then told them that he had made up a small bundle for each of them, and with such articles of clothing as they would find very comfortable at this cold season. He also told them, that I was very anxious to see their country, and learn their language, and by and by be able tell to them some good news. They must have their packs ready to swing up in the morning.

Sir William then gave me just a sketch of what he had communicated to them, and said it was unnecessary to give a minute detail, as he had some days ago given me the purport of what his address to the Seneca chiefs would be, and he was very much hurried in answering some letters of importance lately come to hand, and that he would have as much bean bread and hard buiscuit, put up, as I thought I could carry, my convoy would not carry much for me, as he had loaded them pretty well himself, but he should tell them if any store failed before our arrival, I must share with them.

Jan'y 17. This morning after breakfast, took quite an affectionate leave of Sir William, and set out for the Senecas country. The snow was very deep, and dry, supposed to be four feet. After we had passed the German Flatts, was obliged to put on my snow shoes. I carried my pack of provisions, with a few articles of clothing, and a few books, the whole not weighing more than forty pounds. My convoy was so kind as to carry my two blankets. The first night, we lodged in a log hut on the north side of the Mohawk river. The next night, we encamped in the woods, about twenty miles from Oneida. My convoy unslung their packs, and were very active in making the necessary preparations for a comfortable night's repose. One of them went with his little axe to cutting wood for a fire, the other shoveling away the snow, and then gathering an armful of boughs of hemlock for my bed. I was forbid to do anything but set on a log that was near by, and rest myself. He went now to the assistance of his comrade in packing wood; after the fire was kindled, he ran and brought another armfull of hemlock boughs.

By half an hour after sunset, we had a fine fire, which soon dried and warmed the hemlock boughs, their aromatic flavor seemed to perfume the air, and made it exceedingly agreeable, and pleasant. The one who went to cut fire wood and back (it) to the hut, came in the last time all of a dripping sweat. By this time, we were well pleased to relish a good supper. After they had rested and smoked a pipe, I told them I would take something out of my pack for supper, excepting bread, and asked one of them to take his small kettle, wash it out clean at the brook, and bring it back full of water. A wooden trammel was made and two crotches were put up in a short time. I then took a ham out of my pack, (to tell the honest truth I wish to have it lightened) and cut off a number of slices which I wished to have broiled. They soon cut some sticks about two and a half feet long, sharpened one end, and split the other, part of the way down; they put two or three slices of the ham into one of these sticks, and tied the top with a strip of bark, to prevent their falling out, then stuck the sharpened end into the ground, the top leaning towards the fire, a bark put under to catch the drippings. These were new scenes to me, but highly gratifying. I again opened my pack, and took out a large drinking of tea, which I procured last. I could not immediately get weaned from it. The kettle boiled, and I flung in the tea, and gave it a handsome boiling. The ham by this time was done; my convoy provided bread. The ham (was) put upon clean bark, took the tea kettle off; I asked for wooden spoons; we sat round our dish and ate like brethren; and a better supper I have seldom made. Could I have conversed freely with them, we should have had a sociable evening. One of my convoy was a sensible man, very conversible, and of a good disposition.

The next day we reached Kanonwalohule, the principal town of the Oneidas. There we lodged, and were kindly entertained. After being made acquainted with my mission, they expressed some concern for me, and proposed my tarrying with them till the spring, or for a year, and then visit the Senecas. I thanked them, but told them that I could not relinquish my design, till providence stopped up my path, or hedged up my way. We proceeded on our journey next morning, and it took us two days pretty diligent and smart traveling on snow shoes, to reach Onondaga, some time in the evening. Several of their sachems were convened at the great council house, which was nearly eighty feet long, and contained four fires. They proposed my going to rest, as I appeared to them to be much fatigued, and observed to me, that it was not their custom to receive a message of peace in the darkness of the night, but in the light of day. To-morrow morning (said they,) we will assemble, and hear what you have to say. I acknowledged I was pretty much fatigued with the last two days march, my ankles were swelled, not being much accustomed to travel on snow shoes. My convoy were very kind to help me along, by going before, and making a track for me. This was of considerable relief to me; but if I made a misstep or blundered over a log and fell, three or four rods in the rear, they would look back and stop till I came up. I commonly kept within two yards of the hindmost. I presently observed that the second, took the place of the first, every three or four miles. I offered to take my turn. "No, no," said they, "we are to make a path for you, and not you to make a path for us. Sir William Johnson would be very angry if he knew we let you do so."

The next morning about ten o'clock, they assembled in crowds at this great council house, the mansion of their chief sachem. When they were all seated, and their pipes lighted, the chief sachem made declaration, with an audible voice, that they were ready to hear whatever message

I had to deliver. Sir William had directed the one who had charge of the belt, to communicate his speech, or message, to the Senecas, at Onondaga, as they were the central council fire, of all the Six Nations, and it was a piece of respect, they claimed as due to them, from time immemorial. With this he introduced the subject of his message. One of my convoy arose, taking the belt of wampum in his left hand, that his right hand might be at liberty for action, when necessary to give emphasis. He delivered the purport of Sir William's speech, with a good grace, and by additions, and explanations, spoke nearly three quarters of an hour. At the end of every sentence, they express their assent, if pleasing to them, by crying out one after another, or twenty, all at once, at-hoetogus-ke, (nat-hootogus-keh,) i. e., it is so, very true. When my convoy had finished his address, the venerable old chief replied, and spoke like a Demonsthenes, for more than half an hour. But I lost all the good of it, for want of an interpreter. I found one who understood the Onondaga language pretty well, but spoke English very poorly. So soon as the speech making was over, this venerable old chief rose and was coming towards me. I instantly rose and met him half way. He took me by the hand, and embraced me, kissed one cheek, and then the other. I supposed I must return the compliment; I accordingly kissed his red cheeks, not disgusted at all with the remains of the paint, and grease, with which they had lately been besmeared. He gave me many blessings, while he held me by the hand. Then came one after another, to shake hands with me, perhaps nearly one hundred. The board of sachems all gave me their benediction, in different ways; or the modes of expression varied, by almost every one. The young men said little, only gave me their hands; some of the chiefs congratulated me also.

After the council had broke up, I found I could get a great deal more out of him who spoke poor English, in the way of familiar conversation. He tried to give me some account of the old chief's reply, to the Seneca who produced the belt of wampum from Sir William, but it was delivered in such high language, he could not himself understand it all. He thought it was the most extraordinary speech he ever heard.

In the afternoon we took leave, and proceeded on our journey; encamped about eight miles beyond the town. We rose early and took some refreshment, (but it was not equal to our supper the first night we encamped in the woods,) and the next night we encamped near the outlet of the Nascon lake, a very severe days' march.

We then went on as we could hold it, my fellow travelers or convoy, were very kind and attentive to me, and would have me walk fast or slow, and rise early, and encamp early, just as I pleased. The next night after we had encamped, and I had pulled off my Indian leggins, or stockings, one of them observed that my ankles were very much swelled. He said I must go with him to a small run of water, just at hand, and he would bathe and rub them, and if they were not better by the next night, he should scarify them. This, said he, is our Indian practice, and it always gives relief. The next day we rose early, took some refreshment, and proceeded on our journey. I found my ankles much more limber and pliable, than they were yesterday, which I think I must ascribe to the bathing.

Feb'y. 7th. Arrived at Kanadasegea, their principal town, this side Genesee. According to Indian custom, we halted at the skirts of the town, sat down upon a log, to rest, and lighted our pipes. Presently, a runner was dispatched from the town, and came in full speed to us, and asked whence we came, and where we were going, and what was our desire. One of the convoy answered: we are only bound to this place, and wish to be conducted to the house of the chief sachem. He then told us to follow him, and we soon entered the chief sachem's house, and were cordially received. The speaker, one of my convoy, just informed the chief, that he had a message from Sir William Johnson, to communicate to their chiefs, so soon as they could conveniently assemble. He immediately replied, you must rest yourselves, and take some refreshments. To morrow, I will have the sachems and head warriors, collected in the council house, and we will hear what you have to say. Possess your minds in peace, this night; I am glad to see you. We had a great deal of conversation in the evening, in respect to foreign news, and the state of the colonies. The chief sachem inquired if they were all in peace. The speaker of my convoy entertained the sachems, very agreeably, for some hours in the evening. But I pretty soon lay down to rest me, one of my convoy brought me my blankets, and the sachem's good lady spread them on a bunk, one side of the room, and told me I should sleep there, and loaned me a new blanket to keep me warm.

Feb'y. 8th. The Indians convened a little before noon, when we were invited to the council house, and fortunately for me, a Dutch trader, who had lived many years among the Senecas, had just arrived on his way to Niagara, who had a tolerable understanding of their language, especially for common conversation. He spoke English intelligibly, though very incorrectly. Sir William Johnson's address to them was delivered. It was received with great applause, except by a small minority, whom I observed were silent on the occasion, and I did not quite like their appearance. The head sachem, Sakayengwalaghton, (old king,) made a very handsome, and animated reply. Thanked Sir William for his introducing this young white brother; thanked the minister from Teyorhens, that is, from the east, for sending this young brother to teach them good things, and thanked me, that I had so much love for Indians, as to undertake this long journey, and at such a season of the year, with an unusual depth of snow on the ground. He saluted my convoy, and thanked them for their care of me, through the long and tedious journey; then handed the belt of wampum to the sachem who sat next to him, and it passed round the whole circle; some would strike it up and down with the hand, and perhaps make some remarks; others would look upon it, apparently with the intenseness of thought, and not open their lips, and then pass it to the next. This ceremony took up more than twenty minutes by my watch, as I was determined to notice all their movements on the occasion. I was invited to continue with the head sachem, until some more convenient place could be provided for me. In the course of a week, while this Dutchman tarried with me, I had frequent opportunities of conversing with them, though by a poor interpreter, and they were continually visiting me, and some of them would ask me who put it into my mind, and influenced me to leave my father's house, and my country, to come so many hundred miles, to see Indians, and live among them. I answered them in general, I believe to their satisfaction.

The beginning of the second week, after my arrival, the head Sachem convened a number of the chiefs, and requested me to walk into the council house, and I soon observed that most of his family were present, and were sitting by themselves. In a short time one of their chiefs, who was a good speaker, called for their attention. He had a few words to say to them.

"BROTHERS:—Open your ears, and your eyes, you see here our white brother, who has come from a great distance, and (is) recommended to us by our great chief, Sir William Johnson, who has enjoined it upon us, to be kind to him, and make him comfortable, and protect him to the utmost of our power. He comes to do us good.

"Brothers:—This young brother of ours has left his father's house, his mother, and all his relations; we must now provide for him a home. I am appointed to make this declaration to you, that our head Sachem adopts him into his family. He will be a father to him and his wife, a mother, and his sons and daughter, his brothers and sisters, and conduct towards him agreeable to that relation."

I then rose and took the head Sachem by the hand, and thanked him, and said, I wished the Great Spirit would make me a blessing to his family. I then shook hands with his wife and children, and with the whole who were convened on the occasion, both chiefs and head warriors, and some of the head women were present. A smile of cheerfulness sat on every countenance, and I could not refrain from dropping a tear of joy and gratitude, for the kind providence, which had protected me through my long journey; brought me to the place of my desire, and given me so kind a reception, among these poor savage Indians. After some days, my newly adopted father, Sakayenqwalaghton, took me to a small council, consisting of his chief men, (and) a few warriors. They informed me that Sir William Johnson had given them a strict charge to treat me kindly, and to provide the best house in the village for my stated residence, and make me comfortable as they possibly could, in their present circumstances. We have concluded (said they,) that neither the council house, nor your father's house, would be agreeable, as they are continually exposed to company. Here is a small house, just at hand in full view of both the former, occupied by a small family, the man with his wife, with a niece of theirs, and the man is one of the best in all the town. He is what we call a good man, a sober, and temperate man, and honest; he tells no lies; he is likewise very industrious, always at work, doing something, and a man of few words. We have agreed with him to take you into his house. To-morrow you will move, and change your present unsettled condition, for a stated residence, and (one) much more convenient.

I thanked them heartily, and most sincerely; and I endeavored to tell them, in my broken style, that I always had hoped in God, the Great Spirit, that he would protect and preserve me, and if I might do any good to the poor Senecas, he would give me a kind reception among them, and give them a disposition to hear God's Word, from the Holy Book, so soon as I might acquire a knowledge of their language. That their kind treatment of me, since my arrival, far surpassed my expectations. The next day I moved, accompanied by my adopted father; found everything agreeable. A bunk was ready made for my lodging place, in one corner of the room, and near enough to the fire. Here, I applied myself diligently to learn their language, though I had already acquired the knowledge of the names of things, with some verbs. By the help of these two words, tointashchnay ate, i. e., speak it again, and otkayason, i. e., what do you call this? I daily progressed. But alas! how soon the scene is changed, and my bright prospects are beclouded, and overspread with an impenetrable gloom. The fourth night after I had taken up my lodging with my new landlord, I was waked up out of my sleep about three o'clock in the morning, by the noise of a dismal sobbing. I instantly inquired in Indian, "what has happened?" She (the wife of the landlord,) replied, hawaayou, i. e., "he is dead." I went to the bed, and felt of his pulse, but there was not the least motion, also at the jugular vein, no sign of life, or I would have bled him. I asked if he complained yesterday of being sick. Oh, no, said she, never sick. I tried to speak a word of consolation to her, but I was so overwhelmed by this awful and sudden event, I could scarcely speak for a few minutes, and returned to my bed-side, my thoughts would fly backwards and forwards, foreboding evil to come. I felt the need of immediate Divine aid and support; my heart was full. I could not help crying out, oh my God, and my Savior, I have sinned times and ways without number, yet I am permitted by thy word to inquire of thee concerning thy judgments. What can be thy design in this dark and mysterious providence, by the sudden and altogether unexpected death of the man with whom I had so lately come to reside, for my comfort, and usefulness. Thy ways are a mighty deep! Thy judgments past finding out, I cannot fathom them. But I know thou art holy, and wise. Oh my God, dost thou not approve of my mission. Hast thou not prospered, and comforted me through all my journey to the place of my desire? and can it be that thou hast brought me here to slay me by the hands of savages. That my life must atone, in their view, for the life of this man, who hath died so suddenly, and mysteriously. Oh my God, it cannot be; thou art holy, and thine infinite wisdom, knoweth not to err. Oh most merciful and gracious God, give me a heart to submit to thy decrees, to adore thy providence, and forever praise thee for redeeming love. Oh most gracious God, comfort and support this afflicted family. How long I prayed, I could not tell. I several times thought the sobbing and crying ceased, while I spoke with an audible voice. What ardent desire I had of understanding their language, or having a good interpreter, on this truly afflicting and melancholly occasion.

In the morning my father came in, and addressed the bereaved widow. Then turned to me and said, it was a dark morning; wished me to compose my mind, and possess myself in peace, and it may be we shall see good by and by. You must know, my son, as you understand the word of God, that God in very deed, must do as He pleases. I told him that since the morning, God had given me great composure of mind, and I could rejoice in God, and I myself, as well as others, were in his hands, and that He would do what was right.

When the Indians came in to lay out the body, I

thought it proper for me to withdraw, and visit my father, the head sachem, and try to have a little conversation with him. I was presently given to understand that runners were dispatched to announce the sorrowful tidings to six or seven villages, and that the funeral would not be attended till the clan, or tribe, of the deceased, should have notice, and give their attendance, perhaps they would generally be here by to-morrow noon, and some at a greater distance, by next day morning. I called in at the afflicted house, several times during the day, but did not tarry long; the house was full of mourners. I took a look at the corpse, whenever I went in; I perceived that, attracted their attention, and they seemed pleased with it; and I believe they considered me a hearty mourner. I tried to get in the woods privately, for a little retirement, but soon relinquished my purpose from the depth of the snow, and the Indians were continually traveling backwards and forwards in the beaten paths.

The next day by noon, there was a considerable collection of the friends of the deceased, and they began to counsel. I soon found by prudent inquiry, that the circumstances of this man's death, had given a general alarm; and that there was a party rather unfriendly to me, who intended to charge it upon me. I went into the council house, and sat down at one end for some time, but the countenances of many of them, were very forbidding. I soon determined that was no place for me. My adopted father came out before night, and observed to me that it was good that I went into the council house, and it was good that I did not stay long before I came out. He again wished me to possess my mind in peace, that he should not quit the council house, till all was settled, and done well. He smiled, and appeared cheerful, or at least tried to, but I plainly saw he had a weight upon his mind. The next day by noon, the council house was crowded, though nearly eighty feet long. I once peeped in, to take a view of them, about sun an hour high; the corpse was interred. Perhaps a hundred and fifty women and girls attended; no male, besides myself, except the grave digger, accompanied the corpse to the grave. I saw the corpse just before the lid was fastened, or even put on. He was neatly dressed with a clean white shirt, black shroud blanket, scarlet leggins, a pair of new moccasins, and curiously painted; his pipe, tomahawk, tobacco pouch, flint steel, and punk, were put into the coffin, and placed on both sides of his head. I was careful at the time to make no remarks, nor ask any questions.

When they left the house, and were carrying the corpse to the grave, they sung the most mournful ditty I ever heard; a small number of them seemed to keep the time and rise and fall pretty much together; others followed, and some screamed and yelled like dogs. Such a scene I never beheld before. It produced a variety of feelings in my breast; finally, a feeling of tender pity and compassion toward them prevailed, considering their ignorance, and superstition. I was advised to sleep this evening at the house of my elder brother. They accordingly brought over my bedding and a knapsack, containing my books and clothes. This brother, called Tekanadie, lived in an old block house, built by the direction of Sir William Johnson, in the year 1754–5, with a view to prevent the French influence among them. He intended to have a captain's company stationed there, and occupy this block house, with two or three small field pieces. No sooner was the house built, than they sent a delegation with full powers from their nation, to inform Sir William, that he need not be at the trouble of sending any of his troops there, that they were abundantly sufficient to man it themselves. A very decent way, of forbidding him sending his troops.

My eldest brother only occupied the lower part of this building, except in warm weather. The upper story was rather difficult of access. He told me I might stay there, in peace and quietness, and no one know where I was. He loaned me a bear's skin and blanket, to keep me warm. My sister gave me a small bit of venison, and a dish of samp pottage, just before I went to bed. This was very acceptable, as I had been fasting for nearly thirty-six hours. I plainly discovered by this time, that some of my family, and others who had expressed a friendship for me, were anxious for my safety. But by some means or other, which I believe could be no other than divine aid, the gracious spiritual presence of my Maker, God Almighty, I enjoyed a degree of composure and tranquility of mind, beyond what I ever expected. I was not stupid or insensible, but rather filled with life and self control. I slept sweetly for a few hours, but it was rather a night of reflection, meditation, and self examination. * * In the morning I was informed that they had sat in council a great part of the night, that they had sent to Oswego for a keg of rum, to give a relish to the funeral or burial feast, which was to be celebrated this evening. I could not get sight of my father, he stuck close to the council. In the afternoon, my younger brother, very pleasantly, and with apparent affection, proposed we should take our guns, and go out a mile or two into the woods and kill partridges or squirrels. I readily complied. We traveled first one way, and then another, a kind of circuitous route; a little before sun setting, we came to a commodious sugar hut. Here he proposed kindling a fire, and resting ourselves. I should suppose this cabin, or hut, might be about two miles northwest of the village. After we had sit down to rest, and lit our pipes, my younger brother tells me, that his father said, it would be good for me to sleep in the woods this night, as they expected rum would soon be brought into town, and some might drink too much, and then be looking after me. I thanked him for the good will he had expressed for me, and that I thought the great spirit had put it into his heart to be kind to me. He replied, Kangoendou, i. e., it may be taken for granted. About ten o'clock in the evening, my sister came to our lonely cabin, accompanied by her little nephew, a little lad, and brought with her my blankets, tucked into a large basket, so as not to be discovered; a kettle of corn soup, a little salt in a bark. I made as good a supper as existing circumstances would admit. My sister would try to encourage me, and tell me not to be afraid, my father was constantly in the council house, and they would take care of me. After supper, I proposed singing a psalm, or words out of the Holy Book, if they had no objection. Oh no, said they, we heard you sing a great many times, and love to hear it, we only wish you would not sing so loud, as to make a great noise, we dont want any one should know where we are to-night. I sang with a soft voice, perhaps ten or a dozen hymns and psalms, having no inclination to sleep. My sister and the boy left us about day light in the morning. * * * Spent the day in our cabin, except walking once, about an hour, with my younger brother, to shoot a squirrel or two. In the dusk of the evening, my elder sister came again, with a kettle of soup; told me her heart began to be glad. She believed the council would break up, and be dispersed by to-morrow morning, or before noon; said she heard it went hard in the council. They spoke strong words. They had examined the widow of her late deceased husband; she spoke well of me, said I never did anything bad while I lived there, but was cheerful, and agreeable and (my) her husband began to love him much; again (was) asked if I never came to his bed-side, and whispered in his ear, or puffed in his face. No, never, he always sat, or lay down on his own bed, and in the evening after we were in bed, I could see him get down on his knees, and talk with a low voice; I suppose he was praying to the Great Spirit. They inquired for my knapsack, expecting to find some magic powder. I suspect that they robbed me of some of my papers at that time.

The next day about noon, returned to the town, and I took up my lodgings with my elder brother, in the old block house. The whole family showed marks of joy upon my peaceable return, and a number of my friends came in to see me before night, and told me "all is now only peace." The remaining part of this week nothing material took place. I was pretty diligent in my endeavors to learn their language, and cordially received my friendly visitors; others kept themselves at a distance. When it was not very cold, I would retire into the upper loft, and spend my time in writing. I did not yet begin to visit much.

neither dare to make many inquiries of my father, or elder brother, or urge them to divulge what took place in the late councils. I thought it best some of the rest should be the first movers. I endeavored to appear before them with a degree of cheerfulness, yet sedate. For a number of days, I felt a solicitude, and almost an unconquerable desire to find out what passed in their several days' consulting. I suspected they had enjoined secresy, lest I might make such communications to Sir William, as to produce a remonstrance or reprimand.

My father told me one day, that some of the Indians were afraid of writing, or letters, which would speak for a great many years afterwards. It would therefore be good for me, whenever I wrote to Sir William, or to the ministers, Tegorkunskie, towards the rising of the sun, to call several of their chiefs together, and interpret their contents (letters,) to them. It would please them very much, and make their hearts glad. I replied that I should follow his advice very cheerfully, and with great punctuality. He again observed that I might write a great book, if I pleased, in learning their language, because I frequently read them some parts of it over, for their correction, and that they were sometimes so diverted to hear me give the true Indian pronunciation to some words in their language, which were difficult for a white man to pronounce, that they could not help expressing their admiration with a hearty laugh, and some of them would say, that our white English brother would become a true Indian, in the course of a year or two.

We now lived in great harmony, friendship, and sociability. I suppressed my solicitude of prying into their secret councils. I thought if I pressed on inquiring before a proper time, and should show great anxiety, they might suspect my confidence in their professed friendship, and want of exertion for my safety. I presently found I had enough to do to recognize the goodness of God, the kind interpositions of his providence, for my preservation thus far, and raising up friends in almost every village, as instruments in his hands of doing me good, and it may be, of rescuing my life from the hands of cruel savages. * * *

March 15th, 1765. Provisions are exceeding scarce; the wild game they killed in the winter is nearly consumed, but little corn is in the whole town. Some families entirely destitute; some have been to Cayogou (Cayuga,) to purchase corn, could get but little, and that by giving an enormous price. They planted but sparingly the last year, and that very late in the season, which was greatly injured by a severe and early frost. Indeed, they have but just began to till the ground since they left Niagara, where most of them had been encamped in the vicinity of Niagara, during a great part of the late French war, and were victualed from the King's stores, till the garrison was subdued and taken by Sir William Johnson. The appearance of things at present, seems to threaten a famine among the Indians the ensuing season. Boating from the Mohawk river will be very difficult till some time in the month of May, on condition (supposing) Sir William should be disposed and think himself justified in relieving their necessities, especially that part of the nation, who have so lately been hostile to the colonies.

16th. Informed by some Indians from the westward, that a Mr. Wemp would probably leave Niagara in the course of ten or twelve days, and tarry with me here a few days to rest himself. I may have mentioned this man before. He was in years past employed as a blacksmith for the Indians in this principal town of the Senecas, called Kanadasigea, and sometimes traded among them. He understands their language pretty well, for common conversation, but can but poorly comprehend a public speech, delivered in an oratorical style, and dress. Being of Dutch extraction, he speaks rather broken and incorrect English, and in general, a bad pronunciation of the Seneca. But being a humane, peaceable, and honest man, I find the Indians set a great deal by him. I shall endeavor to detain him when he arrives, as long as will be consistent with his business, and we find anything for him to eat.

March 20th. I this day received a letter from Sir William, which I will here transcribe.

JOHNSON HALL, March 3d, 1765.

"SIR: I received yours, wrote on the way going up. I hope this will find you safe arrived at the Senecas, where I shall be glad to hear you meet with a kind reception, and everything agreeable to you. The enclosed came here under cover to me, with another for Woolley, which I send to him. Peter, of Oghquage, and wife, are gone to Mr. Whelocks, about ten days ago, by whom I wrote. * * The Delaware deputies from Ohigo are here, these eight days past, waiting for Squash Cutter and Long Coat, without whom and all the prisoners in your parts, I will not treat with them, though they seem very well inclined. When you have a good opportunity write me—by Wemp will be a good opportunity. I wish you heartily well, and am

Your Humble Servant,

MR. KIRKLAND. WILLIAM JOHNSON."

This letter I interpreted to the chiefs, for which they appeared much pleased, and to be very thankful. The Squash Cutter mentioned in the foregoing letter, is a noted head warrior of the Delaware nation. He has done a deal of mischief in the back parts of New Jersey and the Susquehanna ; scalped many, and taken many prisoners. He had commonly no more than twenty or thirty men under his command, including his petty officers. His exploits depend much upon stratagem, and surprise. He was acknowledged by the Indians to be bold, and enterprising, but very cruel. He was about six feet two inches high, lean and raw-boned, but all nerve, and a most piercing eye, rather of a serpentine cast. He has been harbored here in this town for some months, being afraid to return to his nation, lest some of their chiefs who are great friends to the white people, should seize him, and carry him a prisoner to Sir William ; upon my first acquaintance with him, he appeared to be jealous of me ; after some time he became quite familiar, and was very fond of conversing with me. He was very sensible, and would speak broken English pretty well, and understood the Seneca.

There are no white prisoners in this village, but there are two children twins in a village about seven miles south of this, on the west side of Seneca lake, called Gaghconghwa i. e., in English, the limb has fallen. One of these children I went to see a few days since, but the little girl perhaps six or seven years old, would neither come to me, nor speak to me, but clung fast around the neck of her adopted grandmother. She had been lost in the woods fourteen days, strayed from a hunting cabin, but found her way back to it, after some days, and there found some deers legs which had been flung out ; the gnawing and sucking of these, with white oak acorns and winter greens, kept her alive till found, by which time she was nearly exhausted. There were perhaps eight or ten prisoners at Genesee and its vicinity. * * *

April 2d. I am frequently visited by several of their young men who I am told by my elder brother are some of the best characters in the town. They are disposed to be very sociable, and appear to be friendly. This I cannot but consider as a favorable circumstance, and enables me to make greater progress in learning their language, and I request them whenever they hear me give a bad pronunciation to any word to correct me, and to repeat the correction or amendment till I give the true Indian pronunciation. When I have been alone, or walked with but one of them at a time, he would disclose some of the secret council, and particularly of Capt. Onongwadekha and some of his violent speeches, and would always enjoin secrecy, and not divulge a word to any of the sachems. I begin to think I have discovered all the principal transactions of this two or three days counseling upon the death of my Indian landlord and its attending circumstances.

April 4th. Mr. Wemp returns from Niagara, made very welcome, particularly by my family and many others. I expressed my earnest desire, and hoped that he would tarry a week, or at least several days with us, to rest himself properly. Had but little conversation with him this evening, and that principally upon common affairs, and the distressed situation of the town, from the great scarcity of corn. I also considered that it would be expected by the chiefs to have the first talk with him, and make all the enquiries they wished, relative to the western Indians, and the news heard at Niagara. In the meantime, I thought it best to absent myself and not appear too forward, of pressing myself into their councils. But they were very civil, and to manifest their confidence in me, they very soon sent for me to come into their council. A great many things were related by piecemeal, and in a broken style, but they were so well augmented with his dialect and mode of speaking, that they could understand him. They thanked him for all the information he had given them, though they found there was very little in it which had any immediate concern in the welfare of their nation; however they were always glad to hear news.

I took the earliest opportunity to take him aside and relate to him what a distressing situation I had been in, on account of the sudden death of my first Indian landlord. He presently replied that he had heard much of it at Genesee on his way down, and was much alarmed. I told him I believed the unfortunate and mysterious event had been pretty generally settled among the Indians, and they appeared to be satisfied, and reconciled except Capt. Onongwadekha, who remained obstinate and revengeful. I now wished him to befriend me so far as to enquire of some judicious Indian, of the arguments urged against me, and those who pleaded for me, as being perfectly innocent respecting that man's death. I thought from his long acquaintance, and the great apparent friendship which had subsisted betwixt him and my adopted father, the head chief, he might easily get from him, the leading traits or general transactions of that council. I told him I thought it was probable that it would be enjoined on him, to disclose nothing to Sir William, only if he asked, to tell him all was peace now. Mr. Wemp replied that he would attempt it, and did not doubt but he could bring it about either with my father or brother-in-law Tekanade, and was willing to set up all night for that purpose. I humbly observed that it might frustrate my object and disappoint my expectations of any aid from Mr. Wemp to be too frequently with him, and express a greater attachment to him, and fondness, for his company, than I manifested to the good Indians, and most of their chiefs, who had been friendly to me from my first arrival. I suggested the idea to Mr. Wemp; he replied it was the very thing he had thought of, and said then when we meet together in the day-time, let it only be, how do you do, and how do you do, and so pass by.

In the mean time, I improved a leisure hour or two when I could be retired, for writing and making minutes. I wrote to Sir William, informing him of the extreme scarcity of bread, corn and very little hunting at this season, and that I did not think I could subsist through the ensuing summer, unless I could procure provisions and some more certain and substantial food than can be obtained among the Indians. I had sold a shirt for four loaves or Indian cakes baked in the ashes; at first sight I thought I could devour them all at one meal, but I immediately concluded on the score of prudence, to be sparing, and to save some of them against a greater time of need. I have eaten but one, and my stomach was so debilitated, it recoiled and emitted the greatest part of it. I kept some part of the remaining three until they began to mould, and gave them to the children who devoured them instantly.

I had it in contemplation to go down the latter part of this month, or the beginning of next. I supposed by this time Col. Butler might have orders from Mr. Wheelock, to furnish me with such articles as I stood in absolute need of.

April 7th, 1765. Mr. Wemp told me he had an opportunity of a long conversation with my father and brother-in-law, separately, upon the subject I had so earnestly requested his aid for investigation. We then laid a plan for being together part of the day and evening ensuing.

April 8th. Mr. Wemp has given me a long narration of the transactions in the afore-mentioned council—sometimes connected and sometimes detached sentences, with curious anecdotes, and added that my father bore down everything in his last speech. He spoke but little for the first and second days, except his introductory address, at the opening of the council."

The whole of this manuscript is interesting, but as it is not strictly connected with the object of our history, must be omitted.

CHAPTER XV.

Several councils were held with the Six Nations during the year 1775, both by Col. Johnson in behalf of the English, and the Commissioners of Indian affairs appointed by the Colonies. Both parties seemed desirous only to secure the neutrality of the Six Nations, and at the same time, to conciliate their friendship.

At a council held in Albany by the Colonial Commissioners, with the Six Nations, in August, 1775, one of the Oneida chiefs spoke thus of Mr. Kirkland, their Missionary :

" Our father, the minister, who stands here, we love, we love him exceedingly. Perhaps in a little time, he may be wrested from us, carried off like a prisoner. Our hearts tremble for him. We tremble greatly. He has been threatened, and should he be taken, it might overthrow the whole Five Nations.

" Our brothers, the white people, would perhaps say that the Oneida Nation had given up their minister ; and that the Six Nations did not regard their missionaries. But truly, we regard our father the minister and missionaries. Therefore, we propose for your consideration, whether it be not wise, that the missionaries retire for a little while, particularly our father, the minister, Mr.

Kirkland, should reside for a short space with his family, as we hope this quarrel cannot subsist long, because you are brothers, both of one nation and blood, and we hope it will soon be settled, and when a reconciliation takes place, let our missionaries immediately return to us." The commissioners were at great pains to explain to the Indians the nature and causes of the quarrel between the king and the colonies. The Indians could not comprehend how it was that "people of one blood" should quarrel. They had never known any thing like it in all their experience. The Indians pledged themselves in the strongest manner, to observe a line of strict neutrality, and to take no part on either side, but "to sit still and see you fight it out," as they expressed it. But they added: "Brothers: we thank you for opening the road. You inform us likewise, that you were determined to drive away, destroy, and kill, all who appear in arms against the peace of the twelve united colonies."

"Brothers, attend: we beg of you take care what you do! you have just now made a good path, do not so soon defile it with blood. There are many round us, Caughnawagas, who are friends to the king. Our path of peace reaches quite to them. We beg, all that distance may not be defiled with blood. As for your quarrels to the eastward, along the coast, do as you please. But it would hurt us, to see those brought up in our own bosoms, ill used. In particular, we would mention the son of Sir William Johnson. He is born among us, and is of Dutch extraction, by his mother. He minds his own affairs, and does not intermeddle in public disputes. We would also mention our father, the minister,* who resides among

*Rev. Mr. Stewart.

the Mohawks, and was sent there by the king. He does not meddle in civil affairs, but instructs them in the way to heaven. He absolutely refuses to attend to any political matters, and says, they do not belong to him. They beg, that he may continue in peace among them. The Mohawks are frequently alarmed with reports, that their minister is to be torn away from them. It would occasion great disturbance, were he to be taken away. The king sent him to them, and they would look upon it as taking away one of their own body; therefore, they again request,•that he may continue to live in peace among them."

Col. Guy Johnson had already removed with a considerable body of his retainers, and some Indians, up the valley of the Mohawk, to Fort Stanwix; where it was rumored, he was collecting a force of loyalists and Indians, to make a descent upon the colonists in the Palatine district. But the active measures of the colonists soon convinced Col. Johnson, that he and his armed retinue would not be permitted to remain at Fort Stanwix; he therefore pushed further interior, and made a stand in the Senecas' country; but still apprehending pursuit, he moved to Ontario, but being unable to procure conveyance across the lake. for all the Indians, he arrived with his rangers and a few Indians, at Montreal, on the 17th day of September, 1775, where he held another council with the Indians, at which he said, they numbered "1700 or upwards."

In his report, to the Earl of Dartmouth, dated Montreal, October 12, 1775, Col. Johnson assigns, as the reason of his flight from the valley of the Mohawk, "that all necessaries for the Indians, were stopped, by ord:r of the committee; and myself, threatened, with an attack from a considerable armed force, "and intimates, that he had secret orders from Gen. Gage, instructing him to that effect.

"Extracts from the records of Indian transactions, under the superintendancy of Col. Guy Johnson, during the year 1775."

"Col. Johnson having early perceived that the different colonies were about to follow the example of Massachusetts Bay, and finding that the various measures taken by New England missionaries, and others, to alienate the affections of the Indians, and spirit them up to bad purposes; he communicated the same to Lord Dartmouth, in March, and soon after sent messengers to call the Six Nations to a general congress. The 14th of May he received by express, an account that a party of New Englanders were on their way to make him prisoner; on which he fortified his house, and kept a large guard at considerable expense. A few days after, he found that his express to the Indians had been stopped, and the purport of his messages altered; and that the provisions, &c., that his agent had provided at New York, had been stopped, together with the ammunition and goods, he was providing for the intended congress. Finding this (to be the case,) and that his communication with the Indians would be totally obstructed, he resolved to proceed to the westward, (with such presents, &c., as he then had,) and meet them in their own country, while it remained practicable; and during his preparation for this, he secretly received a dispatch from Gen. Gage, containing instructions. He then, with such of the Mohawks as were at home, and a body of armed white men, making together about 250, marched to the upper settlements, under every circumstance of difficulty, and leaving all his property at the discretion of the misguided populace. From thence he proceded to Fort Stanwix, where he met 260 Oneidas and Oughquagas, with whom he held a conference, but was obliged to take leave of them, for want of provisions; the whole country being then in arms behind him, and no possibility of obtaining supplies from thence. He accordingly wrote to the commanding officer at Niagara, and Oswegatchie, for vessels, and provisions, and on the 17th of June, he arrived at Ontario, to which place he had directed them to be sent, where one small sloop shortly after arrived, with ninety barrels, which, though all that could be spared from Niagara, was very unequal to supplying the Indians, who assembled there, in a few days, to the number of one thousand four hundred and fifty-eight, with about one hundred white men, including the officers of the department.

"From the state of the country and the villainous stories propagated, it required some time, with great skill and influence, to remove false reports, and fix the Indians heartily in the interests of the crown. He however, had the good fortune at length to bring them to resolve to cooperate with his Majesty's troops, in the defense of the communication and waters emptying into the St. Lawrence river, and in the annoyance of the enemy, and also to send their band of warriors present with him, to Montreal to inspire their dependents there, with the same resolutions. He also procured the like engagement from the Huron chiefs of Detroit, who attended the Congress; which they very faithfully observed, and thereby prevented the design of the Virginians, against that country, as the papers in his hands will show. After which he delivered them a handsome present, and a parcel of new arms, &c., and his provisions being nearly exhausted, prepared to proceed to Montreal. But the Indians having few canoes, and those unfit for crossing the lake, he was obliged to set out, July 11th, with the sloop, and four or five small boats, carrying together two hundred and twenty white men and Indians. The remainder of the latter, being necessiated to return home, for want of craft to transport them, after giving him assurances of their readiness to follow when called upon.

"Col. Johnson, on his landing at Montreal, July 17th, with two hundred and twenty Indians from Ontario, had immediately an interview with General Carleton, to whom he communicated his instructions, and design, to assemble the Indians in that country, to join those that had accompanied him. He also acquainted him with the accounts he had received of the preparations being made, by the New Englanders, at Ticonderoga, and that they considered Canada as an essential object, adding that it would be extremely necessary to put the Indians in motion as soon as possible, as they were unused to remain long idle. The General observed, that he had but a slender force of regular troops, that the province of Quebec mostly depended upon the Canadian militia, that he had hopes, in some little time, of assembling a good body of them, and that in the mean time the Indians must be amused in the best manner that could be found, as he did not think it prudent to let them go beyond the 45th degree of latitude, or over the province line. Col. Johnson had proposed to hold his conference with the Indians at La Chine, to prevent the intemperance to which they must be exposed at Montreal, and the Indians were so sensible of this, that they were prevailed on with difficulty to come into town to oblige Gen. Carleton, who wanted to see them there.

"On the 26th of July, the Indians all assembled, pursuant to Col. Johnson's summons, and finished their business on the last of that month, when their number amounted to sixteen hundred and sixty-four, who readily agreed to the same measures engaged by the Six Nations. After receiving a valuable present, (they) were disposed of, in different camps, on the Island of Montreal. An Indian officer, and thirty men, were also sent to St. Johns, to remain there, at the desire of Gen. Carleton.

"On the 5th of August, the Indian officer at St. Johns, informed Col. Johnson of his having discovered a large body of the enemy, near Port Aufer, (above St. Johns, on lake Champlain,) who fired on his party, and of the eagerness manifested by the Indians to form a large body, and go against them. Col. Johnson immediately communicated this to Brigadier Prescott, who commanded on Gen. Carleton's departure for Quebec. He also told Gen. Prescott, that the warriors of the several Nations, were to assemble that day, when he would give them the war belts, as they appeared very spirited; and in consequence of the rebels approach, would gladly go and dispossess them of any post, they had upon lake Champlain; and that he should be glad to have his sentiments upon it. The General answered that if any parties were sent out to gain intelligence, and see what the enemy were doing, it might be well. But at present, he did not intend acting out of the line of the Province. On Col.

Johnson's remarking that Indians could not be managed as other people, it being necessary at times to keep up their spirits, and encourage them, and therefore he should be glad to know, what to say for their satisfaction on that subject. The General replied that arguments were useless on this occasion, his orders being such, as not to act out of the line of the Province. Col. Johnson observed that this did not appear to correspond with his instructions from Gen. Gage, and that it would be a very difficult matter to manage Indians under such circumstances, and limitations, on which the General concluded with saying, that all in the Provinces, must be subject to Gen. Carleton's orders, and Col. Johnson must act in the best manner he could, without going out of the colony. However, the Indians being assembled, Col. Johnson delivered each Nation a war belt, to be held ready for service, which the Indians cheerfully accepted, but said they were afraid the ax would cut them, if they kept it long without using it.

"Several of the Six Nations, Oughquagus, &c., having waited till the 12th of August, in hopes of some operations, returned with their war belt, to Onondaga, after assuring Col. Johnson that they would be ready to return, whenever there was a prospect of vigorous measures.

"Col. Johnson continued to relieve the party at St. Johns, by detachments from the different Indian encampments, and endeavored by all the means in his power, to render them contented with their situation. The party at St. Johns, continued to scout on lake Champlain, (within the limits prescribed,) and on the 22d of August, four Indians, detached from a larger party, seized a new barge, with which the rebels were reconnoitering, which brought on a skirmish, wherein Capt. Baker, a noted rebel, was killed, whose head, together with his instructions, plans, &c., they brought into St. Johns. In this affair three Indians were wounded.

"For some time past, notwithstanding all the cares to prevent it, some of the inhabitants etc., continued to sell liquor to the Indians, and to strip them of their clothing, propagating also many dangerous reports among them, and telling them that they approved of the rebels coming, as it was for the interest of the colony.

"The Indians complained much of all this, and as they had already waited, inactive, far beyond what they had ever done before, Col. Johnson wrote to Gen. Carleton, representing their urgency to go against the rebels, or attack their communications, with his opinion that it would answer great purpose, whilst restraining men, unaccustomed to inactivity, would abate their ardor, and might occasion their disaffection. To which, the General answered that no one thing had yet happened to make him alter his opinion, in regard to the keeping the savages within the line; Col. Johnson therefore took all possible pains to amuse them, and satisfy them on that head.

"On the 3d of September, in consequence of reports brought by the Indians, that the enemy were advancing, Col. Johnson augmented the party at St. Johns, to four officers, and one hundred and twenty-one Indians; and on the afternoon of the 4th, Gen. Prescott, desired him to stop sending any more parties, but keep them about the town, lest the rebels might make an attempt upon the city of Montreal, by crossing the country. The next day an express arrived from one of Col. Johnson's officers at St. Johns, informing that a scouting party of Indians had discovered the rebel army on Isle au Noix, (sixteen miles from St. Johns,) and that a second scout had fallen in with some of theirs, and exchanged a few shots, by one of which an Indian was wounded. The General immediately ordered the walls of Montreal to be repaired, and summoned the inhabitants to appear armed on the parade that evening, and Col. Johnson sent off an officer and a party of Indians, to cover the King's magazines near La Chine. A body of eighty-six Canesadaga warriors also came in and joined Col. Johnson, who told them that the General requested that they should remain in readiness to march, when their service was most wanted.

"The next day the rebel army came before St. Johns, and on the 7th at daylight, two Indians arrived with letters, giving an account that the day before, the first division, being about one thousand men, under a General Montgomery, covered with vessels, row galleys, &c., began to land about a mile from St. Johns, when the Indians sallied out, and engaged them with so much success, that they obliged them to retire twice, and that they had at length crossed the lake, and afterwards retreated to Isle au Noix. The loss of the rebels, according to the best accounts, was one field officer, two captains, two lieutenants, and thirty men killed, and the wounded were since found to be double that number. On our side Capt. Tice, one of Col. Johnson's officers, was shot through the thigh; Capt. Daniel, a faithful Mohawk, one Canajoharrie, with two Caughnawagas killed, and several wounded, of which three died soon after.

"The Indians complained much that there was no troops to support them, and in the evening a detachment of sixteen of the twenty-sixth regiment, with some of the recruits and volunteers, were ordered out, with whom Col. Johnson sent two officers and seventy Indians.

"On the 10th of September, on the report that some Canadians had assured the Caughnawagas that the rebels would destroy their town, Daniel Claus, Esq., deputy agent, was sent there to remove any fears on that head, to whom the Indians complained that they had lately been much traduced by some of the French gentlemen, who were too apt to be busy about them, and resented that the Indians would not attend to them, observing that at the reduction of Canada, they had been assured that such persons should no longer interfere with them.

"They added that their cause was very hard, as they were threatened with ruin by the rebels, assured by the Canadians that they would not oppose them, and that there appeared no prospect of relief from any other quarter. From all which, Col. Johnson perceived that these people were so circumstanced that they could no longer be depended on. And this day Major Campbell arrived, being appointed agent for Indian affairs for the Province of Quebec.

"The next day a party of Indians reconnoitering, were fired on by a considerable body of the enemy, and Perthus, an interpreter, with an Indian, surprised and killed, at a house on lake Champlain. On the 12th, Col. Johnson held a conference with the Caughnawagas, to remove their apprehensions, and on the 13th, another was held in presence of Gen. Carleton, (then returned from Quebec,) in consequence of intelligence given Col. Johnson, by the Six Nations, that the rebels had employed agents to negotiate a neutrality with the Caughnawagas.

"This day Gen. Carleton gave his thanks to the Indians in general orders, in the words following:

"The General gives his thanks to the Indian Chiefs and warriors who bahaved so gallantly in the action of the sixth instant, near St Johns, and desires that the same may be communicated to them and their nations, by Col. Johnson, their superintendant,

FRAN'S LEMAISTRE,
Maj'r Brigade.

Montreal, Sept. 13, 1775,

"Col. Johnson continued his endeavors, notwithstanding the general discouragement among the Indians, that they might be in readiness, in case the General could raise any force to go against the enemy. On the 20th, one of Col. Johnson's officers, with his party of Indians, was obliged to retire from the prarie, as did the Indians from St. Johns, which was now completely invested, and accounts received, that a certain Col. Livingston, with the inhabitants of Sorelle, had joined the rebels; on which the General, &c., put their papers and baggage on board of vessels in the river. The rebels had now overran all the country, and were in many places joined by the perfidious Canadians. The Indians, thus without prospect of aid, began to provide for their own security, after complaining bitterly of the disappointment of their hopes of succors; and on the 25th, Col. Eathen Allen, crossed to the Island of Montreal, and with a party of about one hundred and forty, partly Canadians, began his march for that city, where he was opposed by a small party of the 26th regiment, some volunteers, and thirty officers, rangers, and Indians of the Indian department. The latter of whom, fortunately falling on the flank where Allen was, he delivered up his sword, and surrendered to one of Col. Johnson's officers, who, with his party, took the most of those made prisoners. On the 27th, Col. Johnson renewed his application to General Carleton, for moving a body of men, in which case he could still get many of the neighboring Indians to co-operate; to which the General answered verbally, (by the secretary of Indian affairs,) that he hoped affairs were taking a more favorable turn, and that he should very soon be able to form a better judgment."

"From this time to October 12th, every art and means was used to assemble the Canadians, and several came in, were clothed and armed, and afterwards joined the enemy. Finding, therefore, the season so far advanced, the Indians almost all withdrew discontended, unwilling to credit any further promises of aid. That those that remained, earnestly solicited for troops to be sent out, and that Col. Johnson should procure them the redress of sundry grievances, they had often represented, and also, at the same time, having received dispatches from the secretary of state, directing that their several grievances should be immediately laid before the king; finding likewise, that Major Campbell's powers, as agent for Canada, must occasion some difficulties, that would effectually obstruct the service, Col. Johnson signified his intention to go to England, and get these points in some measure adjusted before the Indians, from their respective nations could take the field next year. In which resolution, he was confirmed by the Indians, who deputed a faithful young chief to accompany him,* and having posted his officers at such places as they might be most useful to preserve the fidelity of the Indians, with proper

*Joseph Brant.

instructions, he proceeded for Quebec, from whence he sailed for England, the 11th of November."

"The foregoing is a brief abstract from the minutes of Indian affairs, and may serve to give a general sketch of his conduct and success, the last campaign, though laboring under every circumstance of disadvantage; but the points necessary to be enquired into, and regulated, on which the future good conduct of those hitherto faithful people must depend, and the reasonableness and propriety of Col. Johnson's proceedings, will appear from the annexed statement, which is honestly and impartially submitted.

A true copy of extracts from the Indian records.

JOSEPH CHEW,
Sec'y of Indian affairs."

London, June 26, 1776.

CHAPTER XVI.

Col. Guy Johnson, as intimated in his report just referred to, sailed for England, where he arrived in January, 1776. He was accompanied by Joseph Brant, and a Mohawk war chief, named Oteroughyanento. The arrival of Maj. Campbell, as agent for Indian affairs in Canada, whose authority seemed to conflict with that of Col. Johnson, perhaps led to this determination of Col. Johnson, to visit England at this time. He had endeavored to employ his Indian warriors, mostly Mohawks, who accompanied him to Canada; and from the names incidentally mentioned, at least two sons of Sir William Johnson, Peter and William, were employed as officers in the Indian force against the colonists at this time, in the vicinity of Montreal, and took part in the repulse, "and capture of Col. Eathan Allen, after his detachment was routed near Montreal."

Brant, during his visit in England, made a speech to Lord George Germain, one of his Majesty's principal Secretaries of State; setting forth the grievances of the Six Nations in general, and of the Mohawks, his own Nation, in particular. To which Lord Germain made a brief reply, promising attention to the subject of their complaints, which were as usual, in relation to their lands. This speech of Brant, which appears to have been delivered in London, March, 1776, exhibits nothing remarkable, but in all respects shows a mediocre order of talent. It was followed by another, in reply, or as answer from Capt. Brant, as he is styled, on the 7th of May, 1776, in which he says: "We are not afraid Brother, or have we the least doubt but our brethren, the Six Nations, will continue firm to their engagements with the King, their father."

The sojourn of Col. Johnson with his Indian deputies in England, was brief, as we find a letter of his addressed to Lord Germain, dated Staten Island, August 9th, 1776, in which he acquaints his Lordship that he "arrived in the harbor of New York, on the 29th ult., after a long passage, and much molestation from rebel cruisers, one of which attacked us, near Bermudas, but was, after a pretty close engagement of an hour and a half, beat off, with much loss, though she damaged our masts, and rigging so much, that we could not pursue her." * * He adds: "This moment, an inhabitant of the Mohawk river, has found means to reach our camp, and informs that he had heard that Sir John Johnson had reached Gen. Burgoine. That a Col. Dayton, with six hundred men, was repairing fort Stanwix, and that Gen. Schuyler had opened a Congress at the German Flatts, but that only some of the Oneidas and Oughquagys attended it, and adds that 'the rebels had carried off my negroes, &c., and demolished everything on my estate.' The Indians that attended Schuyler, have long been under the influence of New England missionaries, and I found some difficulty with them last year."

This allusion is undoubtedly to the Oneidas, and the

New England missionary, Mr. Kirkland, who we have already seen, had exerted his influence to induce the Indians to take no part in the war. The person alluded to above, by Col. Johnson, as having arrived from the Mohawk river, was undoubtedly the person described in the following declaration, which was reduced to writing, in presence of several persons, one of whom it will be observed, signs himself "Joseph, Indian Chief."

DECLARATION OF DEPUTY COMMISSIONER GUMERSALL.

"That he left the Mohawk river about the beginning of June of the present year, and been for several weeks in that country, where he was acquainted. That Sir John Johnson, through intelligence he had received, partly by means of Gumersall, found it necessary to leave his home, and withdraw to Canada. To effect which, he procured three Indians from the neighboring village, as guides through the woods, and was accompanied by about one hundred and thirty Highlanders, and near one hundred and twenty other inhabitants of the country, attached to government, with whom he proceeded from the house of Mr. McDonnell, called Collaghy, on or about the 13th of May last, for Oswegachy, in Canada. That the said Gumersall, who was instrumental to him on this occasion, accompanied him a few miles further on his route, and then took his leave. After which, and with much difficulty, after secreting himself, and marching by night, after about five weeks, he arrived at Staten Island. * * Mr. Gumersall further declares that he was credibly informed, that John Butler, Esq., who was left at Niagara by Col. Johnson, superintendent of Indian affairs, with other officers, to encourage the Indians to join his Majesty's troops this season, received several letters from Mr. Schuyler, a rebel General, inviting him down, and promising him protection, but at the same time, employed the messenger, (an Indian,) in case he refused, to bring his scalp, for which he was to have a reward of one hundred dollars. That about three days after Sir John's departure, Lady Johnson received a letter from John Butler, Esq., addressed to Sir John, acquainting him that he had, according to Col. Johnson's instructions, assembled a considerable body of Indians, ready to go on service, and only waited to receive news from Col. Johnson, or orders to proceed. And Mr. Gumersall believes, and has heard, that the Indians had proceeded agreeable thereto, and that Lieut. Gray, late of the forty-second, and Mr. Gumersall, helped to raise the men, who accompanied Sir John, and Mr. Gumersall advanced them money on that occasion. THOS. GUMERSALL.

Signed on Staten Island, August, 1776, in presence of John Deas, Gilbert Tice, and Joseph, Indian Chief."

The following correspondence will show the position of Sir John Johnson at this time, as it appears he had remained at Johnstown with his family, surrounded by his tenants and other loyalists.

GEN. SCHUYLER TO SIR JOHN JOHNSON.

Schenectady, Jan. 16, 1776.

SIR: Information having been received that designs of the most dangerous tendency to the rights, liberties, property, and even the lives of those of his Majesty's faithful subjects in America, who are opposed to the unconstitutional measures of his ministry, have been formed in a part of the county of Tryon. I am ordered to march a body of men into that county, to carry into execution certain resolutions of my superiors, and to contravene those dangerous designs. Influenced sir, by motives of humanity, I wish to comply with my orders, in the manner most peaceable, that no blood may be shed. I request therefore, that you be pleased, to meet me to-morrow, at any place on my way to Johnstown, to which I propose then to march. For which purpose, I do hereby give you my word of honor, that you, and such persons as you may choose to attend you, shall pass safe, and unmolested, to the place where you may meet me, and from thence, back to your place of abode. Rutgers Bleecker and Henry Glen, Esqs., are the bearers hereof; gentlemen who are entitled to your best attention, which I dare say they will experience, and by whom, I expect, you will favor me with an answer to this letter. You will please to assure Lady Johnson, that whatever may be the result of what is now in agitation, she may rest perfectly satisfied, that no indignity will be offered her.

I am Sir, Your Humble Servant,

PH. SCHUYLER.

To Sir John Johnson, Baronet.

The next morning after the dispatch of the above letter, Gen. Schuyler resumed his march for Johnstown. He was met, during the day, upon the road, by Sir John, and a few of his friends. The result of the interview, was the offer by Gen. Schuyler to Sir John, and others, that in consideration of their delivering up all arms, ammunition, and military stores of every kind, except that Sir John was to retain his own personal equipments; that Sir John should give his parole of honor, not to leave the county, or the neighborhood of his residence. That on the faithful performance of these stipulations on the part of Sir John and his adherents, they should be protected, in the quiet enjoyment of their property. Gen. Schuyler required that hostages should be delivered up, as a pledge for the faithful performance of these stipulations, and their future good conduct. Sir John asked until the evening of the next day, to consider the matter, which was granted.

On the next day, the 18th, Gen. Schuyler resumed his march to Caughnawaga, where he was joined by Col. Herkimer, and the Tryon county militia. Sir John's answer was not satisfactory, as will appear by the following letter of Gen. Schuyler in reply.

GEN. SCHUYLER TO SIR JOHN JOHNSON, BAR'T., AND OTHERS.

Caughnawaga, Jan. 18, 1776.

GENTS: Messrs. Adams and McDonell have delivered me your answer to my proposals of yesterday's date. The least attention to the articles I offered, when compared with yours, must convince you, that you omitted replies to several of them, and consequently that what you have sent me is very imperfect, and unsatisfactory. I waive pointing out some of the inconsistences in your proposals, as the whole are exceptionable, except the last. I must therefore obey my orders, and again repeat that in the execution of them, I shall strictly abide by the laws of humanity. At the same time assuring you, that if the least resistance is made, I will not answer for the consequences, which may be of a nature the most dreadful. If Lady Johnson is at Johnson Hall, I wish she would retire, (and therefore enclose a passport,) as I shall march my troops to that place, without delay.

You may, however, still have time to reconsider the matter, and for that purpose I give you until twelve o'clock this night, after which, I shall receive no proposals, and I have sent you Mr. Robert Yates, Mr. Glen, and Mr. Duer, to receive the ultimate proposals you have to make. This condescension I make from no other motive than to prevent the effusion of blood, so far as it can be effected without risking the safety of the county, or being guilty of a breach of the positive orders I have received from the Honorable Continental Congress.

I am, Gentlemen, with due respect,

Your Humble Servant,

PH. SCHUYLER.

To Sir John Johnson and Mr. Allan McDonell.

In the interview between Gen. Schuyler and Sir John Johnson, the latter had informed the General, that the Indians were assembled at his house, and would defend him. Gen. Schuyler replied that he should execute his orders, and if opposed by force, would not be answerable for consequences. While the General was waiting for the reply of Sir John, two chiefs of the Mohawks arrived, and assured the General that the Indians would interfere in no other way than as mediators.

Soon after the preceding letter had been dispatched to Johnson Hall, the Mohawk sachems, with all their warriors, together with several from the upper Mohawk castle, visited Gen. Schuyler on a mission of peace. They informed Gen. Schuyler, that Sir John had related to them the terms offered by him for the surrender of Sir John and his party; they assured the General that Sir John had told them that he only desired protection for himself and family, and friends; and protested that he had no unfriendly intentions, against the country. The Indians, therefore, begged the General to accept the terms Sir John had offered. He told the chiefs that he could not accept of those terms, and pointed out the objections. He also recapitulated to them, the terms he had just sent to the Hall. The Indians expressed themselves satisfied with the reasons assigned by the General, and with the course adopted; but requested that more time should be given for Sir John's reply, that they might have time to go and "shake his head," as they expressed it, and bring him to his senses. They also desired, as a particular favor, that Sir John might not be removed out of the country. They apologized for the threats of their own warriors, saying that it was because they were not present at the treaty of Albany; and again repeated the assurance, that they would never take up arms against the colonies.

In reply, Gen. Schuyler informed them, that he should accede to their request, although the conduct of Sir John had been such, that he would be justified in holding him a prisoner. Before the Indians had left the quarters of Gen. Schuyler, (at Caughnawaga,) a dispatch was received from Sir John Johnson, accepting in substance, the terms dictated by Gen. Schuyler, at which the Indians expressed great satisfaction, and retired, with warm expressions of gratification.

The following were the terms of capitulation prescribed

by Gen. Schuyler, and in substance agreed to by Sir John Johnson.

"Terms of capitulation agreed upon between Gen. Schuyler and Sir John Johnson, Jan. 19, 1776:

"Gen. Schuyler's feelings as a gentleman, induce him to consent that Sir John Johnson retain the few favorite family arms, he making a list of them. The General will also consent that Sir John Johnson, may go as far to the westward, as to the German Flatts, and Kingsland districts, in this county, and to every other part of this colony, to the southward and eastward of said districts, provided he does not go into any sea port town. The General, however, believes that if Sir John's private business should require his going to any other of the ancient English colonies, he will be permitted the indulgence, by applying to Congress for leave.

"The General will take six Scotch inhabitants prisoners, since they prefer it to going as hostages. It has been the invariable rule of Congress, and that of all its officers, to treat prisoners with the greatest humanity, and to pay all due deference to rank. He cannot ascertain the places, to which Congress may please to send them. For the present, they will go to Reading, or Lancaster, in Pennsylvania. Nor can he make any promises, with respect to the maintenance of the women and children. His humanity will certainly induce him to recommend to Congress, an attention to what has been requested on that head. Gen. Schuyler expects that all the Scotch inhabitants, of whatever rank, who are not confined to their beds by illness, will attend with their arms, and deliver them on Saturday, at twelve o'clock. If this condition be not faithfully performed, he will consider himself as disengaged from any engagements entered into with them.

"Gen. Schuyler never refused a gentleman, his side arms.

"The prisoners that may be taken, must be removed to Albany immediately, where the General will permit them to remain a reasonable time to settle their family affairs.

"If the terms Gen. Schuyler offered on the 17th inst., are accepted, with the above qualifications, fair copies will be made out, and signed by the parties, one of which will be delivered to Sir John and Mr. McDonell, signed by the General. To prevent a waste of time, the General wishes Sir John and Mr. McDonell immediately to send an answer.

He remains with due respect,
Sir John's and Mr. McDonell's Humble Serv't.,
PH. SCHUYLER."

These terms were acceeded to by Sir John, and on the same day, Gen. Schuyler marched to Johnstown. Sir John delivered up all the arms and ammunition in his possession, both being much less than had been represented. The next day, 20th, Gen. Schuyler paraded his troops and received the surrender of between two and three hundred Scotch Highlanders, who marched out in front, and grounded their arms; and they were dismissed with an exhortation to remain peaceable, with an assurance of protection if they did so.

The energy and success with which Gen. Schuyler executed this expediton, received the approbation of the congress, and a resolution of thanks was passed "for his fidelity, prudence, and expedition with which he had performed such a meritorious service." President Hancock, in his letter transmiting the resolutions of congress, says: "It is with the greatest pleasure I inform you, that the prudent zeal and temper, manifested in your late expedition, met with the warmest approbation of congress."

Notwithstanding the obligations by which Sir John had bound himself to remain a quasi prisoner of war, information was received by Geu. Schuyler, that Sir John was in secret correspondence with the Indians, instigating them to hostilities, and it was thought advisable by Gen. Schuyler, to put Sir John under a stricter surveillance.

For the purpose of securing the person of Sir John, and quelling the rising turbulent spirit of the Highlanders, a force, under Col. Dayton, was dispatched to Johnstown, in May 1776. Sir John received notice of this intention, through sympathising friends in Albany, in time to anticipate Col. Dayton's arrival, and with a large body of his tenants who adhered to the cause of the crown, took to the woods, not daring to take the usual travelled route, and after a most fatiguing march of nineteen days, through the wilderness, having suffered greatly from want of provisions, they arrived at Montreal, considerably diminished in numbers.

In the suddenness of his flight, Sir John left all his property and his family behind. Col. Stone, in his "life of Brant," in a note relates the following: "After the confiscation of the property of Sir John, the furniture of the hall was sold by auction at Fort Hunter. The late Lieut. Governor Taylor purchased several articles of furniture, and among other things, the family bible. Perceiving that it contained the family record, which might be of great value to Sir John, Mr. Taylor wrote a civil note to Sir John, offering its restoration. Sometime after a messenger from Sir John called for the bible, whose conduct was so rude as to give offence. "I have come for Sir William's bible," said he, "and there are the four guineas which it cost." The bible was delivered, and the runner was asked what message Sir John had sent. The reply was, "Pay four guineas and take the book."

Lady Johnson was removed to Albany, where she remained as a kind of hostage for the peaceable conduct of her husband. She subsequently wrote to Gen. Washington, complaining of the detention, asking him to interpose for her release. But the Commander in Chief left the matter with Gen. Schuyler and the Albany committee. Sir John was immediately commissioned a Colonel, in the British service, and raised two battallions, composed of those who accompanied him in his flight, and other American loyalists, who subsequently followed their example. They were called the "Royal Greens."

There have been some doubts entertained as to where the responsibility of engaging the Six Nations in the controversy, between the king and the colonies, should rest. The following letter places that responsibility where it belongs, which, although written in 1775, will be inserted here:

GOV. TRYON TO THE EARL OF DARTMOUTH.

"Ship Dutchess of Gordon, off New York,
7th February, 1775.

MY LORD:

The loyal inhabitants of this province have experienced

a variety of injuries and insults since my dispatch of the 5th of January. The latter end of last month, twelve hundred men from New Jersey, under the command of Col. Hard, went over to Long Island, and after ten days marauding, disarmed upwards of six hundred inhabitants of Queens county and took seventeen of the principal gentlemen prisoners, who have since been marched, under guard, to Philadelphia. The same manouvre has been practised by Gen. Schuyler, at the head of near four thousand armed mob; he marched to Johnson's hall, the 14th of last month, where Sir John had mustered near six hundred men from his tenants and neighbors, the majority highlanders. After disarming them, and taking four pieces of artillery, ammunition, and many prisoners, with three hundred and sixty guineas from Sir John's desk, they compelled him to enter into a bond in one thousand six hundred pounds sterling, not to aid the king's service, or to remove within a limited distance from his house. Such, my Lord, is the degrading situation of His Majesty's faithful subjects in this colony. The rebels have been active in disarming other parts of the colony, and this plan was grounded upon the recommendation of the provincial congress here to the continental congress, to send troops from other parts to the delinquents of this country, as will be seen by the copy of their letter among the enclosures.

I am with great respect, my Lord,

Your Lordship's most obediant servant,

WM. TRYON."

EARL DARTMOUTH.

EXTRACT GOV. TRYON TO THE EARL DARTMOUTH.

"8th February, 1776.

By late secret intelligence from the northward, and as far westward as Detroit, I have the agreeable information that the Indians are firmly attached to the king's interest. The Indians have chosen Peter Johnson, the natural son of Sir William Johnson, (by an Indian woman,) to be their chief. He is intrepid and active, and took with his own hand Eathan Allen, in a barn, after his detatchment was routed before Montreal. The Indian department demands all possible attention, and a commission of General, to Peter, would be politic. To fix and retain the Indians by very liberal presents and encouragement will be of the highest importance to the king's service at the present crisis. Presents sent to them by way of Quebec will be the most certain channel, and an assortment sent to this post, will also be very expedient to be sent up to Albany as soon as the troops arrive in this colony.

"I am assured that the Indian nations will make a powerful diversion on the borders of the lake, very early this spring, cut off all parties going to reinforce the enemy, and probably seize all the vessels, batteaus, and row galleys before they are liberated from the ice; and then join Gen. Carleton in Canada, or come down to Albany, as occasion may require. This my Lord, is the plan of operations for the Indians, and I expect it will be executed, and succeed.

"The enclosures relative to Canada transactions, herewith transmitted, will further explain to your Lordship the happy restoration of his Majesty's affairs in that government.

I am with all possible respect and esteem my Lord, your Lordship's most obedient humble servant,

EARL DARTMOUTH. WM. TRYON."

EARL OF DARTMOUTH TO COL. GUY JOHNSON.

White Hall 24th July, 1775.

"SIR:—I have already in my letter to you on the 5th inst., hinted that the time might possibly come when the King relying upon the attachment of his faithful allies, the Six Nations of Indians, might be under the necessity of calling upon them for their aid and assistance in the present state of America.

"The unnatural rebellion now raging there, calls for every effort to suppress it; and the intelligence his Majesty has received of the rebels having excited the Indians to take a part, and of their having actually engaged a body of them in arms to support their rebellion, justifies the resolution his Majesty has taken of requiring the assistance of his faithful adherents, the Six Nations. It is therefore, his Majesty's pleasure, that you do lose no time in taking such steps as will induce them to take up the hatchet against his Majesty's rebellious subjects in America, and to engage them in his Majesty's service upon such plan as shall be suggested to you, by Gen. Gage, to whom this letter is sent, accompanied with a large assortment of goods for presents to them, upon this important occasion. Whether the engaging the Six Nations to take up arms in defense of his Majesty's government, is most likely to be effected by separate negotiation with the chiefs, or in a general council assembled for that purpose must be left to your judgment. But at all events it is a service of very great importance ; you will not fail to exert every effort that may tend to accomplish it, and to use the utmost diligence and activity in the execution of the orders I have now the honor to transmit to you.

I am, etc.,

DARTMOUTH."

In November, 1776, Col. Johnson writes Lord Germain from New York, as follows :

"I have the pleasure to assure your Lordship that the Indians have faithfully observed the promises they made me, rejecting all the proposals of the rebels, and a considerable number of them proceeded on service. And notwithstanding the artifices practiced by the Indians of the Oneida villages, influenced by their New England missionary Kirkland, the enclosed intercepted letter, communicated to me by Lord Howe, will show the fidelity of the Six Nations, and evince their attention to me. * * * To pave the way for future operations, I have with the approbation of Gen. Howe, lately dispatched (in disguise) one of my officers with Joseph (Brant) the chief, (who desired the service,) to get across the country to the Six Nations, and from their activity and knowledge of the way, I have hopes of their getting through undiscovered."

The following is the intercepted letter spoken of above :

"Copy of a letter from S. Kirkland, a New England Missionary among the Oneidas, to Mr. Schuyler, a rebel General, and manager of their affairs, dated Oneida, 22d May, 1776.

"To the Hon. Philip Schuyler Esq., Commissary, &c., from the Oneida Chiefs.

"BROTHER GOVERNOR :—We the Oneida chiefs, think

proper to acquaint you of the result of the meeting at Niagara with Col. Butler. This we do at our own option, not being desired by the other parts of the confederacy, though it has been reported among them, that General Schuyler ought to be informed.

"We sent two Oneidas to hear what would pass at Niaga. They returned the night before last, and brought the following account:

"The representatives of the Six Nations delivered the answer to Col. Butler's Belts, that was formed and agreed upon at Onondaga, in full council, of which we suppose you have been made acquainted. The purport of our answer was that the Six Nations with the Cagnaagas and the seven tribes in that vicinity, had all united, and resolved to maintain peace, both with the King, and the Bostonians, and receive no ax from either."

Col. Claus it seems also went to England in 1776 ; before returning in the spring of '77, he drew up a plan for the management of Indian affairs, to be adopted upon the restoration of British authority, which was expected as a matter of course. In this document he speaks of the Tsineesios (Genessee) Indians in a note, representing them as having been generally in the French interest, since the French were in possession of Niagara ; it being by their permission and consent, they were allowed to establish themselves there. That nation of Indians claiming the property of the soil. In consideration of which privilege they were much caressed and indulged by the French, and had the liberty to enjoy the emoluments of the carrying place; which were so luciative and considerable to that nation, that in a short time they enriched themselves thereby, and had besides some other advantages of trade, and other necessaries of life. * * Indians not easily forgetting injuries, the Tsineesios still harbored ill-will against those to whom they ascribe their misfortunes and losses, * * and could never be persuaded to attach themselves cordially to the English, till after the unwearied pains and endeavors of the late Sir William Johnson, they about five years ago, declared themselves publicly at Johnson Hall, firm friends and allies to the Crown of Great Britain, and have hitherto behaved as such."

In a letter of Col. Johnson to Lord Germain, dated New York, June 8th, 1777, he says:

"A person whom I employed to carry messages to the Indians, gave a particular account of a large magazine of military stores and provisions collected at Danbury, Connecticut, which I communicated to Sir William Howe, who soon after sent a body of troops there, and effectually destroyed the whole; and also that the Six Nations having called in and assembled all their people, in order to make a diversion on the frontiers of this province and Pennsylvania, agreeable to my messages, since which they have had several attacks along the back settlements from Fort Stanwix to the Ohio, with such success that the rebels have been obliged to detach Gen. Hand with some troops to protect the frontiers which are in much consternation. * * * He also reports that his Secretary, Mr. Chew, was taken prisoner by the rebels, on the east end of Long Island, whither he had gone on business." * *

Joseph Brant having been dispatched to the Six Nations, Col. Johnson writes from New York, July 7, 1777, that they were in readiness, with the exception of the Oneidas, to join Gen. Howe's army, and act as 'one man;'

and that they had cut off a Sergeant and twelve men at Fort Stanwix, and sent several parties to the back of Pennsylvania, to the great terror of the inhabitants, and had cut off a party with fifty head of cattle for the rebel garrison on the Mohawk river; that their main body of about seven hundred Indians was assembled near Owegy (Owego,) on the Susquehanna, which would be much increased as soon as any movement was made to the northward; adding that they would strike a blow; and expresses his conviction that the Indians will join the expedition of Gen. St Leger, by way of Ontario, or the main army under Gen. Burgoyne, before Ticonderoga.

It would seem from the correspondence of Col. Claus with Secretary Knox, dated at Montreal, in October, 1777, that St. Leger's expedition was destined against Fort Stanwix. Col. Claus and Sir John Johnson accompanied this expedition, and it was joined by Joseph Brant at Oswego, with a party of about three hundred, warriors. Brant complained that his party had not been furnished with necessary supplies by Col. Butler, who was in command at Niagara.

After much delay, St. Leger and his army arrived before Fort Stanwix on the 2d of August, 1777, and in the words of his report, "surprised a party of rebels, which had come out to meet them, defeated them with great slaughter, but another party coming out of the fort, plundered the Indian encampment of all their packs, with their clothes, wampum, and silver work, and as the Indians had gone into the battle nearly naked, they found themselves in a destitute condition, as to clothes or covering for the night. The Indians lost thirty-two men in this engagement, among whom were several Seneca Chiefs. The fort was beseiged for nineteen days with little effect ; the Indians becoming dispirited, gradually withdrew, and dispersed to their homes, and Gen. St Leger retreated to Oswego. He arrived there the 26th of August, when he received orders from Gen. Burgoyne to join him, which he proceeded to do by way of Montreal, to procure necessary supplies for his army. * *

The action near Fort Stanwix, happening near a settlement of Oneida Indians, who were considered to be in the rebel interest, the Indians under Brant, with St Leger, burnt their houses, destroyed their fields and crops, killed and carried away their cattle. This so exasperated the Oneidas, that on their retreat they revenged themselves by plundering Brant's sister (Molly Brant,) who resided with her family at the upper Mohawk town, together with others of the Mohawks in the lower town, where the families of those who accompanied Brant in this expedition, resided. Molly Brant and her family fled to the Onondagas, the council-place of the Six Nations, where she laid her grievances before that body.

It does not appear that any lives were lost on either side in this attack of Brant and his Mohawks upon the unoffending Oneidas. Nor does it appear, that the Oneidas in their retaliatory measures upon the Mohawks, did anything more than visit upon the well known individuals who were engaged with Brant in the destruction of their own property, just what they had suffered at their hands ; although by the usages of war among the whites they would have been justified in taking the lives of those who attacked, and destroyed their dwellings, and plundered them of their property. This is believed to be the first instance, in which one of the Six Nations was ever known to make war upon another of their own confederacy.

CHAPTER XVII.

The information given to Gen. St. Leger of the approach of the reinforcements under Gen. Herkimer, was through the instrumentality of "Molly Brant," and led to the surprise, and almost to the defeat, of the entire party under Gen. Herkimer. Thomas Spencer, a half breed sachem, of the Oneidas, brought early news of the expedition under St. Leger, from Montreal, whither he had gone as a secret emmissary, to obtain information; and at a meeting held on his return, he concluded his report in the following speech:

"BROTHERS: Now is your time to awake, and not to sleep longer, or on the contrary, it shall go with Fort Schuyler, as it went already, with Ticonderoga.

"Brothers, I therefore desire you to be spirited, and to encourage one another to march on to the assistance of Fort Schuyler. Come up and show yourselves as men, to defend and save your country, before it is too late. Dispatch yourselves, to clear the brush about the Fort, and send a party to cut trees in the Wood creek, to stop up the same.

"Brothers, If you don't come soon, without delay, to assist this place, we cannot stay much longer on your side. For if you leave this Fort without succor, and the enemy shall get possession thereof, we shall suffer like you, in your settlements, and shall be destroyed with you. We are suspicious that your enemies have engaged the Indians, and endeavor daily yet to strike and fight against you, and Gen. Schuyler refuses always, that we shall take up arms in the country's behalf.

"Brothers, I can assure you that as soon as Butler's speech, at Oswego, shall be over, they intend to march down the country immediately to Albany. You may judge yourselves, that if you don't try to resist, we shall be obliged to join them, or fly to our castles, as we cannot hinder them alone. We, the good friends of the country, are of opinion, that if more force appears at Fort Schuyler, the enemy will not move from Oswego, to invade these frontiers. You may depend on it, we are willing to help you if you will do some efforts too."

Notwithstanding this earnest appeal of the Oneida sachem, and a patriotic proclamation of Gen. Herkimer, who it was said, was a better citizen than soldier, a spirit of apathy seemed to possess the people.

John Jay, in a letter to Governeur Morris, under date of July 21, 1777, says: "The situation of Tryon county is both shameful and alarming. Such abject dejection and despondency, as mark the letters we have received from thence, disgrace human nature. God knows what to do with, or for them."

"The Oneida Indians," says Stone, in his life of Brant, "who were sincerely disposed to favor the cause of the colonists, but who, pursuant to the humane policy of Congress, and the advice of Gen. Schuyler, had determined to preserve their neutrality, beheld the approaching invasion from Oswego, with no small degree of apprehension. The course they marked out for themselves, as they were well aware, was viewed with displeasure by their Mohawk brethren, while the other members of the confederacy, were obviously inclined to side with their "uncle," (the King.) Living, moreover, in the neighborhood of Fort Schuyler, (for that was the name now given to Fort Stanwix,) where St. Leger's first blow must be struck, they were not a little troubled in prospect of what might happen to themselves.

The watchful Thomas Spencer dispatched the following letter to the committee, on the 29th July, which was received the 30th. "At a meeting of the chiefs, they tell me, there is but four days remaining, of the time set for the King's troops to come to Fort Schuyler; and they think it likely they will be here sooner. The chiefs desire the commanding officer at Fort Schuyler, not to make a Ticonderoga of it, but they hope you will be courageous. They desire Gen. Schuyler may have this with speed, and send a good army here. There is nothing to do at New York; we think there is men to be spared; we expect the road is stopped to the inhabitants by a party through the woods, we shall be surrounded, as soon as they come. This may be our last advice, as these soldiers are part of those that are to hold a treaty. Send this to the committee, as soon as they receive it, let the militia rise up and come to Fort Schuyler.

"To-morrow we are going to the Three Rivers, (the junction of the Oneida, Seneca and Oswego rivers,) to the treaty. We expect to meet the warriors; and when we come there and declare we are for peace, we expect to be used with indifference, and sent away. Let all the troops that come to Fort Schuyler take care, on their march, as there is a party of Indians to stop the road, below the Fort, about eighty or one hundred.

"We hear they are going to bring their cannon up Fish Creek. We hear there is one thousand going to meet the enemy. We advise not ; the army is too large for so few men to defend the Fort; we send a belt of eight rows, to confirm the truth of what we say. It looks likely to me the troops are near. Hope all friends to liberty, and that love their families, will not be backward, but exert themselves, as one resolute blow would secure the friendship of the Six Nations, and almost free this part of the country from the incursions of the enemy."

The imminence of the danger, the patriotic appeals of the committee, and the proclamation of Gen. Herkimer, aroused the dormant energies of the people, to a sense of duty; and the ranks of the advancing army under Gen. Herkimer, were speedily augmented, which in a measure atoned for the apathy that had hitherto prevailed; and the General soon found himself in command of between eight hundred and a thousand men, all eager for action, and impatient of delay. Their impetuosity and want of proper precaution, and the observance of discipline, had well nigh proved their ruin. They moved forward in rather a disorderly manner, until they reached the neighborhood of Oriskany, where they encamped.

Gen. Herkimer dispatched a messenger to apprise Col. Gansevoort, who commanded the Fort, of his approach ; and to concert measures of co-operation. The signal agreed upon to inform him of the safe arrival of the messenger at the Fort, was three successive discharges of cannon, there port of which, it was supposed, would be easily heard at Oriskany, the distance of only eight miles. The messenger did not reach the Fort until ten or eleven o'clock the next day. An unusual silence had prevailed in the camp of the enemy, and a body of troops were observed by the garrison, to move along the edge of the woods down the river, in the direction of the Oriskany creek.

The concerted signal was immediately fired, and as Gen. Herkimer was to force a passage to the Fort, if it became necessary, arrangements were immediately made by Col. Ganesvoort to create a diversion, by a sortie from the Fort, upon the hostile camp of the besiegers. For this purpose two hundred men under Col. Willett, were detailed, with one field piece, an iron three pounder. It appears that Gen. Herkimer had some misgivings as to the propriety of advancing, without first receiving reinforcements himself. His officers, however, were eager to press forward. A consultation was held, much excitement and impatience was manifested by some of the officers. High words ensued, during which Cols. Cox and Paris, and others, denounced their commander as a tory, and a coward, to his face. The brave old man calmly replied that he considered himself placed over them as a father, and that it was not his wish to lead them into any difficulty from which he could not extricate them; and told them plainly, that their intemperate zeal, did not augur well for their courage, in face of the enemy; and that he expected to see them run, at his first appearance. But their clamor increased, until at length stung by their imputations of cowardice, and want of fidelity to the cause, the General gave orders to advance, and no sooner than the word forward, was given, than the troops gave a shout, and rather rushed, than marched. They advanced in files of two deep, with scouts in front, and upon each flank. Having proceeded rapidly forward, a distance of only about two miles, the guards both front and flanks, were suddenly shot down; the forest rang with the war whoop of a savage foe, and in an instant the greater part of the division found itself involved in the midst of a formidable ambuscade. St Leger having been informed of the advance of Gen. Herkimer, (in the manner already indicated,) had detached a portion of Sir John Johnson's regiment, under command of Sir John's brother-in-law, Major Watts, Col. Butler with his Rangers, and Joseph Brant with a strong body of Indians, to intercept his approach.

With true Indian sagacity, a position had been selected admirably fitted for the purpose of drawing the Americans into an ambuscade. There was a deep ravine crossing the route which Gen. Herkimer and his undisciplined army was traversing.

The bottom of this ravine was marshy, and the road crossed it by means of a log causeway. The ravine swept round in a semicircle, at that point, and the ground enclosed in that semicircle was somewhat elevated, and level. The ambush lay upon this elevated ground, and was so disposed, as to encircle the ground occupied, with the exception of a narrow segment open for the entrance of the provincials on their approach. The stratagem was successful. The whole army of Gen. Herkimer with the exception of the rear guard, Col. Vischer's regiment, fell into the trap. The baggage and amunition wagons, which had just descended into the ravine, were also cut off from the main body, by the sudden closing up of the circle. Being thrown into irretrievable disorder by the suddenness of the surprise, and the destructiveness of the fire, which was close and brisk, for a time, it partook more of the character of a massacre, than of a battle ; at every opportunity, the savages concealed behind the trunks of trees, darted forward with knife and tomahawk to ensure the destruction of those who fell wounded ; and many, and fierce, were the conflicts that ensued hand to hand.

The veteran Herkimer fell wounded, in the early part of the action ; a musket ball having passed through, and killed his horse, and shattered his own leg, just below the knee. The General was placed upon his saddle against a tree, for his support, continued to order the battle. Col. Cox and Captains Davis and Van Slayck, were severally killed, near the commencement of the battle ; and the slaughter of their broken ranks, from the rifles of the Tories, and the spears and tomahawks of the Indians, was dreadful. But even in this deplorable situation, (says Col. Stone) the wounded General, his men falling like leaves around him, and the forest resounding with the horrid yells of the savages, ringing high, and wild, above the din of battle, behaved with the most perfect firmness and composure.

The action had lasted about forty-five minutes, in great disorder, before the Provincials formed themselves into circles, in order to repel the attack of the enemy, who were concentrating and closing in upon them from all sides. From this moment the resistance of the Provincials was more effective; and the enemy attempted to charge with the bayonet.

The firing ceased for a time, excepting the scattering discharges from the fire of the Indians, and as the bayonets crossed, the contest became a death struggle, hand to hand, and foot to foot. Never, however did brave men stand a charge with more dauntless courage, and the enemy for the moment, seemed to recoil. Just at that instant the work of death was arrested by a heavy shower of rain, which suddenly broke upon the combatants with great fury. The storm raged for upwards of an hour, during which time, the enemy sought such shelter as might be found among the trees, at a respectful distance, for they had already suffered severely, notwithstanding the advantages in their favor.

During this suspension of the battle, both parties had time to look about, and make such dispositions of their respective forces, as they pleased; either for defense, or attack; on the renewal of the conflict, the Provincials under the direction of their General, were so fortunate as to take possession of an advantageous piece of ground, upon which his men formed in a circle, and as the storm abated, awaited the movements of the enemy. In the early part of the engagement, the Indians whenever they saw a gun fired, by a militia man from behind a tree, rushed up and tomahawked him before he could reload. To counteract this mode of warfare, two men were stationed behind a single tree, one only to fire at a time, the other reserving his fire until the Indian ran up as before. The fight being renewed under this new arrangement, the Indians were made to suffer severely, and with the cool execution of the fire of the militia, forming the main circle, the Indians began to give way, when Major Watts came up with a re-inforcement, consisting of another detachment of Johnson's Greens. Many of the Greens who were Loyalists, who had fled from Tryon county, were known to the Provincials, and as they advanced near to each other in the conflict, mutual recognitions, added fierceness to the contest, and it became more bitter than before; mutual feelings of resentment, and revenge, raged in their bosoms; as this force advanced upon the Provincials, they fired upon them, and then rushed upon them, attacked them with their bayonets, and the butts of their muskets, or both parties in closer contest, throttled each other, and drew their knives, stabbing, and sometimes literally dying in each others embrace.

This fierce contest was continued with increased ferocity, for some time, and a remarkable degree of courage, fortitude, and bravery, was exhibited by individuals of the Colonists, whose names have been recorded, and will be embalmed in the memory of a grateful country; it is said that about thirty of the Royal (Johnson's) Greens were killed in this conflict, besides many Indian warriors. Such a conflict could not be maintained long. The Indians finding that the brunt of the battle fell on them, and that their numbers were sadly diminished, a signal was given, in Indian, to retreat, which was obeyed with precipitancy. Firing in the direction of the fort, was heard, the Rangers (Butlers) and the Greens (Johnson's) retreated as precipitately as the Indians had done, leaving the Provincials masters of the field.

Thus ended one of the bloodiest battles of the revolution, considering the numbers engaged. It is said, several of the wounded and prisoners of the provincials, were killed by the savages, after they were brought into Col. Butler's own quarters. Upon the retreat of the enemy, the provincials proceeded to remove their wounded, as best they could; among these, was their brave old

General, who had so nobly vindicated his character for courage, during the day. Though wounded almost in the first onset, he had borne himself during the six hours of the conflict, under the most trying circumstances, with a degree of fortitude and composure, worthy of all admiration. Nor was his example without its influence upon his troops, in sustaining them, in the trying circumstan ces, by which they were surrounded, and through which they were called to pass. It is said that at one time during the battle, while sitting upon his saddle, in the position which has already been described, it was proposed to remove him, to a less exposed situation, he replied, "no, I will face the enemy." "Thus surrounded with a few men, he continued to issue his orders with firmness. In this situation, and in the heat of the onslaught, he deliberately took from his pocket, his tinder-box, lit his pipe, and smoked with the greatest composure."

The loss of the English in this engagement, says Col. Stone, was equally, if not more severe than that of the Americans. Johnson's "Royal Greens," and "Butler's Rangers" must have suffered severely, although no returns were given in the contemporaneous accounts. "I beheld, says an eye witness who crossed the battle field some days afterward,* the most shocking sight I ever witnessed. The Indians and white men were mingled with one and another, just as they had been left when death had first completed his work. Many bodies had been torn by wild beasts."

It has been supposed that the Senecas were inveigled into this conflict, by the artifices of the Johnsons, But-

*Frederick Sammons.

lers, and Claus, the agents or emmissaries of the English government, and that they resisted the importunity of these agents for a length of time, expressing their determination to take no part in the war, as appears by the statement of Mary Johnson, the "white woman," who then resided with the Senecas, at Geneseo. After describing the quiet, and peace enjoyed by the Indians, after the close of the French war, until the breaking out of the revolution, she says, "we, as usual, were enjoying ourselves in the employment of peaceable life, when a messenger arrived from the British commissioners, requesting all the Indians of our tribe, to attend a general council, which was soon to be held at Oswego. The council convened, and being opened, the British commissioners informed the chiefs that the object of calling a council of the Six Nations was, to engage their assistance in subduing the rebels, the people of the states, who had risen up against the good king, their master, and were about to rob him of a great part of his possessions and wealth, and added that they would amply reward them for their services. The chiefs then arose and informed the commissioners of the nature and extent of the treaty which they had entered into with the people of the states, the year before, and that they would not violate it by taking up the hatchet against them.

"The commissioners continued their entreaties without success, till they addressed their avarice, by telling our people, that the people of the states were few in number, and easily subdued, and that on account of their disobedience to the king, they justly merited all the punishment that it was possible for white men and Indians to inflict on them; and added, that the king was rich, and powerful, both in money and men. That his rum was as plentiful as the water in Lake Ontario; that his soldiers were as numerous as the sands upon its shores, and the Indians, if they would assist in the war, and persevere in their friendship to the king, till it was closed, should never want for money or goods. Upon this the chiefs concluded a treaty with the British commissioners, in which they agreed to take up arms against the rebels, and continue in the service of His Majesty, till they were subdued, in consideration of certain conditions, which stipulated in the treaty, to be performed by the British government, and its agents,* as soon as the treaty was finished, the commissioners made a present to each Indian, a suit of clothes, a brass kettle, a gun and tomahawk, a scalping knife, a quantity of powder and lead, a piece of gold, and promised a bounty on every scalp that should be brought in. Thus, richly clad and equipped. they returned home, after an absence of about two weeks, full of the fire of war, and anxious to encounter their enemies. "Many of the kettles which the Indians received at that time are now (1824) in use on the Genesee Flats." In the narrative of Mary Johnson, it is added, "previous to the battle of Fort Stanwix, the British sent for the Indians to come and see them whip the rebels, at the same time stated that they did not wish to have them fight, but wanted to have them just sit down, smoke their pipes, and look on. Our Indians, the Senecas, went to a man, but contrary to their expectations, instead of smoking, they had to fight for their lives, and in the end of the battle, were completely beaten with a great loss in

*The Oneidas were not parties to this treaty.

killed and wounded. Our Indians, the Senecas, alone had thirty-six killed, and a great number wounded. Our town exhibited a scene of real sorrow and distress, when our warriors returned, recounting their misfortunes, and stated the real loss they had sustained in the engagement. The mourning was excessive, and was expressed by the most doleful yells, shrieks, and howlings, and by inimitable gesticulations. During the revolution my house was the home of Col. Butler and Brant, whenever they chanced to come into our neighborhood, (Genesee,) as they passed to and from Fort Niagara, which was the seat of their military operations; many and many a night I have pounded samp for them, from sun set till sun rise, and furnished them with the necessary provisions and clean clothing for their journey."

The following incident is related by Doct. Dwight, in connection with the expedition of St. Leger, against Fort Stanwix, as it has been also connected with the name of a celebrated chief of the Senecas, it will be transcribed here:

"In the autumn when the seige of Fort Stanwix was raised, he following occurrence took place here: Capt. Greg, one of the American officers, left in the garrison, went out one afternoon with a corporal belonging to the same corps, to shoot pigeons. When the day was far advanced, Greg knowing that the savages were at times prowling round the Fort, determined to return. At that moment a small flock of pigeons alighted upon a tree in the vicinity. The corporal proposed to try a shot at them; and having approached sufficiently near, was in the act of elevating his piece towards the pigeons, when the report of two rifles, discharged by unknown hands, at a small distance, was heard; the same instant, Greg saw his companion fall, and felt himself badly wounded in the side. He tried to stand, but speedily fell, and in a moment perceived a huge Indian making long strides towards him, with a tomahawk in his hand. The savage struck him several blows on the head, drew his knife, cut a circle through the skin from his forehead to the crown, and then drew off the scalp with his teeth. At the approach of the savage, Greg had counterfeited being dead, with as much address as he could use, and succeeded so far as to persuade his butcher that he was really dead, otherwise, measures still more effectual would have been employed to dispatch him. It is hardly necessary to observe, that the pain produced by these wounds, was intense and dreadful; those on the head were, however, the most excruciating, although that in his side was believed by him, to be mortal. The savages having finished their bloody business, withdrew. As soon as they were fairly gone, Greg, who had seen his companion fall, determined, if possible, to make his way to the spot where he lay; from a persuasion, that if he could place his head upon the corporal's body, it would in some degree relieve his excessive anguish. Accordingly he made an effort to rise, and with great difficulty having succeeded, immediately fell. He was not only weak and distressed, but had been deprived of the power of self command, by the blows of the tomahawk. Strongly prompted, however, by this little hope of mitigating his sufferings, he made a second attempt and fell. After several unsuccessful efforts, he finally regained his feet, and staggered slowly through the forest, he at length reached the spot where the corporal lay. The Indian who had marked him for his prey, had taken surer aim than his fellow, and killed him outright. Greg found him lifeless, and scalped. With some difficulty he laid his own head upon the body of his companion, and as he had hoped, found considerable relief from this position.

While he was enjoying this little comfort, he met with trouble from a new quarter. A small dog which belonged to him, and had accompanied him in his hunting, but to which he had been hitherto inattentive, now came up to him in apparent agony, and leaping around him in a variety of involuntary motions, yelped, whined and cried, in an unusual manner, to the no small molestation of his master. Greg was not in a situation to bear the disturbance even of affection. He tried in every way, which he could think of, to force the dog from him, but he tried in vain. At length wearied by his cries and agitations, and not knowing how to put an end to them, he addressed the animal as if he had been a rational being. 'If you wish so much to help me, go and call some one to my relief.' At these words, the creature instantly left him and ran through the forest at full speed, to the great comfort of his master, who now hoped to die quietly. The dog made his way directly to three men belonging to the garrison, who were fishing at the distance of a mile from this tragedy; as soon as he came up to them, he began to cry in the same affecting manner, and advancing near them turned and went slowly back towards the point where his master lay, keeping his eye continually on the men; all this he repeated several times. At length one of the men observed to his companions that there was something very extraordinary in the actions of the dog; and that in his opinion they ought to find out the cause.

His companions were of the same mind, and they immediately set out with the intention to follow the animal whither he should lead them. After they had pursued him some distance and found nothing, they became discouraged. The sun had set, and the forest was dangerous; they therefore determined to return. The moment the dog saw them wheel about, he began to cry with increased violence, and coming up to the men took hold of the skirts of their coats with his teeth, and attempted to pull them towards the point to which he had before directed their course. When they stopped again, he leaned his back against the back part of their legs, as if endeavoring to push them onward to his master; astonished at this conduct of the dog, they agreed after a little deliberation to follow him until he should stop. The animal led them directly to his master. They found him still living, and after burying the corporal as well as they could, they carried Greg to the fort; here his wounds were dressed with the utmost care, and such assistance was rendered to him, as proved the means of restoring him to perfect health. 'This story,' says the Doctor, 'I received from Capt. Edward Buckley, who received the account from Greg a few days before.'"

The following official letters written near the close of the year 1777, throws additional light upon the history of this period, particularly as relates to the Indians. The policy of the Indians had undoubtedly been to remain neutral; and from the whole tenor of the correspondence between the agents of the British Government and the government at home, shows that there had been some reluctance at least on the part of some of the officials, to employ the Indians, and suffer them to prosecute the war in their own way, and after their own barbarous manner. But the representations of the agents and officers as the Johnsons and their auxiliaries were called, that it would be easy to restrain and control the Indians to a more humane and civilized mode of warfare, finally prevailed, and the consent of the government was given to the measure, against the judgment and feelings of at least some of the officers of the crown.

EXTRACT OF COL. CLAUS' LETTER TO SECRETARY KNOX.

Dated Montreal, Nov. 6th, 1777.

"It is the opinion of several that had I not appeared at the expedition, and Joseph (Brant) acted so indefatigably and cleverly, with his party, as to cause an emulation, the Six Nations would not have been encouraged to act, (when the rebels advanced upon us) by Col. Butler, they having declared publicly, that they were not called to war, but to a congress to be held at Oswego, and receive presents." * * *

In November, Col. Guy Johnson writing to Lord George Germain, makes a general report of his proceedings as general Superintendent of Indian Affairs, of which the following is an extract:

This letter is dated New York, November 11, 1777.

"The greater part of those men from the Six Nations, with my officers in that country, joined Gen. St Leger's troops, and Sir John Johnson's Provincials, and were principally concerned in the action, near Fort Stanwix, when the rebels lost their General, and several of their principal officers, and a large number of their men, and the Indians had about thirty of their principal warriors killed ; and undoubtedly had the number of men under Brigadier General St Leger been adequate to the service and the difficulties, they met with, the Indians would have rendered more material service.

"On the other communication, Gen. Burgoyne has testified for them, to whom the Mohawk tribes were obliged to retire, after the unlucky affair at Bennington, which raised the drooping spirits of the rebels, who have since burned the Mohawk villages, of which I shall avail myself, as it will strengthen the resentment of the several Nations.

"The rebels have also completed the destruction of my property, and parcelled out my estate. The Six Nations complain much of the Oneidas ; the manner in which they have been seduced by the New England Missionaries, I long since represented. I know they are much more inclined to neutrality, than to war, but they are too inconsiderable, to deserve much notice, whilst the loyality of the rest, under so many disagreeable circumstances, merits everything I can say for them." * *

The Senecas seem now to have been entirely committed to the interest of the King. They had been led to believe that the colonists were poor, and weak, while the King was rich, and powerful. Guy Johnson had impressed this idea strongly upon their minds, in his speech to them at Oswego, in which he was seconded by Brant, who had been to England and seen the evidences of the wealth, and power, of the British Nation. The liberal distribution of valuable presents, which the colonists were unable to do, confirmed them more fully in the belief that it was their true policy to adhere to the cause of their great father, the King.

In the same month the following letter was written by Cols. Bolton and Butler to Gen. Clinton:

Niagara, 23d Nov. 1777.

"SIR:—Joseph (Brant) and myself are ready to wait your orders. We wish to know your situation, and when we can be of use to you, and where. We only wish to know the time, and place, as we are confident of being well supported.

"The bearer is faithful, and of abilities, your excellency may confide in him; our friends are determined to be so in the worst of times.

MASON BOLTON.
JOHN BUTLER,
Dep'ty Sup't Ind'n Affairs.

Gen. Clinton or officer commanding on the Hudson river, or Sir Wm. Howe."

It would seem from the correspondence about this time that some objection had been made by Lord George Germain to employing Indians, and permitting them to carry on the war in their own savage and unrestrained manner. But Col. Johnson assured his Lordship, that there was no difficulty in restraining the Indians in this respect; that the tomahawk and scalping knife are not to be so much dreaded, as he has been led to suppose. That the former "is seldom used except to smoke through, or to cut wood with, and that they (the Indians) are very rarely guilty of anything more than scalping the dead, in which article they may be restrained," and says "some of the American Colonies offer a price for scalps."

CHAPTER XVIII.

Almost simultaneously with the expedition of General St Leger against Fort Stanwix, was that of Gen. Burgoyne against Ticonderoga. Had both these expeditions proved successful, it was the intention that the two should unite at Albany, and open communication with New York, and thus cut off the connection between New England and the south or middle states. It was the policy of the British government however, to conceal the real object of this expedition. Its destination was supposed to be against Boston.

Sir Guy Carlton who was Commander-in-Chief of the forces in Canada, it is said was strongly opposed to the employment of the Indian forces to act in conjunction with regular soldiers; and for this reason it was said the command was transferred to General Burgoyne, who was less scrupulous as to the character of the forces to be employed. It is certain however, that Sir Guy Carleton exhibited no such scruples, when in 1775 he courted the alliance of the Mohaws under Brant. The Indians accompanying Gen. Burgoyne to the number of several hundred, were all Canada Indians, probably Massasaugas and Hurons, and the cruelties which are recorded as following in the track of this expedition, are in no way chargeable to the Indians of the Six Nations. They, were employed at the time, in the expedition of Gen. St Leger, as a comparison of dates will show. Among the cruelties practiced by the Indians accompanying Gen. Burgoyne's army, none has excited greater sympathy than the fate of Miss McCrea. Every circumstance connected with this unnatural and bloody transaction (says Col. Stone) around which there lingers a melancholy interest to this day, served to heighten alike its interest and its enormity. Miss McCrea belonged to a family of Loyalists which resided at the village of Fort Edward. She was engaged to a young English Officer in Burgoyne's army of the name of Jones. It had been agreed between the parties that when the British forces should advance to the place of her residence, she would join him, and they would consumate the union to which they had mutually pledged themselves. The impatient lover anxious to possess himself of his bride, sent forward three Indian chiefs, to bring her to the British camp. The reluctance of her family and friends to her trusting herself to such an escort, created some delay. But her affection triumphed over her prudence, and in spite of the entreaty of friends and relations, she set forward with no other attendants than her savage conductors. She was on horseback. They had proceeded but a short distance, before her conductors stopped to drink at a spring. In the mean time her lover impatient at the delay, dispatched a second party of Indians upon the same errand. The two parties met at the spring, where it is said they became engaged in a controversy about the promised compensation for their services, for bringing her in safety to her betrothed. Both parties claimed it, which it was said, was a barrel of rum. In the heat of the controversy, one of the chiefs, to put an end to the controversy, struck her down with his hatchet. "Tradition reports that the Indians divided the scalp, and that each party carried half of it to the agonized lover." Before the Indians had left the spring, they were attacked by a pursuing party of Provincials, and at the close of the skirmish, the body of Miss McCrea was found among the slain, tomahawked, and scalped, and tied to a pine tree, which is yet standing, a sad memorial of this terrible deed of blood.

A correspondence passed between Gen. Gates, and Gen. Burgoyne, relating to this transaction, which in justice to the parties concerned, should be copied. After charging the British Commander with encouraging the Indians to acts of cruelty, and the murder of defenceless women and children by offering a price for scalps, he thus speaks of the case above related:

"Miss McCrea, a young lady lovely to the sight, of virtuous character and amiable disposition, engaged to an officer of your army, was with other women and children taken out of a house near Fort Edward, carried into the woods, and there scalped and mangled in the most horrid manner. Two parents with six children were treated with the same inhumanity, while quietly resting in their own peaceful dwelling. The miserable fate of Miss McCrea was particularly aggravated, she being dressed to receive her promised husband, but met her murderer, employed by you. Upward of one hundred men, women, and children, have perished by the hands of the ruffians, to whom it is asserted you have paid the price of blood."

Gen. Burgoyne replied to this letter, repelling with indignation, the charge of encouraging the outrages of the Indians, in any manner whatever. But asserted that from the first, he had refused to promise, or pay anything for scalps. The only rewards he offered were for prisoners brought in, and hoped by the adoption of this course, to encourage a more humane mode of warfare on their part. He said "I would not be guilty of the acts you presume to impute to me, for the whole Continent of America, though the wealth of worlds was in its bowels, and a paradise upon its surface." In regard to the hapless fate of Miss McCrea, Gen. Burgoyne remarked :

"Her fall wanted not the tragic display, you have labored to give it, to make it as severely abhorred, and lamented by me, as it can be by the tenderest of her friends. The act was no premeditated barbarity. On the contrary, two chiefs who had brought her off for security, not of violence to her person, disputed which should be her guard ; and in a fit of savage passion, in one from whose hands she was snatched, the unhappy woman became the victim.

"Upon the first intelligence of this event, I obliged the Indians to deliver the murderer into my hands, and thought to have punished him by our laws, or principles of justice, would have been perhaps unprecedented, he certainly should have suffered an ignominious death, had I not been convinced from my circumstances, and observation, beyond the possibility of doubt, that a pardon under the terms which I presented, and they accepted, would be more efficatious, than an execution, to prevent similar mischiefs.

"The above instance excepted, your intelligence is false."

The expedition under Burgoyne proved even more disastrous, to the cause of the Loyalists, than that under St Leger. Although everything seemed to favor him, and he had advanced to, and captured Fort Edward, he began to experience a series of defeats and repulses, in which his army was greatly weakened by losses, while that of the Americans was contiually strengthened by additions. It was on the 17th of September, 1777, that a general battle was brought on, it is said more by accident, than design, on the part of either of the commanding Generals, which proved one of the most obstinate, and bloody of the revolution. It continued a good part of the day, and was only terminated by the darkness of the night. Gen. Wilkinson, who himself participated in the battle, says:

"Neither, attempted a single manouvre during one of the longest, warmest, and most obstinate battles, fought in America. Gen. Gates believed his antagonist intended to attack him, and circumstances seemed to justify a like conclusion, on the part of Burgoyne; and as the thickness and depth of an intervening wood, concealed the position of either army from its adversary, sound caution obliged the respective Commanders to guard every assailable point. Had either of the Generals been properly apprised of the dispositions of his antagonist, a serious blow might have been struck, either on the left of the American army, or on the enemy's right."

The loss on the part of the Americans, in killed and wounded, was between three and four hundred, while that of the British was from six hundred to one thousand killed, wounded, and prisoners.

Early in October Gen. Burgoyne finding his army

greatly reduced by the losses he had sustained, his supplies getting short, and his communications with his base of supplies being threatened, began to feel that his situation was becoming critical. His entire Indian force had left him. In this critical state of affairs, a council of war was called in the camp of Gen. Burgoyne ; some of his officers recommended a retreat, others an attack upon the American works. Burgoyne himself expressed strong aversions to a retreat, and proposed to lead an assault in person. The attack though made with vigor, and under disguise, was seasonably discovered by the Americans, and repulsed, with great loss on the part of the British, who lost more than four hundred officers and men, killed wounded, and prisoners, including the flower of his army, while the loss of the Americans was inconsiderable. Burgoyne now commenced his retreat. Gen. Gates lost no time in disposing his forces so as to intercept this movement, by throwing a force in his rear, upon all the routes by which it was possible for him to escape.

Thus surrounded with difficulties, his effective force reduced to less than thirty-five hundred men, short of provisions, the American army increasing every moment, and now forming almost an entire circle around him, no alternative was left Gen. Burgoyne but to negotiate the best terms of surrender he was able, which was done with the unanimous consent of his surviving officers. Terms of capitulation were soon agreed upon, and on the 17th of October, 1777, the Royal army surrendered prisoners of war. The first meeting of Burgoyne with Gates is thus described by Gen. Wilkinson :

"Gen. Gates being advised of Gen. Burgoyne's approach, met him at the head of his camp. Burgoyne in a rich royal uniform, and Gates in a plain blue frock; when they had approached nearly within a sword's length, they reined up and halted. I then named the gentlemen, and Gen. Burgoyne raising his hat most gracefully said: 'The fortune of war, Gen. Gates, has made me your prisoner,' to which the conqueror returning a courtly salute, promptly replied: "I shall always be ready to bear testimony that it has not been through any fault of your excellency."

Gen. Burgoyne with all his general officers were treated with the courtesy and consideration due to brave, but unfortunate men. They were received into Gen. Gate's quarters, and entertained by him at a dinner, where the conversation was affable and free. The whole conduct of Gen. Gates was highly honorable to his generosity, which Gen. Burgoyne and his officers duly appreciated, and publicly acknowledged.

CHAPTER XIX.

The year 1778 was an eventful one for the Senecas; and in order to a full understanding of these events, a few extracts from the official correspondence of this period, will introduce the notice of them.

Extract of a letter of Col. Guy Johnson to Lord Germain, dated New York, 12th March, 1778.

My Lord:—"I have now the pleasure to inform your Lordship, that notwithstanding the events of last campaign to the northward, the Indians are as firm as ever, and eager for service; a courier having just arrived here, with messages to me, and a billet to the General, signed by Lieut. Col. Bolton, commanding at Niagara, and by my deputy Mr. Butler, of which the enclosed is a copy; which briefly shows their zeal, readiness, and abilities. On this subject, I have by direction of Sir Henry Clinton wrote at large to Sir Wm. Howe, whose commands I hope shortly to receive, that I may send back such messages, as he approves or such as will prepare them (the Indians) to meet me, agreeable to the proposal I submitted to your Lordship, and to him, at such time, and place, to the northward, as should be approved of for the purpose of keeping the Indians out of the reach of rebel emissaries, and of employing them in the way most serviceable to the government.

"In my letter of November last, I explained the general design I had in view, and although from the nature of this war, the best schemes may be rendered abortive. I think I can rely upon the advantages to be derived, from what I have proposed ; as it will keep the Indians out of the reach of the rebel arts, and employ them in some servicable manner. For until we have possession of some direct communication to the Six Nations, we cannot have them better occupied, than as I have mentioned, until the arrival of more troops ; unless they are let loose to carry on the Petitte Guerre (small war) in their own way. Indians, with small bodies of troops, are often exposed to what appears to them, as very discouraging difficulties ; in which cases, they cannot be expected to keep together, like British troops ; nor can they ever do so, after the beginning of October, because of the hunting season. They do not adopt the same ideas of bravery, nor can they feel so much interest in our cause, as Britons do; but, in all other respects, they afford much security to an army, and strike a terror into the enemy.

"The French system of management, by several distinct agents, was calculated for that government, and the state of the domesticated tribes near their cities in Canada ; but suits no others, as Sir William Johnson fully demonstrated, to his Majesty's ministers. No uniform system, could be pursued, on such a plan, and the French after much expense and trouble, lost the Indians by it. They entered into the fullest treaty with me at Ontario, and in Canada, in 1775 ; they have hitherto adhered, and will still adhere, to the same, if duly attended to ; but to render them truly serviceable, the nature of the service, and the time it is likely to take up, are necessary considerations, as well as under what restrictions they are to act, since it appears they are so much misrepresented in the article of cruelty. It is well known my Lord, that the Colonists, solicited the Indians early in 1775, that they proposed to make me prisoner, that they carried some Indians then to their camp, near Boston, as they did others since, who were taken in the battle on Long Island. That the tomahawk, that is so much talked of, is seldom used, except to smoke through, or to cut wood with, and that they are very rarely guilty of cruelty, more than scalping the dead, in which article even, they may be restrained. It is also certain, that no objection was made to them formerly, that the king's instructions of 1754, to Gen. Braddock, and many since, direct their being employed, whilst some of the American colonies went further, by fixing a price for scalps. Surely, foreign enemies have an equal claim to humanity with others. Perhaps some of these hints are not amiss, my motives, I hope, will apologise for them. I am persuaded that I am by no means destitute of the feelings of humanity, and that I can restrain the Indians, from acts of savage cruelty; but as I must be ignorant of the intended operations, I can only humbly propose, as I have already done, to collect the Indians in some fitting place, out of the reach of the rebel agents, till the arrival of more troops, or till some movement can be made, that will give us the possession of the important communication, between this and the lakes; and if, in the mean time, I can be honored with your Lordship's commands, or be directed to give any further agreeable appearances to the

Indians, it will be highly pleasing to them, and useful to his Majesty's service.

I have the honor to be, with great respect,

My Lord, your Lordship's

Ob't and most hmb'l servant,

G. JOHNSON."

How well these promises were kept, or these restraints upon the savage mode of warfare practiced by the Indians were realized, the history of the unrestrained Indian war instigated by the agents and officers of the British government, during this year, furnish the melancholy evidence. The slaughter of Wyoming, was perpretated by a party consisting of loyalists, or tories, and Indians, under Col. John Butler. The expedition was organized at Niagara, and was undoubtedly largely augmented in its march through the country, both by additions of whites and Indians. There have been published, several different versions of this affair, most of which assume that Joseph Brant led the Indians on the occasion. But the official report of Col. Guy Johnson, shows that Brant was not present, but engaged, at the time, on another expedition. It is equally certain, that the Indians engaged were principally Senecas, and were led by their own war chiefs, to whose skill and bravery the success of the enterprise was mainly attributable. The original force, consisted of about three hundred white men, principally refugee loyalists, under Butler, and about five hundred Indians. The expedition left Niagara the latter end of June, 1778, passing by way of the Indian settlement, on the Genesee river, to Tioga point, where the forces were embarked on floats, and rafts, and descending the Susquehanna, landed at a place called Three Islands, whence they marched about twenty miles, and crossing a wilderness, entered the valley of the Wyoming. The inhabitants, on being apprised of the advance of the invaders, retired into a fortification, called "Fort Forty." Col. Zebulon Butler, who was in command of the colonial forces, was desirous of waiting within the Fort, for reinforcements, which were hourly expected. But, being overruled by his officers, in this prudent resolution, he marched out, with about four hundred men, to meet the advancing foe, whose force was greatly under estimated by the colonists.

Col. John Butler had encamped with his forces, at some miles distance, from the fort; and it was the intention of the Americans, by a sudden movement, to surprise their camp ; but their approach was discovered by an Indian scout, who immediately gave the alarm. They however pushed forward rapidly, but found the enemy formed in line of battle, in front of his camp, on a plain thinly covered with pine, shrub-oak, and underbrush, and extending from the river to a marsh, at the foot of the mountain. On coming in view of the enemy, the Americans, who had advanced in single column, immediately deployed into line, of equal extent. The right wing, commanded by Col. Zebulon Butler, the left wing by Col. Denison. The left of the enemy rested on "Witermoot's Fort," already in flames, and was commanded by Col. John Butler, who, divested of his uniform, appeared on the ground, with a handkerchief tied round his head. His division was composed of refugees and loyalists; a company of Johnson's Royal Greens, under Capt. Caldwell, formed on Butler's right, with Indian sharp shooters filling the space between. The main body of the Indians forming the right wing, extended to the morass, or swamp. This appears to have been the disposition of the forces, as gathered from the most reliable and authentic sources of information. There is no doubt that the Americans were greatly deceived as to the actual Birtish and Indian forces, which had been greatly increased, by the addition of numbers of tories, still residing in the neighborhood, and also by a large number of Indian warriors, who joined the expedition in its passage through the Senecas' country. The attack was begun by the Americans, at about four o'clock in the afternoon; the order was for the men to advance one step, at each discharge. The firing along the whole American line was rapid and steady, and as they advanced, the British line gave way, in spite of the exertions of their officers to prevent it. The Indians on the right of Butler's command, who acted as sharp shooters, appeared to be divided into six bands, or squads, and cheered each other at intervals, by a yell at one end of the line, and repeated responsively by all the rest. As the battle waxed warmer, the fearful yell was renewed, again and again, with more and more spirit. It appeared to be, at once their animatnig shout, and their signal of communication. The battle had raged for half an hour, when the vastly superior force of the enemy began to show itself. Hitherto, a large portion of the Indians had been concealed from view; but their fire, from their covert in the swamp, had proved destructive to the lives, of several valuable officers. But now they rose from their concealment, and commenced a flanking movement on the left of the American line. Nothing could withstand the impetuosity of the Senecas, under their brave leaders; Col. Denison's wing was thrown into confusion, and all efforts to form a new line at right angles with the first, to meet this new attack, proved unavailing. The rout became general. On seeing this, the Indians throwing away their guns, rushed in with horrid yells, using only their tomahawks, with terrible execution. No quarter was given, and many are the records of personal bravery exhibited on that bloody field that day. So terrible was the slaughter, that it is said "that less than sixty of the Americans escaped, either the rifle or the tomahawk. Although there have been many thrilling narratives of the "massacre" said to have been perpetratad at this time at Wyoming, yet the truth of history compels the conclusion, that these for the most part were mere fictions. Stone in his life of Brant says, "it does not appear that anything like a massacre followed the capitulation." Capt. Walter Butler, in his letter to Gen. Clinton states positively, that no massacre of prisoners or women and children took place at Wyoming; and it does not appear that the truth of this assertion was ever questioned. The attack upon Wyoming, as well as that upon Cherry Valley, both of which occurred in the same year, may be considered the legitimate fruit of the measures recommended by Col. Guy Johnson, and adopted by the British government, to subdue the rebellion. After the affair at Wyoming, Col. John Butler returned to Niagara, and the Senecas to their homes, at Kanesadaga or Genesee. Early in October, Mr. Dean, the Indian interpreter and agent, wrote Major Cochran, commanding at Fort Stanwix, as follows: "A Seneca chief, called Big Tree, who was all the summer past with Gen. Washington, returned through Oneida; he gave our friends there the most solemn assurance, that upon arrival in his country, he would exert his utmost influence to dispose his tribe to peace and friendship with the United States; and that should his attempts prove unsuccessful, he would immediately leave his nation, and join the Oneidas with his friends and adherents. A long time having elapsed, without hearing from Big Tree, the Oneidas, a few days since, dispatched a runner to him, desiring an account of his success. The express returned yesterday with the following intelligence, which the sachems immediately forwarded to me, by three of their warriors, namely: that upon his arrival in the Seneca country, he found that people in arms, and the two villages Kanadaseago and Jennessee, where he was, crowded with their warriors; collected from the remotest settlements. That upon Big Tree's first arrival, appearances seemed to promise him success; but that a rumor being circulated that the Americans were about to invade them, they had all flown to arms. Big Tree was there, and determined to chastise the enemy that dared presume to think of penetrating their country. That they are to be joined by all the Indians as far as Onondaga, a small party of whom has gone to meet them, and likewise by those of the several settlements upon the branches of the Susquehanna. That the Senecas were to march the 8th, and the others the 9th instant. That the whole party were to rendezvous at Kanakals, a place situated on the branch of the Susquehanna, called Tioga branch, and from thence were to proceed against the frontiers of Pennsylvania or the Jerseys. Our Oneida friends rely on the authenticity of the above intelligence, and beg that it may not be neglected." On the 6th of November, the following letter was sent from Fort Stanwix to Col. Alden, who commanded at Cherry Valley, "Sir, we are just now informed by an Oneida Indian, arrived at their castle, from one of the branches of the Susquehanna, called the Tioga; that he was present at a great meeting of Indians and tories, at that place; and their result was, to attack Cherry Valley, and that young Butler was to head the tories. I send you this information that you may be on your guard. Col. Alden immediately acknowledged the receipt of the above by the return messenger. Capt. Walter Butler, son of Col. John Butler, had accompanied Col. Guy. Johnson in his flight to Canada. He visited the Mohawk Valley early in the summer of 1778, where he was arrested and sent to Albany a prisoner, and confined in the Albany jail. Being sick, or feigning it, he was taken to a private house in the city, and placed under guard. Through the connivance, or co-operation of the family, the guard was stupefied with liquor, and Butler escaped on horseback to Niagara, and joined his father. It is said that he projected the expedition against Cherry Valley, to avenge the wrongs he supposed himself to have suffered in his capture and imprisonment. For this purpose he procured from his father who was then in command at Niagara, the command of a part of his regiment, called Butler's Rangers, together with authority to employ the forces under Brant, who had spent most of the summer on the Susquehanna, and its vicinity. On his way he met Brant, who, with his forces, was returning to winter quarters at Niagara. Brant was displeased at being placed under Walter Butler, but was prevailed upon to join the expedition. The united force consisted of about two hundred rangers and five hundred

Indians. The season was so far advanced, and Brant and his Indians having left the country, the inhabitants, many of whom had left in the summer, in consequence of the repeated attacks of the Indians upon the frontiers, had now returned to their homes, where they hoped to remain in security, during the winter. A fort had been built at Cherry Valley, by order of Gen. Lafayette, who visited the Mohawk valley, in the spring of this year, and on the first intimation of the approaching invasion, the inhabitants requested permission to remove with their valuable effects into the fort. But Col. Alden not giving full credit to the information given by the Oneida Indians, refused the request, and treated their apprehensions as groundless; saying that he should keep out scouts, who would apprise them in season, to secure themselves in case of real danger. But, it was to the carelessness, or criminality of these scouts, in which they confided, that ruin was brought upon them. The scouts sent down the Susquehanna, carelessly kindled a fire at night, and foolishly, or criminally, lay down to sleep. The fire was discovered by the enemy, and before daylight, the Americans were surrounded, and all taken prisoners, without any alarm being given.

Having obtained all the information they desired from their prisoners, on the morning of the 11th, twenty-four hours after the capture of the scouts, the enemy moved from his encampment toward the fort. Having learned from the scouts that the officers of the garrison lodged in different private houses out of the fort, their forces were so disposed that a party should surround every house in which an officer lodged. A storm of snow in the night, which gradually changed to rain towards morning, creating a thick, hazy atmosphere, favored their approach. The Rangers, who were approaching cautiously, in advance, stopped, to examine their pieces, the powder being exposed to wet by the rain. This gave the Indians an opportunity to rush by, and commence the assault. The advance body was composed principally of Senecas. Col. Alden had escaped from the house at the moment the Indians came up, and ran for the fort. He was pursued by an Indian, with tomahawk in hand, and challenged to surrender, which he peremptorily refused to do, but, drew his pistol upon his pursuer. It missed fire, upon which the Indian hurled his tomahawk, with such deadly aim, that it struck him on the head, he fell, and was scalped, being one of the first victims of his own most criminal neglect of duty.

Others of the officers were taken prisoners. The indiscriminate massacre of the inhabitants immediately commenced, in which, if the accounts are true, the savages were exceeded in barbarity by the tories of Butler's Rangers. A party of Indians had entered a house and killed and scalped a mother and a large family of children. They had just completed their work of death, when some royalists belonging to their party came up, and discovered an infant alive in the cradle. An Indian warrior, noted for his barbarity, approached the cradle with uplifted hatchet. The babe looked up into his face and smiled, the feelings of nature triumphed over the ferocity of the savage. The hatchet fell from his hand, and he was in the act of taking the infant in his arms, when one of the royalists, cursing the Indian for his humanity, took it up on the point of his bayonet, and holding it up, struggling in the agonies of death, exclaimed "this too is a rebel."* Whole families were indiscriminately slaughtered. The family of Mr. Robert Wells, consisting of thirteen persons, was barbarously murdered. "One of the tories boasted that he killed Mr. Wells while at prayer."* He, and his family, were not active partisans, but remained quietly, yet always performing military duty when called upon, to defend the country. The father of Mr. Robert Wells, then deceased, had been one of the Judges of Tryon county, and in that capacity, had acted with Sir William Johnson, and also with Col. John Butler, who had also been a Judge; hence there existed an intimacy, and friendship, between the families; and it is said Col. John Butler expressed great sorrow and remorse at their melancholy fate. In conversation relative to them, he remarked, "I would have gone miles on my hands and knees, to have saved that family; and why my son did not do it, God only knows."*

The circumstances of the death of Miss Jane Wells, the sister of Mr. Robert Wells, were peculiarly aggravating. During the slaughter of the whole family to which she was an unwilling spectator, she fled from the house, and sought shelter behind a large pile of wood, near by. Here she was pursued by an Indian, who, as he approached, deliberately wiped his bloody knife upon his leggins, and then placed it in his sheath; then drawing his tomahawk, he seized her by the arm; she possessing some knowledge of the Indian language, remonstrated, and supplicated, in vain. Peter Smith, a tory, who had formerly been a domestic in Mr. Wells' family, now interposed, saying, that she was his sister, and desiring him

*Campbell's Annals of Tryon County.

to spare her life. He shook his tomahawk at him, in defiance, and then turning round, with one blow, smote her to the earth.

A Mr. Mitchell, who was in his field, beheld a party of Indians approaching; he could not gain his house, and was obliged to flee to the woods. Here he evaded pursuit, and escaped. A melanchollу spectacle presented itself on his return. It was the corpse of his wife, and four children. His house had been plundered, and set on fire. He extinguished the fire, and by examination, found life existing in one of his children, a little girl of ten or twelve years of age. He raised her up, and placed her in the door, and was bending over her, when he saw another party approaching. He had barely time to hide himself behind a log fence, near by, before they were at the house. From this hiding place he beheld an infamous tory by the name of Newberry, extinguish the little spark of life, which remained in his child, with a blow of his hatchet.* Newberry was arrested as a spy the following summer and tried by a court martial, found guilty and was executed.

The house of Col. Campbell was surrounded, and Mrs. Campbell and four children were taken prisoners. Col. Campbell was absent, but hastened home in time only to witness the destruction of his property, and the loss of his family without knowing their fate. Many others were killed, some few escaped to the Mohawk river, and the remainder were made prisoners. Thirty-two of the inhabitants, mostly women and children, and sixteen continental soldiers, were killed. Mrs. Clyde, the wife of

---

*Annals of Tryon county, p. 113.

Col. Clyde, fled with her children to the woods, and thus escaped.*

It should be recorded to the credit of Joseph Brant, that on this occasion he exhibited traits of humanity which seemed to be wanting in some, at least, of the white men present. "In a house which he entered, he found a woman engaged in her usual business. 'Are you (said he,) thus engaged, while all your neighbors are murdered around you?' 'We are King's people,' she replied. 'That plea will not avail you to-day. They have murdered Mr. Wells' family, who were as dear to me as my own.' 'There is one Joseph Brant, (said she,) if he is with the Indians he will save us.' 'I am Joseph Brant, but I have not the command, and, I know not that I can save you, but I will do what is in my power.' While speaking, several Senecas were observed approaching the house. 'Get into bed and feign yourself sick,' said Brant hastily. When the Senecas came in he told them there was no person there but a sick woman and her children, and besought them to leave the house, which, after a short conversation, they did. As soon as they were out of sight, Brant went to the end of the house and gave a long, shrill yell. Soon after, a small band of Mohawks were seen crossing the adjoining field, with great speed. As they came up he addressed them, 'where is your paint, here put my mark upon this woman, and her children.' As soon as it was done, he added, 'you are now probably safe.'"*

---

*Annals of Tryon county.

CHAPTER XX.

Much obloquy has been cast upon Capt. Walter Butler, for planning, and the manner in which this expedition was executed. It will be remembered that his mother, the wife of Col. John Butler, and her children, were detained as prisoners of war, by the committee of safety; and the capture of Mrs. Campbell and her children, and that of Mrs. Moore and her children, afforded Capt. Walter Butler an opportunity to procure the release of his own relatives, by an exchange, which was in fact subsequently accomplished.

On the second morning after their capture, all the captive women, and children, (except Mrs. Campbell and Mrs. Moore and their children,) were released, and sent back, with the following letter from Capt. Walter Butler, addressed to Gen. Schuyler.

CAPT. BUTLER TO GEN. SCHUYLER.

Cherry Valley, Nov. 12th, 1778.

SIR: I am induced by humanity, to permit the persons whose names I send herewith, to return, lest the inclemency of the season, and their naked and helpless situation, might prove fatal to them; and expect that you will release, an equal number of our people, in your hands, among whom I expect you will permit Mrs. Butler, and family, to come to Canada. But if you insist upon it, I engage to send you, moreover, an equal number of prisoners of yours, taken either by the Rangers, or Indians, and will leave it to you to name the persons. I have done every thing in my power to restrain the fury of the Indians, from hurting women and children, or killing the prisoners that fell into our hands, and would have more effectually prevented them, but that they were much incensed at the destruction of their village at Anguaga,* by your people. I look upon it beneath the character of a soldier, to wage war with women and children. I am sure that you are conscious, that Col. Butler or myself, have no desire that your women, and children, should be hurt; but be assured, that if you persevere in detaining my father's family, with you, that we shall no longer take the same pains to restrain the Indians from prisoners, women and children, that we have heretofore done.

I am your Humble Servant,

WALTER N. BUTLER,

Capt. Com. of the Rangers.

GEN. SCHUYLER.

Mrs. Campbell and her children were taken to Kanesedaga, (near Geneva,) where she was separated from her children, and placed in the family of a Seneca chief, to fill the place left vacant by the death of one of its members. This family was composed of females, with the exception of one aged warrior, who no longer went forth either to the chase or to war; this circumstance enabled

*One of the old names of Unadilla.

her to render herself useful to them. The Indians knew little of the most common arts of life; few of the Indian women, could make an ordinary calico garment; she made garments not only for the family to which she belonged, but also for the neighboring families, who in return, sent corn and venison, for their support. By reason of these services, she was under no restraint, but was free to go and come, as she pleased.

The Indians paid no regard to the Sabbath, but pursued their usual avocations on that day. On her informing them that she kept that day sacred, they no longer asked her to do any work, and gave strict orders to their children to remain silent, while in her presence.

An Indian came into the house one day, and asked her why she wore caps, saying, "Indians do not wear caps." She replied that it was the custom of her country women. "Well, (said he,) come to my house and I will give you a cap." Her adopted mother told her to follow him. As soon as they entered the house, he pulled from behind a beam, a cap of a smoky color, and handed it to her, saying in English, "I got that cap in Cherry Valley. I took it from the head of a woman." On examination, she recognized it as having belonged to the unfortunate Jane Wells, and was no doubt the one she had on when she was barbarously murdered, as it had a cut in the crown, made by the tomahawk, and was spotted with blood. She could not but drop a tear to the memory of one she had known from her infancy, as a pattern of virtue and loveliness. In the Indian who stood before her, she saw the murderer of her friend, and turned from him with horror."*

---

*Annals of Tryon county.

"Returning to her cabin, she tore off the lace border, and washing it carefully, though she could not efface the stains of blood, laid it away with the intention of giving it to some of the relatives of Miss Wells, if any of them had been fortunate enough to escape. She afterwards gave it to Miss Ramsey, a cousin, whom she found at Fort Niagara, and who, together with her mother, melted into tears, as they beheld this little relic, spotted with the blood of their deceased relative."*

The letter of Capt. Butler to Gen. Schuyler reached the hands of Col. Campbell, who, of all others, felt the greatest interest in carrying out the arrangement proposed; who lost no time in placing it in Gen. Schuyler's hands. It was not answered immediately, for the reason that Gen. Schuyler was not then in command of the District. Subsequently, however, it reached the hands of the proper authorities, and was answered by Brigadier General James Clinton.

GEN. CLINTON TO CAPT. BUTLER.

Albany, Jan. 1st, 1779.

SIR: A letter dated 12th of November last, signed by you, and addressed to Gen. Schuyler, and which was delivered by John Campbell, is come to hand. As its contents related to persons who were citizens of this State, with which the military do not interfere, the letter was not delivered to Brig. Gen. Hand, who commands in this Department, but transmitted to his Excellency, Gov. Clinton, that his pleasure might be known on its contents. He has authorized me to make the exchange you request. I am at a loss to know not only where to address you,

*Annals of Tryon county.

but also in what part of the country the unhappy prisoners from this State have been carried. I therefore send the bearers A. B., and C. D., with a flag, to carry this letter, to any place where they may learn you are, or any other officer who can accomplish the exchange in your absence. Should the prisoners be in any of the Indian villages, and in condition to be removed, you will please to send them to the nearest of our settlements. Or if you do not choose to do that, I will send proper persons to meet, and receive them, at any place you may appoint. I am not informed if Mrs. Butler, her family, and such others as will be given in exchange for those you have in captivity, and those you have suffered to return, as mentioned in your letter, would choose to go at this inclement season. If they do, they shall be sent; if not, they may remain till spring, and then they may go to Oswego, or Canada, at their option. Should the prisoners taken at Cherry Valley, or any others belonging to the State of New York, be at Niagara, it will be impossible for them to return until Spring; and then I request, that they may be sent to Oswego, or Fort Schuyler, (Fort Stanwix,) and that you will send notice of your determination, that provision may be made accordingly. Do not flatter yourself, sir, that your father's family have been detained on account of any consequence they were supposed to be of; or that it is determined they should be exchanged in consideration of the threat contained in your letter. I should hope for the sake of human nature, and the honor of civilized nations, that the British officers, had exerted themselves in restraining the barbarity of the savages. But it is difficult even for the most disinterested mind to believe it, as numerous instances of barbarity, have been perpetrated, where savages were not present; or if they were, the British force was not sufficient to restrain them, had there been a real desire to do so.

The enormous murders committed at Wyoming and Cherry Valley, would clearly have justified retaliation, and that your mother did not fall a sacrifice to the resentment of the survivors of those families, who were so barberously massacred, is owing to the humane principles which the conduct of their enemies evinces a belief they are utterly strangers to.

The flag will carry their arms with them, that they may furnish themselves with provisions, should, what they set out with, be expended before they reach any places where they can be supplied. As Capt. Butler may be absent, I enclose a copy of this letter to Gen. Schuyler.

I am, &c.,

JAMES CLINTON.

To Capt. Walter Butler, or any officer in the British service to whom this may be handed.*

This letter was dispatched with a flag of truce, in the middle of winter, through the Seneca's country, to Niagara; and called forth the following reply:

CAPT. BUTLER TO GEN. CLINTON.

Niagara, Feb. 18th, 1779.

SIR: I have received a letter dated the 1st of January last, signed by you, in answer to mine of the 12th No-

*Stones Life of Brant.

vember. Its contents I communicated to Col. Bolton, the commanding officer of this garrison, &c., by whom I am directed to acquaint you, that he had no objection that an exchange of prisoners, as mentioned in your letter, should take place; but not being fully empowered by his Excellency, Gen. Haldimand, to order the same immediately to be put in execution, has thought proper I should go down to the Commander-in-Chief for his direction in the matter. In the mean time, Col. Butler, as he has ever done, on every other occasion, will make every effort in his power, to have all the prisoners, as well those belonging to your troops, as the women and children in captivity, among the different Indian nations, collected, and sent into this post, to be forwarded to Crown Point, should the exchange take place by way of Canada or at Oswego, if settled there.

In either case Col. Bolton desires me to inform you, that the prisoners shall receive from him, what assistance their wants may require, which prisoners have at all times received at this post. The disagreeable situation of your people in the Indian villages, as well as ours amongst you, will induce me to make all the expedition in my power to Quebec, in order that the exchange may be settled as soon as possible. For the good of both, I make no doubt that his excellency, Gen. Haldimand will acquiesce in the proper exchange.

The season of the year renders it impossible that it should take place before the 10th or 15th of May next. However I shall write you by the way of Crown Point, Gen. Haldimand's determination ; and when, and where, the exchange will be most agreeable to him to be made. I could wish that Mrs. Butler and her family, including

Mrs. Scheehan and son, and Mrs. Wall, were permitted to go to Canada, in the spring, even should the exchange be fixed at Ontario.

"It is not our business, sir, to enter into an altercation, or to reflect on the conduct of either the British, or the Continental forces, or on that of each other; but since you have charged (on report I suppose) the British officers, in general, with inhumanity, and Col. Butler and myself in particular; in justice to them, and in vindication of his, and my own honor, and character, I am under the disagreeable necessity to declare the charge unjust, and void of truth; and which can only tend to deceive the world, though a favorite cry of the Congress, on every occasion, whether in truth or not. We deny any cruelties to have been committed at Wyoming, either by whites or Indians; so far to the contrary that not a man, woman, or child, was hurt after the capitulation, or a woman or child before it, and none taken into captivity. Though should you call it inhumanity to kill men in arms, in the field, we in that case plead guilty. The inhabitants killed at Cherry Valley, does not lay at our door. My conscience acquits (me.) If any are guilty, (as accessories) it is yourselves; at least, the conduct of some of your officers. First, Col. Hartley of your forces sent to the Indians the enclosed, being a copy of his letter, charging them with crimes they never committed, and threatening them and their villages with fire, and sword, and no quarters. The burning of one of their villages, then inhabited only by a few families, your friends who imagined they might remain in peace and friendship with you, till assured a few hours before the arrival of your troops, that they should not even receive quarters, took to the woods; and to complete the matter, Col. Denniston and his people, appearing again in arms, with Col. Hartley, after a solemn capitulation, and engagement, not to bear arms during the war; and Col. Denniston not performing a promise to release a number of soldiers belonging to Col. Butler's corps of Rangers, then prisoners among you, were the reasons assigned by the Indians to me, after the destruction of Cherry Valley, for their not acting in the same manner as at Wyoming. They added that being charged by their enemies with what they never had done, and threatened by them, they had determined to convince you it was not fear, which prevented them from committing the one, and that they did not want spirit to put your threats against them, in force against yourselves.

"The prisoners sent back by me, or any now in our or the Indians hands, must declare, I did everything in my power to prevent the Indians killing the prisoners or taking women and children captive, or in any wise injuring them.

"Col. Stacey, and several other officers of yours, when exchanged, will acquit me, and must further declare that they have received every assistance before, and since, their arrival at this post, that could be got to relieve their wants. I must however beg leave by the by, to observe that I experienced no humanity, or even common justice during my imprisonment among you.

"I enclose you a list of officers and privates, whom I should be glad were exchanged likewise. The list of the families, we expect for those as well sent back as others in our hands, you have likewise enclosed. Col. Stacey and several officers and others (of) your people are at this post and have leave to write.

I am your very humble servant,

WALTER N. BUTLER,

Capt. Corps of Rangers.

Brigadier General Clinton of the Continental forces.

Capt. Butler obtained the assent of Gen. Haldimand to the proposed exchange, and his father, Col. Butler lost no time in repairing to the Seneca castle at Kanedesaga to procure the release of Mrs. Campbell and her children. This was a matter of some difficulty, as the Indians were very reluctant to part with those they have adopted, and the family which had adopted Mrs. Campbell, interposed strong objections to entertaining any propositions for her release.

Her cause however was warmly espoused by the old chief sachem, Sayenquaraghta, and as a part of the family to which Mrs. Campbell belonged had removed to Genesee, whither she herself, was to go in a short time; the aged chief made a journey from Kanedesaga, at the foot of Seneca lake, to Genesee, on foot, and succeeded in obtaining the consent of all the members of the family to her release. On his return home, and before Mrs. Campbell was removed to Niagara, the old chief came to see her, and bid her an affectionate farewell, and wish her success on her journey. The following is his address to her, as repeated to her by an interpreter: "You are now about to return to your home and friends; I rejoice; you live a great way, many day's journey from here. I am an old man, I do not know that I shall live to the end of this war. If I do, when the war is over, I will come and see you."

The following extraordinary exhibition of the strange vicissitudes of war, from the "Life of Mary Jemison," (the white woman,) is inserted here, as connected with the history of the Cherry Valley massacre: "The same year at Cherry Valley, our Indians (the Senecas,) took a woman and her three daughters,* prisoners, and brought them on, leaving one at Canandaigua, one at Honeyoye, one at Canawagus, and the other (the woman,) at Little Beardstown, where I resided. The woman told me that she and her daughters, might have escaped, but that they expected the British army only, and therefore made no effort. Her husband and sons got away. After some time they were all taken to Niagara, where they were redeemed by Col. Butler, well clothed, and sent home, except one daughter, who was married to a British officer by the name of Johnson. Johnson was of the party who captured her, at which time he very unceremoniously, took from her finger, a gold ring, and appropriated it to his own use. When he saw her again at Niagara, he recognized her, restored the ring so impolitely borrowed, courted, and married her; and although the marriage ceremony was celebrated in a wilderness, far from the rendezvous of civilized society, and destitute of the facilities of obtaining the elegancies, conveniencies, or even the necessaries of life, they were singularly provided with a wedding ring."†

Two of the sons of Sir William Johnson, by Molly Brant, it will be remembered, were officers under Sir John Johnson, and the young captive maiden, captivated her captor, and under these strange circumstances, was

*This must be Mrs. Moore and her children.—Ed.
†Life of Mary Jemison, p. 115.

thus transferred from a bondage of force and fear, to one of liberty and love.*

In the narrative of Mrs. Campbell, she thus speaks of a female who occupied a very prominent and influential position among the Indians. She says: "Among the persons driven into the Fort (Niagara,) by the American army, was Catharine Montour, who had signalized herself by her inhumanity at Wyoming. She had two sons, who were leaders of bands, and who, consequently, imparted additional consequence to her. This creature, was treated with considerable attention by some of the officers. * * A son of Catharine Montour, took prisoner in Cherry Valley, Mr. Cannon, the father of Mrs. Campbell. Mr. Cannon was severely wounded by a musket ball, and was also advanced in life; but he had been a committee man, and had taken an active part in the war. He was therefore taken along, a prisoner, for the purpose of exchange. On the return of the party into the Indian country, Catharine, addressed her son in English, and in the presence of Mr. Cannon, reproaching him for having acted humanely, 'why did you bring that old man a prisoner? why did you not kill him when you first took him.' * * Catharine Montour, who might be well termed a fiend, acted a conspicuous part in this tragedy. She followed in the train of the victorious army, ransack-

*This romantic story lacks the element of entire accuracy. In Stone's Life of Brant, it is said that on the occasion of this wedding, Brant being present, insisted upon being married after the Episcopal form, to his third wife, with whom he was then living, but says it was Capt. Powell, who courted and married Miss Moore. In the narrative of the Gilbert family, it is stated that the wife of Capt. Powell interested herself strongly in behalf of Elizabeth Peart, the mother of the young child captured, "and inasmuch as she herself had also been a prisoner among the Indians, she claimed some relationship in their way, and her request was granted." This confirmation of Col. Stone's statement, was not discovered until after the account of Mary Jemison had been written. This correction is therefore added in a note.

ing the heaps of slain, and with her arms covered with gore, barbarously murdering the wounded, who in vain supplicated for their lives."

Mrs. Campbell was transferred from Niagara to Montreal, having recovered three of her children at the former post. On her arrival at Montreal she met Mrs. Butler, who had already been released, who had in charge Mrs. Campbell's fourth child, a little son, who although he had not forgotten his mother, had forgotten his mother tongue; he could speak only Indian. He was dressed in the uniform of Butler's Rangers. From Montreal, Mrs. Campbell was sent to Albany by way of lake Champlain, where she joined her husband.*

The truth of this statement in regard to Catharine Montour, is doubted by Col. Stone. He says, "from the antecedent character of that remarkable woman, the story can hardly be credited."†

The question as to who led the Indians at the battle of Wyoming, is one that has been of rather difficult solution. Brant, for many years, was the reputed leader, but this was denied by Brant himself, and it is a matter of record, that John Brant, the son of Joseph Brant, visited the author of "Gertrude, of Wyoming," and exhibited to Mr. Campbell documents, to prove that his father was not present at the battle of Wyoming, which were entirely satisfactory to Mr. Campbell, who did not hesitate to correct the error into which he had fallen, in the next edition of his work, and in a letter over his own signature, dated London, Jan. 20th, 1822.

Col. Stone, in his life of Brant, (see note to the 4th edition, p. 342,) says: "The Indians engaged were chiefly

*Annals of Tryon county.
†Stone's Life of Brant, p. 339, v. 1.

Senecas. Their leader was a chief named Gi-en-gwah-toh." This does not at all relieve the subject of difficulty. Gi-en-gwah-toh, in Seneca, is identical with Say-en-qua-ragh-ta in Mohawk, and is the name, or title, of the same individual—and means the bearer of the smoking brand, from the great council fire of the Six Nations, to kindle that of the Seneca Nation. "His official name, (says Rev. Asher Wright, in a manuscript letter,) was Gui-yah-gwaah-doh, which I understand to mean, the smoke has passed by, but the idea intended to be conveyed was smoke bearer."*

The following is an extract of a letter written in answer to one of inquiry, written by the author to Rev. Ashur Wright. Mr. Wright has been long a resident among the Senecas, and unquestionably has a better critical knowledge of the Seneca language, than any white man now living. Speaking of "Young King," he says: "That son was a chief of some distinction, and held the important office of internuncius between the grand council of the Six Nations and the Seneca Nation. He bore the smoking brand from the great council fire to kindle that of the Senecas. His official name was Gui-yah-gwaah-doh, which I understand to mean the smoke has passed by, from gwaah, smoke, and oahdoh, it is passed, or has passed by; but the idea intended to be conveyed was "smoke bearer." Hence the white people finding that the idea of smoke was in his Indian name, gave him that appellation, and called his father "Old Smoke," not knowing that father and son can never bear the same name among the Indians, for they belong to different clans or tribes; and all names are clan property, so to speak. The parents must always be of different clans, because they must not bear a blood relationship to each other. The children always belong to the clan of the mother, and may bear the offices of that clan and no other. Chieftianship was inherited from the mother's brothers, never from the fathers. How the name of "King" came to be applied to the smoke bearer of those days, I have not been able to learn; but having obtained it, and the father and the son both dwelling in the same house, he was called "Young King," and his father "Old King," to distinguish them from each other. I have not seen the Johnson manuscripts, but the name you give from them for Old King, appears to be the Mohawk mode of pronouncing the official title of Young King, and without doubt, belonged to his predecessor in office, (all the names of chiefs are names of office, and are handed down from generation to generation.) Probably his maternal uncle or grandfather, was his immediate predecessor. It could not have been his father; and if that name was applied to the father by white people, it must have been through ignorance of Indian custom; * * but my knowledge of the Indians, makes

*Some say it is from o yah-gwaah, smoke, and oh-wah-doh, it is extinguished, or it has disappeared; in other words, it has gone out of sight. This may be a better definition.

"Old King," or "Old Smoke," as he was familiarly called by the whites, was the chief sachem of the Senecas at Kanesadaga, (Geneva,) from about 1655 to the time of the destruction of that town by Gen. Sullivan, in 1779. It was in the spring of this year, that he is mentioned in connection with the liberation of Mrs. Campbell, as an "old man," and we learn from the narrative of the Gilbert family, that he, with his family, were at Niagara in 1780, and that he came to Buffalo Creek with his daughter, the wife of Rowland Montour, and the rest of his family, in the spring of 1781, and subsequently died, and was buried at "Smoke's Creek." Now it is impossible that he should have been the leader of the Indians at Wyoming in 1778. The question then arises, who was the Gui-yah-gwaah-doh that led the Indians on that occasion? It could not have been "Young King," who bore that title in 1825, for at the time of the battle of Wyoming, he could have been no more than nine years of age. Some other individual bearing that name or title, for such it was, must have been the leader. The Indians say that old "Black Snake," was one of the leaders on that occasion. He died a few years since at Alleghany, aged over one hundred years.

It is very certain that the statement made by "the in-

---

it certain to me, that whoever bore that Mohawk name, was some maternal relation of 'Young King.' The dates will help to determine whether he was his immediate, or some more distant predecessor in office. Very likely, if the name occurs through a period of many years, several different persons were intended by it, but no one of them should have been called "Head Chief" of the Senecas, for each one of them, all from the organization of the confederacy downward, was simply in his day, the messenger of the confederate council, to kindle the Seneca council fire, on business of the confederation. Personally, he might be a man of great influence, and thus be a head man, but officially, he could only be an internuncius; and I suspect it is the nature of his official business that gives him, in the manuscripts, the appearance of being a Head Chief, to those unacquainted with the Indian mode of doing business."

dustrious gleaner of border warfare reminiscences, the author of the history of Schoharie," in regard to the following certificate, which it is said, was found among the papers of Capt. Machim, who is said to have been at the head of the engineers in Sullivan's expedition, is erroneous: "This may certify that Kayingwaarto, the Sanakee chief, has been on an expedition to Fort Stanwix, and taken two scalps, one from an officer and a corporal. They were gunning near the fort; for which I promise to pay at sight, ten dollars for each scalp. Given under my hand at Buck's Island.

JOHN BUTLER,

Col. and Sup't. of the Six Nations, and the allies of His Majesty."

The "industrious gleaner of border warfare reminiscences" adds, "this Kayengwaarto, was a principal Seneca chief at Kanadesago; he was killed by a scouting party of Gen. Sullivan's army, and in his pocket the certificate was found. The history of those scalps is one of the most melancholy tales of that era of terrible savage warfare."

The remarks which have already been made, to show that Sayenquaraghta, the principal Seneca chief at Kanadesago, could not have been the leader of the Indians at Wyoming, will apply with equal force against the truth or probability of this statement about the above certificate. It is historically certain that the age, if nothing else, would preclude the possibility of Sayenquaraghta's being the person who wounded and scalped Capt. Greg, and his corporal, near Fort Stanwix, in 1778. And it is equally certain that Sayenquaraghta was not killed by a scouting party of Sullivan's army in 1779, but was alive and well, at Niagara, in 1780, and came to reside at Buffalo Creek in 1781.

It has been stated that this certificate bore evidence on its face of its spurious character. The certificate purports to be given by Col. John Butler, and is signed by him as "Superintendent of the Six Nations, and the allies of his Majesty." Now Col. John Butler had for many years before, and up to the time of the breaking out of the Revolution, been a magistrate, and Judge, in the county of Tryon. Of course, he was a man of education. He understood and spoke the Indian language, at least the Mohawk, as all accounts show. He had often written the name of the "principal Seneca chief," named in this certificate, which in the Mohawk is uniformly written by Sir William Johnson, and all his cotemporaries, Sayenquaraghta, while in this certificate it is spelled Kayingwaurto—which spelling it would be absurd to attribute to Col. Butler. So also the word "Sanake," is liable to the same criticism. None of the copies of this certificate bear any date; but inasmuch as the certificate purports (very absurdly,) to specify the persons to whom these scalps belonged, the allusion of course, as is very plain, refers to the case of Capt. Greg and his subordinate, who were scalped near Fort Stanwix, as has been already related, in 1778. Col. Butler did not hold the office of Superintendent of the Six Nations at that time. That office was held by Col. Guy Johnson, in 1778, and for several years afterwards. Again, there can be no reason assigned why such a certificate should be given at all. It promises "to pay at sight, ten dollars for each scalp." If he was to pay it, why did he not pay it? Moreover, this is not the way military officers make disbursements for the government they serve? The absurdity of the whole thing is too apparent on the face of it, and may be explained by what is added by the "industrious gleaner of incidents of border warfare," who says: "It having been asserted in Congress, after the war, that there was no evidence of the fact, that the British government authorized the payment of money for scalps, the certificate of Col. Butler to Kayinguarto, known by one of the New York members to be in Machin's possession, was sent for; and was accordingly forwarded to the seat of government; the evidence it contained was satisfactory, that Britain did buy American scalps, and thus the controversy ended."

The statement made by Col. Stone, "that Brant had been advanced to the situation of principal war chief of the confederacy," in 1776, is undoubtedly erroneous. In the first place, there was no such office recognized in the confederacy; each nation had its own warriors and war chiefs. There was but one office that was an office conferred by the confederacy, and that was the chief speaker at Onondaga, where the councils of the Six Nations were held. It was an office similar to that of our Speaker in the House of Representatives at Washington, or in our Assembly at Albany, and conferred no authority beyond that of presiding over, or opening the great council of the confederacy, or the duties connected with it.

But we have other evidence that even the Mohawks, who accompanied Sir John Johnson in his flight to Canada, did not recognize Brant as their head, or chief warrior. For we see that they actually chose Peter Johnson, a natural son of Sir William Johnson, to be their leader, and that Col. Guy Johnson recommended that he should be commissioned as such, to give encouragement to the Indians. In a note, Col. Stone admits that it has been denied, that Brant ever received the appointment of "principal chief," but reiterates the statement on the authority of "David Cusick," a very unreliable authority for any historical fact."

CHAPTER XXI.

In the spring of 1779 a deputation of a principal Onondaga chief, Teyohagweanda, and three Cayugas, were induced to visit his excellency Gen. Haldimand, at Quebec; and in his answer to the messages they were charged with, he said:

"With regard to your inquiring why Oswego was not established, I am to tell you that when I sent you my speech, early this spring, of my intending so to do, and in consequence had appointed your patron, the late Sir William Johnson's son, Sir John Johnson, to march with his regiment for that purpose, I then had intelligence that the rebels were preparing boats, at Saratoga, and Albany, to go up the Mohawk river, with intention to post at Oswego. But in the course of a few weeks, I received a different account that that was not their intention, but that a large rebel army was coming up Connecticut river, under the command of the rebel General Hayzen, with an intention to invade this Province, which according to events in war, made me put a stop to Sir John's proceedings, at the same time, to throw some additional force into the garrisons of the Indian country.

"I sent a re-inforcement to Detroit, another to Niagara, and one to Carleton Island, and kept some light companies ready upon the first notice, to send to your relief. At the same time, let me tell you, that the great King your father, is not sparing of his troops, nor lets you fight his battles by yourselves. If you were to see the numerous armies along the sea coast, and their vigorous operations, you would stop such reflections, and rather acknowledge that your country's safety, greatly depends upon that, for you know very well, that the rebels in 1774 attempted to dispossess you of your country, and if they once got the better of the King's troops, they would soon pursue their encroachments upon your country, and drive you a great distance in the back country.

"As to your apprehensions of the rebels coming to attack your country I cannot have the least thought of it; if they mean anything, it is to secure their frontiers against your incursions and depredations, and in order to the better enable you to keep them at bay, I shall give my leave, and encourage the Seven Nations of Canada, to co-operate with, and join you in opposing your enemies the rebels."

In writing from Halifax in February, 1779, he says:

"Mr. Butler, my deputy, (to whom as formerly mentioned I have transmitted instructions,) continued when we heard last from New York, to make a very useful diversion on the frontier with a good party of Loyalists and Indians, and Joseph the Indian has with a large body of Indians, struck some capital strokes, which obliged the rebels to detach part of their force that way, and has greatly disconcerted them, and by those who carried dispatches to General Haldimand, I sent instructions for meeting the Indians, soon after the waters become open, hoping to leave this place so as to arrive at Quebec about the second week in May. * * I mentioned in my last that many good woodsmen had been lately enlisted for my service, as the late Sir William Johnson expressed, and I have experienced the utility of incorporating them with the Indians, I persuade myself it will meet your approbation."

For various reasons not given, it would appear Col. Johnson did not leave Halifax for Quebec until June, 1779, and arrived on the 17th July of that year.

Under date of 5th September, 1779, writing from Montreal, he says:

"When I arrived in this Province, I found a deputation of the Six Nations had newly come down, who were particularly solicitous about troops and the re-establishment of the important post at Ontario, which the General had under contemplation, but from the difficulty that attended the transportation of provisions, he did not think it practicable this season.

"The Indians were the more urgent on this point, as there were certain accounts that the rebels were marching in a considerable body into their country, of which we have since had more particular information; and that my deputy, Major Butler was advancing to the relief of the Senecas. I herewith enclose a copy of the proceedings with the General, and shall take another with me to the Indians, but since my arrival in this city, the General has from further accounts, judged it proper to order up a body of troops with Sir John Johnson, to support and encourage the Indians, which I consider as a very necessary measure; and I heartily wish it could have been undertaken sooner, for I may venture to affirm, that the Six Nations are now from situation, and circumstances, of such superior consequence to the government, that should they receive a blow of a capital nature, the rebels might do what they pleased on the frontiers, and we should very soon lose the possession of the lakes, and communications, as well as the friendship of the other Indian Nations, the effects of which I need not point out.

"If the rebels are not able to effect anything material very soon, I hope to furnish a reasonable re-inforcement to oppose them, and I am confident, if I was armed with a proper authority to encourage the many white people who constantly retire from the rebels to the frontiers, and are good woodsmen, I could soon have a respectable body of men, fitting to be incorporated with the Indians. Sir John could do the same, and such bodies might be formed on the spot, capable of much larger undertakings than can be expected from the present force in that country. * * I am by no means doubtful of success (if the present inroad of the rebels fails) so long as I am supported in the authority, and field rank, essential to my station; and which always accompanied it, and should they even succeed in some measure, I am not without resources."

COL. GUY JOHNSON TO LORD GERMAIN.

Niagara, 11th Nov. 1779.

"My Lord:—Previous to my departure from Montreal the beginning of last September, I had the honor to inform your Lordship of my destination at that time, a duplicate of which accompanies this dispatch; a few days after I went up the river St Lawrence, with about one hundred and thirty whites and Indians, who were augmented to two hundred and twenty, on my arrival at Carleton Island, where accounts had just been received that the rebels had hastily retreated out of the Indian country, after destroying almost all the villages and corn-fields of the Six Nations ; and that Major Butler, my deputy, with a considerable body of Indians had retired to Niagara. As this in a great measure defeated the object the General had in view in ordering up Sir John Johnson with about five hundred men to their support, the next consideration was, whether anything further could be undertaken with those troops, assisted by Indians, on which subject Sir John and I conferred, and it was proposed to rendezvous at Aserotus (Sodus Bay,) about thirty-five miles west of Oswego, to call some Indians from Niagara to that place, and thence proceed according to circumstances, and information. And to that end, a detachment was sent in boats, along the south side of the lake, accompanied by Capt. Frazer, and the Canada Indians, who were to send a large party to the neighborhood of Fort Stanwix, to bring off cattle and provisions, while Sir John and myself with the rest proceed directly to Aserotus, in the vessels ; but were forced by a hard gale to go to Niagara, when without loss of time, we proceeded to collect the Indians and return to Aserotus. But this was a work of some days, and from the accounts received at Niagara, there appeared little prospect of effecting anything beyond the harrassing the frontiers with detached parties. However Sir John's zeal for the service, induced him to make every effort, and accordingly he left this place on the 10th of October, and proceeded for Oswego, where it was thought best from accounts received, to collect the whole, and where we were joined by the Indians etc., from Aserote, but a considerable body of the Indians were obliged to march from this place for want of craft to transport them, under the care of Capt. Brant, and other of my officers, for whom we waited a considerable time, during which, it was found that the Canadian Indians were, notwithstanding all the pains taken by Capt. Frazer, very little attached; that they had declined going towards Fort Stanwix, and that they opposed any measures against the Oneidas, the only object then in contemplation with any prospect. At the same time the General's despatches arrived, with distribution of winter quarters, and orders to Sir John Johnson to return, accompanied with his approbation of the measures that had been pursued, and a letter to me for the dividing the Indians between Niagara, Carleton Island, etc., on account of provisions. About this time an officer of my department, with five Indians who were advanced a few miles in front of a body of rangers, captured three Oneida rebels, who had been reconnoitering, and another party took a rebel Sergeant, from whom we learned that the rebels had reinforced the environs of Fort Stanwix, with six hundred men, and had notice of our motions, mentioning particularly my own.

"Sir John Johnson in consequence of his orders, as well as that the party by land had not been able to come up, accordingly decamped, and returned to this place, on the 28th ult., where I have been a good deal occupied in endeavoring to prevail on the Indians to send a large body of their people down to Carleton Island, for the winter, which they do not much incline to, as their late losses induce them to be more united, however, their number is now reduced to two thousand six hundred and twenty-eight, the majority of whom will remain hereabouts, and from the situation to which they have been reduced through their attachment and services to government, I humbly conceive they are entitled to every mark of attention, that can be afforded, as well from principles of justice, as from policy. I propose to employ them usefully on the communications, through the winter, and to use every endeavor for keeping up their spirits, and preserving their attachment to government, which has hitherto proved to be of so much use to his Majesty's interests, and on which the safety of the country so much depends. It is an arduous undertaking, since their late losses, but I enter on it with confidence, and the expectation of your Lordship's continuance, and I persuade myself if measures can be taken next spring, for reestablishing Fort Ontario, (Oswego) which they have much at heart, and supporting his Majesty's arms with a proper body of troops, they will not a little contribute to their success.

I cannot conclude without recommending the good conduct of all my officers to his Majesty. Because I am convinced they have in their respective stations acquitted themselves, with as much zeal and performed as much as any other subjects of the King ; and whilst the good of the service requires my recommending what was mentioned in my last respecting myself to his Royal consideration, I cannot avoid doing that justice to their merits which they have faithfully deserved.

I request to be honored with your Lordship's commands, and I am with very true regard, my Lord, your Lordship's most humble and most obedient servant,

G. JOHNSON."

The following letters written about this time, will throw

light upon the transactions of this period from a different stand point than that from which we have been accustomed to view them. In September, 1778, Col. Guy Johnson writes from New York to Lord Germain as follows:

"Your Lordship will have heard before this can reach you, of the successful incursions of the Indians and Loyalists from the northward. In conformity to the instructions I conveyed to my officers, they assembled their force early in May, and one division under one of my deputies (Mr. Butler) proceeded with great success down the Susquehanna, destroying the posts and settlements at Wyoming, augmenting their numbers with many Loyalists, and attaining all the country, while another division under Mr. Brant the Indian chief, cut off two hundred and ninety-four men near Schoharie and destroyed the adjacent settlements with their magazines, from whence the rebels have dervied great resources, thereby affording encouragement and opportunity to many friends of government to join them."

Col. Johnson soon after the date of this letter set out to go by water to Quebec; but meeting contrary winds in the Gulf of St Lawrence, was compelled to put into Halifax for safety, where the vessel was compelled to remain all winter.

CHAPTER XXII.

There is very little doubt that if Gen. Sullivan had pushed his successes to Fort Niagara instead of being satisfied with the destruction of the Indian towns, he would have captured that post, and thus inflicted a punishment upon those who deserved it far more than the poor Indians.

The history of Catherine Montour whose name occurs frequently in the Indian history of this period, is somewhat involved in obscurity. Col. Stone in his "Life of Brant," says:

"It is related in the unwritten history of this battle (Wyoming) that the celebrated Catherine Montour was present with her two sons; and that she ranged the field of blood, like a chafed tigress, stimulating the warriors of her adopted race, to the onslaught, even in the hottest of the fight. But from the antecedent character of that remarkable woman, the story can hardly be credited.

"She was a native of Canada, a half-breed; her father having been one of the early French Governors, probably Count Frontenac, as he must have been in the government of that country about the time of her birth. During the wars between the Six Nations, and the French and Hurons, Catherine when about ten years of age was made a captive, taken into the Senecas country, adopted and reared as one of their own children. When arrived at a suitable age, she was married to one of the distinguished chiefs of her tribe, who signalized himself in the wars of the Six Nations against the Catawbas, then a great nation living to the south westward of Virginia. She had several children by this chieftain, who fell in battle about the year 1730, after which, she did not again marry.

"She is said to have been a handsome woman when she was young, genteel, and of polite address, notwithstanding her Indian associations. It was frequently her lot to accompany the chiefs of the Six Nations to Philadelphia, and other places in Pennsylvania, where treaties were holden; and from her character and manners, she was greatly caressed by the American ladies; particularly in Philadelphia, where she was invited by the ladies of the best circles, and entertained at their houses. Her residence was at the head of Seneca lake."*

That her father was one of the early French Governors seems to be merely conjectural. We have better evidence as to her parentage, gathered mostly from the Colonial Documents.

The first historical notice of the name of Montour is, that Mons. Montour was wounded by the Mohawks in the neighborhood of lake Champlain, in 1694. He was undoubtedly an officer in military service of the French at that time. In a letter of M. de Vaudrieul to M. de Pontchartrain, dated Nov. 17th, 1709, he commends M. de Jonciare for "making his men kill, not three weeks before, one Montour, a Frenchman by birth, but entirely devoted to the English, and in their pay."

*Stone's Life of Brant, vol. 1, p. 339–40.

In a communication of Lord Cornbury to the Board of Trade, dated about the same time or a little previous to the foregoing, he says :

"There is come to Albany one Montour, who is the son of a French gentleman who came above forty years ago, to settle in Canada. He had to do with an Indian woman, by whom he had a son, and two daughters. The man I mention is the son. He had lived all along like an Indian; some time ago, he left the French, and had lived with the far Indians, and it is chiefly by his means, that I have prevailed with those far Nations to come to Albany."

It is quite certain that this is the son of the first Montour spoken of as being killed by order of Mons. Vaudreuil, as he distinctly justifies the act, and says Montour would have been hanged if he could have been taken alive, and brought to Canada.* "Mrs. Montour," is mentioned as interpreter at a council held at Albany with the Six Nations in 1711. This Mrs. Montour was probably one of the two daughters of the first mentioned "French gentlemen." In the manuscript journal of Rev. Samuel Kirkland, Sally Montour, probably the other daughter, is spoken of, as residing in the vicinity of Fort Stanwix in 1764.

Capt. Andrew Montour, appears to have been an interpreter at numerous councils and treaties with the Six Nations, from 1756 to 1757, &c., and Henry Montour, Indian interpreter at Johnson Hall, on several occasions in 1765. These were all descendants of the first named "French gentleman," who came to settle in Canada more than forty years prior to 1708.

---

*M. Vaudreuil to Gov. Burnett 1721.

It appears to have been the custom to call the children of a white father, by the name of the father, as is the custom among the whites; hence the children of Montour were known by that name for several generations. Catherine Montour disappears from history about 1780. It is hardly possible therefore that she could have been the Mrs. Montour mentioned as interpreter at Albany in 1711; but perhaps her mother, who may have been called by that name. Catherine Montour must have been born about the beginning of the eighteenth century, and it is more than probable that she was the daughter of a Mohawk, or a woman of some other one of the Six Nations. It is stated in the Kirkland manuscript that Lucy Montour was related to the celebrated Oneida chief Skenando. Her mother may have been a sister of that chief. It appears that at the time, or prior to, the battle at Wyoming Catherine Montour lived at an Indian settlement called Sheshequin, and her house was known as "Queen Esther's Palace." She being known by the name of Queen Esther among the common people at that time.

She is charged with having accompanied, and by some with having led, the Indian warriors in the attack upon Fort Forty, and that she officiated at the torture of the prisoners, the night after the battle in the terrible scenes described as having been enacted at "Bloody Rock;" the truth of which statements have been doubted, and seem too revolting, to have been perpetrated by any human being, much less by a woman possessing the least spark of humanity. It is said that "in October after the massacre of Wyoming, Col. Harpley of the Pennsylvania line, joined Col. Z. Butler, and they proceeded with one hundred and thirty men, to Sheshequin where they met the Indians in a battle, burned the Indian settlement, and destroyed Queen Esther's Palace, and laid waste her plantation."

It would seem that she immediately removed to the head of Seneca lake, where an Indian settlement was formed known as "Catherine's Town," which was destroyed by Gen. Sullivan in 1779. She then fled to Niagara, where she is spoken of as being, at the time of the arrival of the Cherry Valley prisoners that same year. She had two sons, Rowland and John, both active participants in the border war, during the Revolution.

These two were the leaders of the band that captured the Gilbert family in 1780, according to the "Narrative of the captivity and sufferings of Benjamin Gilbert and his family," a family of fifteen persons were captured by a party of only eleven Indians, of whom it is said Rowland Montour was Captain, and John Montour was second in command. Benjamin Gilbert was a Quaker, as were most of his family. They had settled in 1775 upon the Mahoning Creek in Northampton county, Pennsylvania, where Benjamin Gilbert had erected a Mill. Their own account of the capture, is as follows :

"About sunrise on the morning of the 25th of fourth Month 1780, the family were alarmed by a party of eleven warriors, whose appearance struck them with terror. To attempt an escape was death, and a portion of distress and suffering, not easy to be endured, was expected to be the inevitable consequence of the most patient submission to become captives to the Indians.

"Although Benjamin Gilbert was a friend to the natives, and on this occasion offered them his hand as a brother, yet it had no effect to induce them to relinquish their hostile measures."

"The Indians who committed this depredation, belonged to different tribes or nations, but were of those who abandoned their settlements on the approach of Sullivan's army, and fled within the command of the British forts in Canada. Here they had settled promiscuously, and according to the Indian custom of carrying on war, they frequently invaded the frontier settlements of the white people, making captives of the weak and defenceless, and carrying off plunder. The names of these Indians and their respective tribes, are as follows: Rowland Monteur, first captain; John Monteur, second captain; Samuel Harris, John Huston, and his son John Huston, Jr., Cayugas; John Fox, of the Delaware Nation; the other five were Senecas."

After giving the names and ages of the captives, fifteen in all, the account proceeds: "The men prisoners, were bound with cords, which the Indians had with them, and in this melancholy condition, a guard was placed over them, for about half an hour, while the rest of the Indians were plundering the houses, and packing up such goods as they chose to carry off. When they got sufficient loading for three of Benj. Gilbert's horses, which they took, and also compelled the distressed prisoners to carry part of their plunder, they began their retreat, and hastened away to a considerable distance in the woods. Two of the Indians were then detached to set fire to the buildings, as if to aggravate the distress of the prisoners, for although they were urged forward by the party, and not suffered to look back, yet they could observe the flames, and the falling in of the roofs, from an eminence called Summer Hill.

From this place the Indians hastily pushed forward,

expecting to be pursued by the inhabitants. At their next halting place, they prepared moccasins for such of the children as had no shoes, there being six children, one an infant about nine months old. Considering themselves out of danger of being pursued, they partook of a hearty meal, from the provisions taken from the houses of the prisoners. They continued their flight over mountains, and through swamps, choosing the most unfrequented, and difficult routes, to avoid their fancied pursuers; lodging the first night in a pine swamp. The day's march was a very fatiguing one, and some of the prisoners were nearly exhausted. The manner of securing their prisoners is thus described: "They cut down a sapling about five or six inches in diameter, and therein cut notches, large enough to receive the ankles of their victims. After fixing their legs in these notches, they place another pole over the first, and thus secure them as in the stocks. This upper pole, was then crossed at each end, by stakes, driven into the ground, and in the crotches of these stakes, they placed other poles, to keep them firm, and thus effectually confined the prisoners on their backs. Besides which, they put a strap or thong (of raw hide,) around their necks, and fastened it to a tree, bush, or stake. Their beds were hemlock branches, strewed on the ground, and they were covered with blankets, this last, an indulgence scarcely to have been expected, from those who were esteemed unfeeling, cruel men. In this manner, they passed the night, but it may be reasonably supposed, that in this melancholy situation, sleep was a stranger to their eyelids. It should be understood that it was the adult males who were thus confined every night, for the children, and the female captives, were suffered to lie down to sleep among the others, without being tied, or otherwise restrained."

The second day, the prisoners were separated, and two being placed under a single guard, pursuing their route by different paths, the better to avoid or embarrass, their pursuers. Towards evening however, the different parties again met, and encamped as on the preceding night; but, as they were becoming more accustomed to the temper, and treatment of the Indians, they both rested and slept. On the morning of the third day of their captivity, the prisoners were all painted, according to the Indian custom. Some with red, and some with black, paint. Those who are painted black, are devoted to death, and although this cruel purpose may not be executed immediately, yet it denotes the purpose of their destruction. When they had been about ten days out, Andrew Harrigar, a young German, who was employed as a laborer by Benjamin Gilbert, made his escape, just after dark, and before he had been secured for the night. He was immediately pursued, but under cover of the darkness, he was able to elude his pursuers, and ultimately returned in safety to the settlements of the whites, giving the first authentic intelligence of the fate of the captives.

The party arrived at "Kettarinetown," which had been destroyed by Sullivan's expedition. They found a little further on, a deserted cabin, covered with bark, which they took possession of, and remained three days. Here they found potatoes and turnips, which had remained undisturbed in the ground, while everything else, had been destroyed. They also found game plenty; deer, and wild turkeys, are mentioned as having been killed, while fish, called "suckers," were caught in the neighboring streams, constituting with the vegetables mentioned, an abundant supply of food.

On the 15th of May, the party arrived at Kanasedaga, which had been destroyed the year before by Gen. Sullivan. Here they painted Benjamin Gilbert, the father, black, which was the evidence of their intention to dispatch him, and exceedingly alarmed the family. In the evening they were visited by two white men, (one a British soldier, the other a prisoner,) who supplied them with some food, of which they were in great want. On the 17th, they crossed the Genesee river, on a raft of logs, bound together with hickory withes. They encamped near the bank of the river. On the 18th, one of the Indians left the company, on horseback, to procure food. After some hour's delay, he returned with a large piece of meat. It was boiled and distributed among the prisoners, the Indians eating sparingly. It was eaten without bread, or salt, with a good relish, under the supposition that it was fresh beef. It was afterwards ascertained to be horse flesh. Capt. Rowland Montour also returned with the wife of John Montour, and some other Indians, with provisions, bread, and Indian corn, which was also distributed among the prisoners. Capt. Montour had been absent several days, and appeared glad to see the prisoners, and shook hands with all of them, with expressions of kindness. Early on the morning of the 21st, they heard the report of the morning gun at Fort Niagara, and a messenger was immediately dispatched to the fort, for provisions. On the 22d, having approached so near the Indian encampments, in the vicinity of the fort, the whoop of the Indians, was answered by their friends, and soon after, they were met by the wife of Rowland Montour.

'She was the daughter of Siangorochti, king of the Senecas, but her mother being a Cayuga, she was ranked as of that nation.'* A party accompanied her, among whom was John Montour, the brother of Rowland, who had previously arrived at Niagara. They brought a supply of provisions from the fort. Capt. Rowland Montour, being at some distance in the rear, when his wife arrived, a halt was made until he came up; after saluting her, he informed her, that Rebecca Gilbert, the daughter of Benjamin Gilbert, about sixteen years of age, was now her daughter. As the party were in great distress for food, they did not advance to the settlement until the next day, remaining where they were to partake of the food brought by John Montour, and his party. On the 23d, they proceeded on towards the fort, the Indians whooping and yelling in the most frightful manner. As they passed through an encampment near the fort, the captives experienced the compliment of blows, inflicted by men, women and children, with sticks, clubs, and stones; and taunting them with horrid grimaces, to show their contempt, or to gratify their revenge, for the loss of their relatives, slain in battle. On arriving at the village, or encampment, where Capt. Rowland Montour resided, the assaults of this kind, upon the captives, was very severe, many of them receiving serious wounds, and bruises. Two of the women who were on horseback, were much hurt, by being thrown from their horses, which became frightened at the unusual assault. This sanguinary proceeding was kept up, until arrested by the principal chief, who came out and forbid it. "The poor prisoners were in a piteous condition. Their hair had been cropped close, the blood

*Gilbert Narrative, p. 59.

trickled from their heads in streams, and the clothes they had on, being in rags, were smeared with blood."*

The Indian village or encampment to which these prisoners were brought, was situated on the bank of the river, between Lewiston and Fort Niagara. Two officers from the fort (Capt. Dace and Capt. Powell,) visited the camp to see the prisoners, and proposed to come next day and remove them to the fort, in a boat, as many of them were rendered almost incapable of traveling. To this Capt. Rowland Montour objected, and insisted on their going on foot. The next day they set out in charge of members of the respective families, to which they had been respectively assigned, or by whom they had been adopted. On leaving the Indian settlement, they were again assailed, as upon their arrival, with sticks, and stones, and pursued to some distance, with yells and screeches, but were in some measure protected by those who accompanied them.

They were soon met by Capt. Powell, who with some difficulty, persuaded the Indians to get into his boat with the prisoners, and thus they reached the fort on the 24th. Here they were introduced to Col. Guy Johnson, and Col. Butler, who asked the prisoners many questions, in presence of the Indians. On the 25th, just one month after their capture, Benjamin Gilbert, and Elizabeth his wife, and Jesse Gilbert their son, about nineteen years of age, were given up to Col. Johnson. None of the other captives were liberated at this time, but remained with the Indians." It has been traditionally asserted, that when the British authorities in Canada, understood that

*Gilbert Narrative, p. 64.

the Gilbert family were Quakers, they used great exertions for their release from captivity.*

The wife of Jesse Gilbert being about his own age, still remaining in captivity, her liberation became an object of great interest to the British officers at Fort Niagara. It was ascertained that she was among the Delawares, and unsuccessful efforts were made, to obtain her release. Soon however, a party of Delawares came to the fort, and brought Sarah Gilbert with them; and further efforts were made to obtain her release. The next day the officers visited the camp of the Indians, which was about two miles from the fort, but returned unsuccessful. Early the following morning, Capt. Robeson generously and kindly undertook to procure her liberty. In this he persevered with much solicitude, and close attention, until by the aid of Lieut. Hilliard, he happily succeeded. To effect the benevolent object, they made the Indians several small presents, and gave them thirty pounds, as a ransom." * * There were now four of the prisoners at Col. Johnson's, in the enjoyment of liberty. During their stay, they were treated with kindness by Col. Johnson's housekeeper, who procured clothing for them from the King's stores.† A few days after their arrival at Niagara, a vessel came up from Montreal with orders for the captives who had been released. In this vessel came one Capt. Brant, an Indian chief of high rank, among them, who promised to use his endeavors to obtain the release of the children of Elizabeth Gilbert, who still remained in captivity.

Several of the members of the Gilbert family were

*Gilbert Narrative, p. 84.
†Gilbert Narrative.

brought to Buffalo Creek by their captors, and the account given by Rebecca Gilbert, is interesting, as marking the period of the first permanent settlement of the Indians on Buffalo Creek. It will be borne in mind that Gen. Sullivan's expedition was directed more particularly against the Senecas. We find that he destroyed their towns on the Susquehanna, and Tioga rivers, at the head of Seneca lake, and Kanesadaga, at the foot of that lake, and at Canandaigua, Honeyoye, and Genesee river. At that time they had no permanent settlement in this State west of that point. Their settlement upon the Niagara river had always been temporary, not permanent. Their huts or wigwams were found on the south shore of the Niagara river, between Fort Niagara and Lewiston, by the first Europeans who visited that locality; but they were there, for the purpose of fishing. Their permanent residence was thirty leagues distant, in a southeasterly direction, where De Nonville found them in 1686, when their principal town was destroyed, and never again rebuilt. After the settlement of Europeans, and the opening of trade with the western Indians from Quebec, and New York, the carrying place, around the Falls of Niagara, began to assume great importance. This was in the territory of the Senecas; their two castles, or principal towns were, one at the foot of Seneca lake, (Kanesadaga,) the other was at Genesee river, (Chenisseo.) The carrying place, being nearer to the Chenisseos, was under their more immediate control, and it is probable that it was a source of profit or revenue to them, up to the final surrender of Canada to the English, or at least the surrender of Fort Niagara in 1759. In their negotiations, both with the French and the English, they frequently refer to it as theirs, and their claim to it was recognized. Sullivan's army swept over their country, carrying destruction everywhere. Nothing was spared. Mary Jemison, who then resided at the Chenisseo village, (Little Beard's Town,) says: "In one or two days after the skirmish at Conesus lake, Sullivan's army arrived at Genesee river, where they destroyed every article of the food kind that they could lay their hands on. A part of our corn they burnt, and threw the remainder into the river. They burnt our houses, killed what few cattle and horses they could find, destroyed our fruit trees, and left nothing but the bare soil and the timber. But the Indians had eloped, and were not to be found."*

---

*Life of Mary Jemison, p. 123.

CHAPTER XXIII.

The campaign of Gen. Sullivan was a terrible blow to the Senecas, and indeed, to all the Six Nations; although the Senecas were by far the greatest sufferers. "From this blow, (says Doct. Dwight,) they never recovered;" and after this disaster, they never exhibited their former lofty independent spirit. Their towns were all destroyed, together with all the provisions they had provided for their winter consumption, and they were driven to the necessity of starving, or fleeing to their friends, the British, at Niagara. Great numbers of them actually perished during the winter of 1779–80, from starvation and exposure; this was particularly true of women and children. Add to this great numbers of them died from disease induced by exposure and want. They appear to have been provided for at Niagara, or at least those of them who were able to reach that post, so far as the means provided would allow; but, the unexpected addition of the Indians to the ordinary number of troops at the Fort, rendered their supplies entirely inadequate to the emergency, and it was found necessary to make other provision for the supply of food for the Indians. The following correspondence will show the condition of things at Niagara at this time.

COL. GUY JOHNSON TO LORD GERMAIN.

Niagara, 26th July, 1780.

My Lord:

In my letter of the 4th of May, I gave a brief account of the faithful and successful services of the Indians, under my superintendency, against the rebels during the winter, and of the endeavors of the latter, to draw off the Six Nations through the negotiations of four disaffected Indians, sent to this place for that purpose. I have now the honor to acquaint your Lordship, that the major part of the disaffected tribes, are come in, and at length restored to the British interest, and I shall also lay before you the good conduct, and success, of the Indians since my last. Being sensible that those Oneidas and others, who had, during the war, remained at the rebel frontiers, and under their influence, were rather governed by situation, and imposed on by artifice, than led by inclination to espouse their interest, and finding that their continuance in that quarter, exposed our motions, and served to cover that part of the country, our Indians however, averse to their conduct, not inclining to cut off a part of their own confederacy, I improved a favorable occasion last winter, to intimate that if they ever expected to be restored to the favor and protection of government, they had no time to lose. In consequence of which, I received last month, a message from them informing me, that they had approved of my advice, and were preparing to leave their country and join me, which they did the beginning of this month, to the number of about three hundred and thirty souls;

of whom above one hundred are men, more than seventy of whom, have since marched with my war parties, and will I expect, do their utmost to efface the remembrance of their past conduct, having told them that they owed their reception to His Majesty's clemency, but they must merit his favors by their actions.

The particulars of my proceedings with them, are transmitted to the Commander-in-Chief, and I am assured that the small remainder still with the rebels, will soon follow their example; and thereby lay open the rebel frontier towards the Mohawk river, which will promote the service by facilitating parties, and encouraging the Six Nations, as much as it must distress, and disappoint the rebels. The success that attended those I sent out at a season when it had not been usual to go to war, encouraged others. The number of killed, and prisoners, amounted, early in June, to one hundred and fifty-six, and is now much enlarged; besides which, many houses, and graineries, from which the rebels drew supplies, with many cattle, were destroyed, and interruption given to their planting, as well as recruiting on the frontiers.

The parties have been ranged along the rear of New York, Pennsylvania and Virginia, and although unaccompanied with troops, their mode of warfare does not admit of any thing capital, it is still of much importance to His Majesty's service, in keeping the rebels in a continual state of alarm, and apprehension, and destroying their resources. It is with great satisfaction, that I can add, that these services have been effected, without acts of cruelty, and although three of the Indians were treacherously murdered, they have, at my entreaty, withheld their resentment, and suppressed their darling passion, revenge, in an unusual manner. From principles of humanity, I could wish their example had been imitated by the rebels, who in many instances, have exhibited a very different conduct.

The number of men of the Six Nation confederacy, (exclusive of their people to the southward,) is about sixteen hundred, above twelve hundred of whom, are warriors; and of the latter, eight hundred and thirty-six, are now on service against the frontiers, and more in readiness to follow them, which far exceeds what has ever been out at one time, without the army; few or none remaining except those necessary to assist in planting, and providing for their families. I hope soon to have favorable accounts from them, as so great a number must prove very distressing to the rebels, and contribute much to favor the operations of the campaign.

The large body that was to be provided for at this post, during the last winter, in consequence of the rebel invasion, and the destruction of many Indian towns, occasioned much expense, and great consumption of provisions, which I have endeavored to restrain as far as consistent with the service, and the Commander-in-Chief afforded his assistance for re-establishing them, and enabling them to plant, as early as he could; to promote which, as well as to forward parties, I have lately visited their new settlements; one on the Ohio route, is increasing fast, and I have already induced above twelve hundred of their people to settle and plant at these places, which will lessen the burden of expense. At the same time, I have no doubt that should any material operations be undertaken from hence, that notwithstanding the Indians have been constantly employed all the season, they will readily and cheerfully assist.

Since my arrival here last September, I have not omitted anything in my power, for promoting His Majesty's interests with the Indians, and rendering their services useful to government. I am highly gratified in being honored with the Commander-in-Chief's approbation of my conduct, and that of those faithful people, and I shall study, by every possible exertion in the discharge of my duty, to merit your Lordship's favorable endeavors to His Majesty.

I have the honor to be, with much respect, my Lord, your Lordship's most humble Servant,

G. JOHNSON.

The principal settlement on the "Ohio route," mentioned above, was Buffalo Creek. In the Gilbert narrative, we have the account of the arrival of the first settlers from Niagara. They first landed at Fort Erie, where the British had a garrison; "thence they continued their journey, about four miles further up Buffalo Creek, and pitched their tent for settlement."* This may be considered the first permanent settlement of the Senecas on Buffalo Creek. It took place probably late in May, or early in June, 1780, the precise date is not given. This party consisted of "Siangorochti," (as it is spelled in the narrative,) or Old King, and his family; including his daughter and her husband, Rowland Montour.

They commenced immediately "to clear the ground, and prepare it for a crop of Indian corn. While the women were engaged about the corn, the men built a log house or cabin, for the residence of the family, and then

†Gilbert Narrative, p. 143.

went out hunting. * * During the summer, this family raised about one hundred skipples of corn. A skipple being equal to three pecks, would make about seventy-five bushels. * * While their corn crop was growing this summer, they drew their provisions from the stores at the forts, (Erie and Niagara,) which occasioned the Indians frequently to visit them. * * About the beginning of winter, (1780–1,) some British officers came among the Indians, and remained with them till towards spring, using all their endeavors, for effecting the discharge of the two captives, Rebecca and Benjamin Gilbert, Jr., but without success. Some time after, another British officer, attended by Thos. Peart, (one of the captives,) came among them, with provisions, and hoes, for the Indians. These officers, we learn from the narrative of Thomas Peart, were Capt. Powell, and Lieut. Johnson, the former the husband of Miss Moore, and the latter one of the sons of Sir William Johnson, by Molly Brant.

Elizabeth Peart, another of the captives of the Gilbert family, was brought to Buffalo Creek. The following extracts from her narrative, will further illustrate the history of this period. Elizabeth Peart was the wife of Benjamin Peart, the son of Mrs. Elizabeth Gilbert, Senior, by a former husband. At the time of their capture, Elizabeth Peart had a child about nine months old. She was separated from her husband soon after their arrival in the Indian settlement, but had been allowed to retain her child. She was taken within about eight miles of Niagara, where she was adopted by the usual ceremony, into one of the families of the Seneca Nation. The family that had adopted her, received her very kindly, and she was given to understand that the members of it were to be considered her parents, brothers and sisters. "After Elizabeth had been with the family two days, they all left their habitation, and taking her with them, went to Fort Slusher, where they staid several days. This Fort is about one mile above the great Falls of Niagara. As Elizabeth Peart was much indisposed, the Indians continued several days at the Fort, on her account. But as they cared little for her comfort, she was obliged to lie on the damp ground, which undoubtedly increased her illness and suffering. As soon as the violence of her disorder abated, they set out in a bark canoe, which they had provided, and paddled their course towards Buffalo Creek, and as they went slowly, they had opportunity of taking some fish for their food. When they arrived at the place of their intended settlement, they went ashore and built a cabin. A short time after they came to this new settlement, they returned with Elizabeth to Fort Slusher, and told her that her child must be taken away from her. This was a very affecting circumstance; but all remonstrances, and entreaties, on her part, were unavailing. They however suffered the child to remain with her, till they got to Niagara. Shortly after, they set out from Fort Slusher, and traveled on foot, Elizabeth Peart having to carry her child all the way to Niagara, being eighteen miles, and the weather warm and sultry, rendered the journey very fatiguing and painful; and the more afflicting, in anticipation of having to part with her infant child.

As one object of the journey to the Fort was to procure provisions, their stay at Niagara was of several day's continuance; during which, Capt. Powell afforded Elizabeth an asylum in his house. The sympathy of Capt. Powell's wife towards Elizabeth Peart, was so much moved at the prospect of her child being taken from her, that she prevailed with her husband to intercede with the Indians, that it might remain with her. But his arguments and appeals were in vain; for they took the child from her, and went with it over the river, in order to have it adopted into the family they had assigned for it. As it was so young however, they returned it to its mother (after it was adopted,) to be kept with her until it should be convenient to send it to the family, under whose care it was to be placed. After obtaining provisions and other necessaries, which they came to Niagara to trade for, the Indians and their prisoners returned to Fort Slusher on foot. Thence they embarked in their canoes for Buffalo Creek, their new settlement, and it being near the time of planting, they used much expedition in this journey.

In the Indian families, the labor and drudgery of raising provisions, falls to the share of the women, and Elizabeth had to assist the squaws in preparing the ground, and planting corn. Their provisions becoming scant, they suffered much from hunger. As their dependance for a supply, sufficient to last until the gathering of their crop of corn, was on what they could receive from the British fort, they were under the necessity of making another journey to Niagara. This they performed in two day's traveling. A short distance before they came to the fort, they took Elizabeth's child from her, and sent it to the family that had adopted it, and it was several months before she had an opportunity of seeing it again. * * After the Indians had disposed of their peltries, and obtained a supply of provisions, they returned to their wigwams, by the same route they had gone. With a heart oppressed with grief, Elizabeth trod back her steps mourning her lost infant, for this idea, was continually present to her thoughts. But as she had found how fruitless, and even dangerous it was to apply for redress on behalf of her child, she endeavored to dry up her tears, and thus mourned in secret."

Soon after they reached their settlement, Elizabeth Peart was attacked with sickness, which incapacitated her for labor, and the Indians built a small cabin for her beside the corn field, where they placed her to mind the corn. Here she was visited by a white man, also a prisoner, who informed her that her child was released, and was with the white people. This information greatly relieved her anxiety, and contributed to her speedy recovery. She remained in this employment until the corn was ripe, and then assisted in the harvest, when she was permitted to live again with the family. The release of Elizabeth Peart's child, was effected through the influence and unremitted exertions of the wife of Capt. Powell. Near the close of the winter, their provisions again failing, they were under the necessity of going to the fort for a fresh supply; their corn being so nearly exhausted, that they had all been on short allowance for some time, of only one meal a day. Elizabeth accompanied the party to the fort. They were four days making the journey, through snow and severe frost, suffering much from the cold. When they came near the fort they built a temporary wigwam, where a part of the family, with prisoners, were to stay until the return of the men from the fort.

As soon as Capt. Powell's wife heard that the young child's mother had come with the Indians, she desired to see her, and inasmuch as she herself had also been a prisoner among the Indians, she claimed some relationship in their way, and her request was granted. When Elizabeth came to Capt. Powell's, she was informed that her husband was returned to the fort, and that there was some expectation of his release. This unexpected intelligence was a cordial to her mind, and her happiness was increased by a visit from her husband the same day. But they were not permitted to be long together, for the Indians insisted on her returning with them to their cabin, a few miles back.

Elizabeth Peart was not allowed to leave the cabin for several days; but at length a white family who had bought her child from the Indians that had adopted it, offered the party with whom Elizabeth was confined, a bottle of rum if they would bring her across the river to her child. This offer they accepted, and the fond mother was delighted with this happy meeting; for she had not seen her infant for the space of eight months, since it was taken from her as aforesaid. She was permitted to remain with the family where her child was, for two days, and then returned with the Indians to their cabin.

After some time she obtained a further permission to go to Niagara fort, where she had some needle work to do for white people, and this furnished her a plea for frequent visits there. At length Capt. Powell's wife prevailed with the Indians to let Elizabeth continue a few days at her house and work for the family. At the expiration of the time agreed on, the Indians came for her in order to return with them to the cabin. But she pleaded indisposition, and by this means they were several times dissuaded from taking her away.

"When the season for planting approached, Elizabeth made use of a little artifice in order to prolong her stay at the fort. Having a small swelling on her neck, she applied a poultice, which induced the Indians to think it was improper to remove her, so they consented to leave her, and proposed coming again for her in two weeks. It should have been mentioned that her child was given up to her soon after her arrival at the fort, where she continued to lodge at Capt. Powell's—the kindness of him and his wife demands her acknowledgment and grateful remembrance. * * At the time appointed, some of the Indians came for her again, but she still feigned indisposition, and had confined herself to her bed. One of the Indian women had interrogated her very closely, but did not insist on her going back with them. In this way, several months elapsed; she contriving delays as often as they came for her. She continued at the fort until the vessel was ready to sail, that was to convey the prisoners to Montreal, among whom were her husband and child. The officers at the fort permitted her to go on board with the rest. At Montreal, the prisoners were visited by 'one Thomas Gomerson, (Gumersal,) who hearing of the captives, came to see them.'" This is the person whose statement regarding his agency in the flight of Sir John Johnson, from Johnstown, was made in 1776. It is said "he had been educated among the Friends, and after he arrived at manhood, had been a merchant in New York. He also had traveled as companion to Robert Walker, a ministering Friend from England, in his religious visits to Friends in America, about the year 1773. But, upon the commencement of the Revolutionary war, he had deviated from his peaceful principles and profession, and had now lost all the appearance of a Friend, so as even to wear a sword, * * but he behaved respectfully towards the prisoners, and made Elizabeth a present."

Two of the captives, Abner Gilbert, and Elizabeth Gilbert, aged respectively, the former fourteen, and the latter twelve years, were separated from the rest of the captives, on their arrival in the vicinity of Fort Niagara, and adopted into the family of John Huston, one of the captors. John Huston, his family, and the two captives, removed to a place near the great Falls of Niagara, which is about eighteen miles from the fort. Here they loitered three days more; they then crossed the river and settled near its banks. Their first business at this new settlement was to clear a piece of land, and prepare it for being planted with Indian corn, and this was done with hoes only; so that it was three weeks before the planting was done. While the crop was growing, they had to depend principally on the fort for a supply of provisions. After remaining here about three weeks, they packed up their moveables, (which they generally carry with them in their rambles,) and went down the river to Butlersbury, a small village on the opposite side of the river from Niagara Fort. They staid but one night at this village, taking great care that none of the white people should converse with the prisoners. Next day, after transacting their business, they returned to their settlement, and continued there only a week, before they concluded that they must go again to Butlersbury. * * In the morning, the whole family, and John Huston's brother, went on to Butlersbury, and arrived there before night. They all went to the house of an Englishman named John Secord, who was styled brother to John Huston, as he had lived with him sometime before. After some deliberation, it was agreed that Elizabeth Gilbert, junior, should continue in John Secord's family, until she was sent for by the Indians. * * Abner Gilbert returned from Butlersbury with the Indians to their settlement, where his business was to fence and take care of the cornfield. * * They continued at their settlement until the fall of the year, and as it was not far distant from the fort, they could easily apply there for provisions. So they were not so much distressed for provisions between the failing of their old crop and the gathering of the new one, as those who lived at a greater distance from the fort."

In the spring of 1781, "the family removed about forty miles and encamped, in order for a new settlement near Buffalo Creek, which empties into lake Erie. As they intended this for their summer residence, they went to work to clear a piece of land, and when prepared, they planted it with Indian corn, pumpkins, and squashes. At this place Abner Gilbert heard of his sister Rebecca, who still remained in captivity, and lived not far from this new settlement, but it does not appear that he had liberty to visit her. * *

Thomas Peart having obtained his release from the Indians, he and Capt. Powell, with several others, came among the Indian settlements with provisions and hoes, to distribute among them. The news of their coming soon spread among the Indians, and the chiefs of every tribe came to receive their shares. For this purpose, they each brought as many little sticks as there were persons in their tribes, to express the number of each, in order to obtain a just and equal proportion of the provisions and hoes, that were to be distributed. * *

In the 7th month, 1781, the Indian family again went to Butlersbury, for the purpose of trading and getting a supply of provisions. While there, Col. Butler treated with the Indian woman, who was the head of the family, for the release of Abner, which she at length consented to, on receiving some presents; but she said he must return home with her, and she would deliver him up in twenty days. After they returned to their settlement, (at Buffalo Creek,) she told Abner that he was to be given up to Col. Butler. * *

Some days before the time agreed upon, they proceeded to Butlersbury, and went to the house of John Secord, where his sister Elizabeth had remained ever since the time mentioned in the early part of this narrative.

Abner Gilbert was delivered up by the Indians according to contract, soon after they arrived at the English village; and John Secord permitted him to live in his family with his sister. With this family they continued about two weeks; and as they were under the care of the English officers, they were allowed to draw clothing and provisions from the King's stores. Afterward Benjamin Peart and his brother Thomas who were both released, came over the river to John Secord's for Abner and Elizabeth, and took them to Capt. Powell's at the fort that they might be nearer the vessel in which they were to sail for Montreal with four of the other captives who had been released where they subsequently arrived as has been already related.

The following letter of Col. Guy Johnson was written at this period, and is inserted as part of the history of current events :

COL. GUY JOHNSON TO LORD GERMAIN.

"Niagara, Oct. 11th, 1781.

MY LORD :—I had the honor to address your Lordship

by letter the 20th of November last, and having since frequent communications with his excellency, Gen. Haldimand, who would doubtless inform your Lordship of any thing material in my department, I have deferred writing till this season when military operations are nearly at an end in this quarter.

"The transactions of the present year, and the proceedings of my Indian parties, correspond in many respects with the last, and the Pettite Guerre (small war) in these parts, have never appeared to me to be of sufficient importance to lay a minute detail of them before your Lordship.

"The Six Nations Confederacy have, however, more than ever distinguished themselves this year in several smart actions with the rebels, in which through the good conduct of the Indians and of my officers, they have every time been successful, and in several different actions have killed and taken several noted partizans, and laid waste a country abounding in supplies for the rebels, which has compelled the latter to contract their frontiers, and confine themselves within little forts. A large detachment is lately gone with a body of troops ordered on service by the Commander-in-chief, and I have just sent off two large parties to co-operate with them. In a former letter I informed your Lordship of having prevailed on many of the Indians (who for their faithful services and sufferings, expected to be maintained here during the war) to go upon planting grounds at convenient distance from hence, and the great expense and difficulty attending the transportation of provisions to this post having made it necessary to get as many as possible to withdraw, I have been indefatigable in my endeavors for that purpose, and can now assure your Lordship that I have re-established near four thousand of them, though at much expense, as by the destruction of their country in 1779, they were in want of everything, and their demands greatly increased; but by settling them, I have not only reduced the consumption of provisions, but also of all other expenses, which will in future be very low. * *

"Some endeavors have been made lately by the rebels to draw them into a neutrality, which most of them disdain. I hope shortly to put an end to such attempts, as well as to reconcile the Indians to the plan of economy now entered upon, for reducing expenses, which however enormous, was for a time unavoidable. The accomplishing this, will afford me much satisfaction, for the expenses which were only occasional, before they were drawn out of their country, and whilst they lived at considerable distance, increased so much, by their residence here, as to require immediate attention.

"Some of the principal chiefs now here, request that I should make favorable mention of their zeal, and fidelity to his Majesty, which I constantly tell them is done, as every such assurance is very flattering to them, and indeed their conduct deserves it, having seldom less than five hundred on service, who are generally successful, without cruelty.

"As the Commander-in-chief is fully acquainted with the state and service of my department, it is needless for me to add more than that I am with very great respect, your Lorship's most obedient, and most humble servant,

G. JOHNSON."

CHAPTER XXIV.

Most of the members of the Gilbert family were brought to Niagara and its vicinity. The Indians seem to have had their residence on and near the Niagara river between Schlosser and Fort Niagara, where they had located themselves after their expulsion from their settlements by Gen. Sullivan's expedition; some of the captives were taken to Genesee river, upon the head waters of which some settlements had been made. Two places are mentioned in the narrative, one called Caracadera, and the other Nundow. The settlements made during 1780–1, at these places as well as at Buffalo Creek, Cattaraugus Creek, Allegany, &c., were made in pursuance of the policy shadowed forth in the official correspondence of Col. Guy Johnson, already noticed. It would seem that Col. John Butler with his followers, including his Rangers, and a large number of tories with their families had settled upon the opposite side of the river from Fort Niagara, and the village thus formed was called "Butlersbury." The names of several of the inhabitants of the place in 1780–1, are given in the Gilbert narrative, many of which will sound familiar to those acquainted on the Canadian frontier forty years ago. The jurisdiction over the territory here was still claimed by the English, and the Indians came here under the patronage of the English government. The settlement of the Indians at Buffalo Creek drew along with them, the Indian traders and other white men, who had identified themselves with the Indians; and it is easy to see that the first white settlers were of a very mixed character. President Dwight said of the inhabitants of Buffalo in 1804:

"The inhabitants are a casual collection of adventurers; and have the usual character of such adventurers, thus collected, when remote from regular society, retaining but little sense of government or religion."

It will be remembered that two sons of Sir William Johnson by Molly Brant, had accompanied Col. Guy Johnson to Canada in 1775. We occasionally hear of them as officers in the command of small parties of Indians, or serving in some more subordinate capacity under the command of others. The Lieut. Johnson spoken of in the Gilbert Narrative as visiting the Senecas with other British officers, in the first settlement of the Indians at Buffalo Creek in 1781, was unquestionably one of these sons. Their names were William and Peter. The latter had been chosen by the Indians who were with Col. Johnson in Canada, as their commander. The former is the one who came to reside with the Senecas subsequent to 1781. He had allied himself to the Senecas probably by marriage, and had been adopted by them as was their custom. He had the influence and address, to obtain from the Senecas a conveyance of all the lands at the mouth of Buffalo Creek, including of course the lands upon which our city stands; and he was sustained with such pertinacity by the Indians in that claim, although not recognized by law, that the Holland land company, when they came to exercise their right to the land, they had purchased of Robert Morris, including the land upon which our city is built, that they were obliged to make terms with Johnson, by buying his claim also. This was paid for in part by a deed to Johnson, of forty acres of land now in the heart of the city, bounded north by Seneca street, west by Washington street, south by the (then) little Buffalo Creek, now the Hamburgh Canal, extending east far enough to make forty acres which carried the eastern boundary beyond what is now Michigan street. The company also conveyed to Johnson other lands upon Buffalo Creek, besides making him other compensation. William Johnson (or Johnston as it appears he wrote his name) had a son John, who married a daughter of one of the earliest settlers in Buffalo, as will be related when the period in which it occurs comes under observation.

The Indians although driven to seek shelter and protection under the walls of Fort Niagara, by the expedition of Gen. Sullivan, no sooner than he had left the country, began to make warlike excursions in small parties to different points of the frontier settlements, killing and capturing all that fell in their way, without distinction of age or sex. Early in the year 1780, the Oneidas were attacked, and their village, their castle, and their church were utterly destroyed, and they were driven to seek shelter within the white settlements.

A party under Brant, consisting of Indians and tories, destroyed Harpersfield, and took Capt. Alexander Harper and ten others prisoners. Harper was well acquainted with Brant, who, upon recognizing him, said Harper I am sorry to find you here; why are you sorry, Capt. Brant, replied Harper ; because, said Brant, I must kill you, although we were schoolmates in our youth. The threat was not immediately put in execution, but the prisoners were shut up in a pen of logs, and guarded by the tories, during the night. The question whether they should be put to death or carried to Niagara, was discussed, and the latter finally agreed upon.

In the morning Brant informed Capt. Harper that he and his companions should be spared, on condition of their accompanying him to Niagara ; and they immediately commenced their journey. Their route lay along the road travelled by Sullivan's expedition the year before ; they suffered greatly for the want of provisions, neither warriors nor prisoners had more than a handfull of corn each per day ; and they were forced to feed upon the remains of a horse which had been left by Sullivan's expedition, and had perished from the severity of the winter. They procured a fine fat horse at Genesee river, which was immediately killed, dressed, and devoured among the famishing company, which was eaten with great relish by all the company, although eaten without bread or salt. The prisoners fared just as well as the warriors. On arriving at Genesee river, Brant sent on a messenger to Niagara, to apprise of his approach, and the number of his prisoners. But this was not all the object of sending the messenger forward. Miss Jane Moore the Cherry Valley prisoner, whose marriage to Capt. Powell at Fort Niagara, has already been mentioned, was a neice of Capt. Harper, a fact known to Brant. Harper however knew nothing of her marriage or even of her being at Niagara. Brant was anxious to save Capt. Harper from the cruel ordeal of running the gauntlett. He therefore despatched a runner with a message to Capt. Powell, advising of his approach, and asking his aid in accomplishing his desire.

Capt. Powell managed to have the Indians enticed away from the neighborhood of the fort, where they were encamped, to the landing about nine miles distant, for a frolic, the means for holding which, it is said, were supplied out of the public stores, and upon emerging from the woods, and approaching the first Indian encampment, the prisoners were agreeably surprised at finding the Indian warriors absent from the encampment, and their place supplied by a regiment of British soldiers. There were only a few boys and a few old women in the camp, and these offered no violence to the prisoners, excepting one of the squaws, who struck a young man named Patchin, over the head with a club, which caused the blood to flow pretty freely. But the second encampment, lying nearest the fort, and usually occupied by the fiercest and most savage of the Indian warriors, was yet to be passed. But here too, the Indians were gone, and another regiment of troops were paraded in two parallel lines to protect the prisoners. Patchin however, received another severe blow in this camp, and a young Indian aimed a blow at him with a tomahawk, but as he raised his arm, a soldier snatched the weapon from his hand and threw it into the river. The prisoners were thus brought into the fort almost unscathed, and had cause of gratitude at their unexpected deliverance from the fearful and bloody ordeal through which they had expected to be called to pass, and Capt. Harper, in particular, met with an altogether unexpected source of pleasure, in meeting his niece, Miss Jane Moore, now Mrs. Capt. Powell.

The character of Jane Moore shines out with a brilliant

lusture in the history of the transactions of this period. The womanly sympathy, and persevering exertions in behalf of the helpless prisoners of all classes, in which she seems to have been seconded by her noble husband, Capt. Powell, entitle her name to a record on the roll of fame, with that of the noblest patriots, the bravest heroes, and the purest of philanthropists. Prompted by her untiring zeal, her husband visited the prisoners among the Senecas, at Buffalo Creek, several times during the time they remained there, not only to encourage them by his counsel and sympathy, but to administer to their necessities, and to procure their release; which was ultimately accomplished, mainly through his efforts, assisted by other officers at the fort, which the example and interest of Jane Moore, the Cherry Valley captive had influenced to co-operate in this work of mercy.

The release of Rebecca Gilbert, and Benjamin Gilbert, Jr., the young girl and boy who were brought to Buffalo Creek by the family of "Old King," was not effected until the 6th of June, 1782, and is thus described in the narrative: "As the time approached, when according to agreement, the Indians were to return to Niagara, and deliver up the captives, they gave Rebecca Gilbert the pleasing information, in order to allow her some time to make preparation for the journey, and also for the enjoyment of her freedom. So she made a quantity of bread for them to eat on the way, with great cheerfulness. On this occasion, about thirty of the Indians set out to go to Niagara fort with the two captives. They went as far as fort Slusher in bark canoes, the remainder of the way they went slowly on foot; so that it was several days before they reached Niagara. When they arrived, they went to Col. Butler's, and held a conference on the occasion; and at length, in consideration of some valuable presents that were made them, they released the last two of the Gilbert captives, namely, Rebecca Gilbert, and Benjamin Gilbert, Jr. As speedily as it could be accomplished, their Indian dress was exchanged for the customary clothing of the white people, by whom they were kindly entertained and provided for—and on the 3d day of the 6th month, 1782, two days after their happy release from upwards of two years captivity, they sailed for Montreal, in order to join with the others who had obtained their liberty as before mentioned."*

Fort Niagara is described at this period, as being a structure of considerable magnitude, and great strength; enclosing an area of from six to eight acres. Within the enclosure was a handsome dwelling house for the residence of the Superintendent of the Indians. It was then occupied by Col. Guy Johnson, who held that office. Col. Butler and his Rangers lay upon the opposite or northern side of the river. Col. Guy Johnson is described as a stout, short, pursy man, about forty years of age, of stern countenance and haughty demeanor, dressed in a British uniform, powdered locks, and a cocked hat. His voice was harsh, and his speech betrayed evidence of his Irish extraction.

The same authority (Capt. Snyder,) says of Brant at this time: "He was a likely fellow, of a fierce aspect, tall, and rather spare, well spoken, and apparently about thirty (forty) years of age. He wore moccasins elegantly trimmed with beads, leggins, and breech cloth, of superfine blue, short green coat, with two epaulets, and a

*Gilbert Narrative, p. 155.

small, laced round hat; by his side hung an elegant silver mounted cutlass, and his blanket of blue cloth, purposely dropped on the chair, on which he sat, to display his epaulets, was gorgeously decorated with a border of red."*

Col. Stone, in his "Life of Brant," has evidently either mistaken the true character and position of Brant, or made him too much a hero. It is very evident that he did not possess those elements of character which constitute greatness in the eyes of uncivilized men. His importance and conceded influence, rather grew out of those qualities which civilized man approves and admires. Or rather he had influence with the Indians, because they supposed he had influence with white men. He could be useful to them, because he was civilized and associated with civilized people, but in those traits of character which constitute greatness in the eyes of Indians, Brant does not seem to have been eminent. He had more showy, than substantial qualities; all accounts of him seem to indicate this. That he was a gentleman in his manners and address, and kind and humane in his disposition, is also apparent. He was probably superior to most of those around him in this respect, when the observations above were made.

The difficulty of sustaining such a body of Indians as had concentrated at Niagara, led to active efforts on the part of the officers at that post, under instructions from the British government, to induce the Senecas to settle upon lands which they might cultivate, and by that means, furnish their own subsistence. They appear to have been

*See Narrative of Capt. Snyder, by C. H. Dewitt, Esq.

located at Buffalo Creek, Cattaraugus Creek, Allegany, Nunda, and at two or three points on the Genesee river, and at Tonawanda Creek. The Mohawks were settled upon the Grand river in Canada. They all of course looked to the British government for support, and expected to be sustained at these settlements by material aid, and in general, some officer, or agent, of the government, resided at the principal points of these settlements. It would seem that William Johnson came to reside at Buffalo Creek, in that capacity, and exercised considerable influence over the Indians. But this influence, like that of Brant's, was awarded him on account of his usefulness to the Indians in their communications and intercourse with the whites, rather than for the qualities which commanded influence among the Indians themselves.

It was said of Molly Brant, that she had her children educated quite equal to the children of the best families of the whites in the valley of the Mohawk, at that day, and Johnson seems to have been a leading man at Buffalo Creek, so far as related to all the transactions of the Indians with the whites at least, for many years. It was stated by Cornplanter, at a council held at Canandaigua, as late as 1794, that " Johnson had the care of the Senecas at Buffalo Creek," and he was at the council as a delegate, by their invitation, or procurement. But Col. Pickering, who was the representative of the government at that treaty, treated Johnson " as a British spy," and he was compelled to retire in much mortification.* There are some letters and papers to which his signature is attached, where his name is written Johnston, but it is no

*See journal in life of William Savery, p. 116.

unusual thing for members of the same family to spell their names differently. This has however, led many to suppose that this was evidence that the "Johnston" who resided at Buffalo Creek, with the Indians, was not of the family of Sir William Johnson.

The journal of William Savery, who was a member of a delegation of Friends, who attended the treaty at Canandaigua, by appointment, is interesting, and that part of it which relates to Johnson, is inserted here:

JOURNAL OF WM. SAVERY, 1794, WHO ATTENDED AN INDIAN COUNCIL AT CANANDAIGUA.

"This morning, the 25th, snow was seven or eight inches deep, and having been out in it yesterday, I was unwell. Abundance of deer are killed by the Indians, perhaps not less than one hundred to-day, within a few miles of this place, some in sight; one man killed three in a short time. A man named Johnson, having arrived two days ago from Fort Erie, with a message from Captain Brant, a Mohawk chief of the Six Nations, assembled some chiefs yesterday, and delivered it to them. Being in the character of a British interpreter, he appeared at the council with the Indians to-day, and seemed very intimate with them. Cornplanter rose to vindicate his coming, being privy to the great uneasiness it had given Col. Pickering; he expressed his surprise that ever since the conclusion of the peace with the British nation, such an antipathy had existed, that the United States and the British could not bear to sit side by side, in treaties held by the Indians. He said Johnson had the care of the Senecas at Buffalo Creek, and had brought a message to the Six Nations, assembled at this council fire, from Brant, whom he left with Governor Simcoe, at Fort Erie; they having just returned together from Detroit; that when he went some time ago to see the western Indians, he sat in council with the Delawares, Shawnese, Wyandots, and Miamis, and the western Indians expressed great joy at seeing the Six Nations represented by him among them; they told him he recollected that the business of the treaty last year did not go on, but the fault was not theirs, it was that of other people, and the Indians were led astray, for which they were sorry. The misfortunes that have fallen upon them were very heavy, and our brothers, the British, who were sitting by, gave us no relief. We allow you who are listening to us, to be the greatest, we will therefore hear what you say. We desire a council fire may be kindled at Sandusky, for all nations of Indians. Capt. Brant sends his compliments to the chiefs at Canandaigua, and says you remember what you agreed on last year, and the line we then marked out; if this line is complied with, peace will take place; and he desires us to mention this at Canandaigua. After the council at Canada is over, it is my earnest desire you will immediately come to Buffalo Creek, and bring Gen. Chapin with you. I will wait here till your return.

Col. Pickering rose and said, he was sorry anything should happen to interrupt this council fire, but it is now interrupted by the coming of Johnson, whom he considered as a British spy, and that his being here, was an insult to him, to their friends, the Quakers, and to the fifteen fires.

"That the intrusion of this man into our councils, betrayed great impudence, and was a proof of British insolence. It was perhaps as well that there was no council yesterday, for he could not say how far the first emotions of his mind at seeing this fellow here, might have carried him; he hoped he was now a little cool, and would endeavor to moderate his expressions as much as he was capable of. He begged their patience, for he must be obliged to say a great deal to inform them of many of the reasons of his indignation at this step of the British government, and why it was totally improper to go on with business while a British spy was present. He then went into a very lengthy detail of the ill-treatment of that government to the United States, for several years past, and concluded with saying that either this man must be sent back to those who sent him, or he, Col. Pickering would cover up the council fire, for his instructions from Gen. Washington were, to suffer no British agents at the present treaty.

"The Indians appeared in amazement at the warmth with which the Commissioner delivered himself, and said when he sat down, the council fire grows warm, the sparks of it fly about very thick. As to Johnson, he appeared like one that was condemned to die, and now rose and left us.

"The Indians requesting we would withdraw counseled among themselves about half an hour, and sent for us again. Cornplanter rose and said the reason why the council fire has not been uncovered to-day is because of a British man being present. It was caused by us. We requested him to come here it is true, but the fault is in the white people. I am very much surprised and deceived by what you told us at Fort Stanwix, when you laid before us a paper which contained the terms of peace agreed on, between you and the English nation; and told us it was agreed on in the presence of the Great Spirit, and under His influence. We now discover that what the commissioners then told us is a lie, when they said they made the chain of friendship bright; but I now find there has been antipathy to each other ever since. Now our sachems and warriors say what shall we do. We will shove Johnson off; yet this is not agreeable to my mind, for if I had kindled the council fire, I would suffer a very bad man to sit in it, that he might be made better, but if the peace you made had been a good peace, all animosities would have been done away, and you could then have sat side by side in council. I have one request to make, which is that you furnish him with provisions to carry him home.

"The council having sat about five hours, adjourned till to-morrow. We dined by candlelight with the commissioner and about fifteen chiefs, among whom were Cornplanter, Red-Jacket, Little-Beard, Bigs-ky, Farmers-Brother, Fish-Carrier, Little-Billy, &c.

"Many repartees of the Indians which Jones interpreted manifested a high turn for wit and humor. Red Jacket has the most conspicuous talent that way; he is a man of a pleasing countenance, and one of the greatest orators amongst the Six Nations. * *

"26th, first day. The council being assembled, the first business was the preparation of a letter which the Indians having got prepared since yesterday, they thought proper for the commissioner to see it, as they intended to send it by Johnson to Capt. Brant. The contents of it were not altogether agreeable to the commissioner. They expressed their sorrow that Johnson could not be permitted to stay, the reasons for which he would doubtless inform them when he got home. It assured Brant that they were determined to insist on the line agreed to last year, and expressed the sense they now had, that they were a poor despised, though an independent people, and were brought into suffering by the two white nations, striving who should be greatest. The Indians were pretty high to-day, and little was done but clearing up some misunderstanding respecting the cause why the treaty was not held at Buffalo Creek agreeably to the Indians request; the disposition of the Senecas appeared rather more uncompromising than heretofore. * *

"28th * * Yesterday many of the chiefs and warriors were very uneasy at Cornplanter's frequent private visits to the commissioner, and Little Billy spoke roughly to him, told him he should consider who he was, that he was only a war chief, and it did not become him to be so forward as he appeared to be; it was the business of the sachems more than his to conduct the treaty. He (Cornplanter) told them he had exerted himself for several years, and taken a great deal of pains for the good of the nation, but if they had no further occasion for him he would return home, and he really intended it; but Col. Pickering and Gen. Chapin exerted themselves to detain him. The dissatisfaction of the Senecas rose so high that it was doubtful whether a council would be held to-day, but about three o'clock they met, Cornplanter not attending."

The council proceeded, but it does not appear that Cornplanter participated in the proceedings, if he was even present. He had evidently incurred the displeasure of some at least of the chiefs of his own party. In the progress of the business, Col. Pickering had endeavored to exonerate Cornplanter from all blame, on account of his visits to his guests, for the Commissioner had invited him, and if there was any impropriety in it, he alone was to blame. William Savery, in his journal, under date of the 31st, says "the interpreter says, parties rise high against Cornplanter, that he is in a difficult situation with his nation; and they are not able to conceive what he has done with eight hundred dollars received in Philadelphia, from the Pennsylvania government, and what induced the government to give him fifteen hundred acres of land for a farm; these things have created jealousy."

Joseph Brant, like Cornplanter, was recognized by the Indians as a war chief only. His early education was less, than has generally been supposed. Indeed, the time he spent in Dr. Wheelock's school, was insufficient to give him only a very superficial knowledge, of even the elementary branches of education. A letter of his, written in 1777, which has been preserved in the "Annals of Tryon County," shows that neither in his chirography, (which is copied,) his orthography, or his composition, had he attained to a mediocrity of proficiency. The following is a copy of the letter:

Tunidilla,* July 6, 1777.

MR. CARR, SIR: I understand that you are a friend to government with sum of the settlers at the Butternuts, is the reason of my applying to you & those people, for sum provision, and shall be glad you would send me

*Unadilla.

what you can spare no matter what sorte, for which you shall be paid, you keeping an account of the whole, from your friend and Hum. Serv't,

JOSEPH BRANT.

To Mr. Persofer Carr.

Johnson, being a nephew of Joseph Brant, was in constant and intimate communication with him, and although Brant had left the territory of the United States, he was in intimate communication with that portion of the Six Nations which chose to remain in the state of New York, by means of messengers or runners, as well as by letters, which he made the means of communication with persons holding official relations to the Indians, and by this means keeping himself "rectus incuria" with them, while he was in quasi hostility to the government.

The following is a letter written by him to Gov. Geo. Clinton, dated Niagara, 18th June, 1789:

Sir: Having before written to some of your principal people on the subject of our lands at Canajoharie, which we have never as yet had any answer to, probably owing to their not having received, having a safe opportunity, beg leave to mention to your excellency, we are informed a Mr. Clock whom we found troublesome before the commencement of the late war, is again striving to take advantage of us in order to deprive us of our right in that part of the country, which when at the last treaty at Fort Stanwix in 1784, you was with a number more of your principal people kind enough to assure us, as our lands were not confiscated at the close of the war, we should not be deprived of our right; we therefore look up to your excellency for justice and which from your character we have no doubt but we will obtain. The reason of our not exerting ourselves relative to this matter before now was owing to our being employed in business in the different parts of this country, being obliged to attend at the different treaties, which has made us neglect paying that attention to our private concerns, which we otherwise should have done. From the great scarcity of cattle at present amongst us, owing to our having lost numbers this last winter, we would wish to dispose of our Canajoharie lands, and would take part cattle in payment and give a just deed of the same. Your Excellency being at the head of the State, we have thought proper to first mention it to you and shall wait your answer, which we hope will be soon, that an end may be put to the business. I flatter myself we will give you every satisfaction in any purchase which may be made from us, as what we ourselves do we shall wish to abide by. I have the honor to be your most ob'dt Humb'l Serv't,

JOSEPH BRANT.

In behalf of the Mohawk Nation, Geo. Clinton, Esq., Governor of the State of New York.

The following answer to Brant's letter, was returned by Gov. Clinton:

Albany, July 14th, 1789.

SIR: I have received your letter of the 18th June last, and have to inform you in answer to it, the lands at Canajoharie are claimed by private individuals, many others, as well as Clock, produce deeds from the Mohawk Nation, for different parts of the lands there. Whether these deeds were fairly obtained, or whether the lands there remain unsold, I am not able to determine. But if the lands unsold are particularly pointed out to me, I will cause an inquiry to be made into the matter, and see that the Indians have all the justice done them that they have any right to expect. It is unfortunate, and what I could not have expected, after the explanation which took place between us at Fort Stanwix, that the Indians continue to treat and make contracts for lands with individuals, without the consent of our government, and against our laws; and more especially as this conduct never fails to end to their disadvantage and injury. I have only to add that I shall always be ready with the greatest cheerfulness, to hear and redress any grievances the Indians within this State may have cause to complain of, and that I am with regard,

Your friend, and most Obedient Servant,

GEO. CLINTON.

To Capt. Joseph Brant.

It is evident by this reply of Gov. Clinton, to the letter of Brant, that the true position that chief and the Mohawks, whose interest he assumes to represent, held in respect to the government, was well understood by him. His intimation that the complaints of the Indians residing within this State would at all times receive his attention, is significant. Brant however, did not desist from his efforts, but sent a lengthy reply to the Governor, not only to the subject of the letter, but also in relation to other matters of complaint, to which he obtained the names of nearly forty chiefs, mostly residing at Buffalo Creek. Brant himself was rather reluctant to venture upon this side of the lines dividing the territory of the United States and Canada, after the close of the war, and it is probable these signatures were obtained through the agency or instrumentality of Johnson, his nephew. It has been stated that Brant did not like to visit or pass through the country of his former residence, from fear of his own personal safety.

The following letter exhibits what his apprehensions were on this subject:

Grand River, July 2d, 1797.

"DEAR SIR: It is some time since I received your letter, and I have already answered it by way of Fort Erie, but I did not mention in it the particulars of my jaunt to the States. In the first place, I met with a very cool reception, insomuch that I did not see any of the great men of Philadelphia. I suppose by this, they must have forgot that I was a yankee when I was there before, and also at the last meeting we had at the foot of the rapids, when it was reported among you gentlemen of the Indian department, that I was favoring the yankee interest. I expected they might have paid a little more attention to me, after the great service you supposed I had done them. I was greatly insulted on the road between Philadelphia and Jersey, by a yankee Colonel, whose name I don't recollect, insomuch that the affair was nearly coming to blows. At New York they were very friendly, and likewise in Connecticut (in New England,) they were civil. At Albany there were several people who threatened to kill me behind my back; so that the great men there thought it necessary to send a man with me, as a protector, to the end of the settlement at German Flatts.

I suppose that these people have also forgot that I was a yankee."

Joseph Brant had a large family of children, and two of his sons seem to have been in school at Dartmouth College. In his correspondence with James Wheelock, Esq., (son of the Dr. Wheelock of Moor's Charity School,) in 1801: some of the letters of Brant are dated at Buffalo Creek, but most of his letters at this period are dated at Grand River, (Brantford:) showing that that, was his residence at this period. He subsequently removed to what was familiarly called "the beach," at the head of lake Ontario. The beach separates Burlington Bay and the lake. Here he built a large commodious house, and here he closed his extraordinary and eventful life, on the 24th of November, 1807, at the age of about sixty-five years. His remains were interred at the Mohawk village at the Grand river, near what is now the city of Brantford.

CHAPTER XXV.

It was in May of this year, 1780, that Sir John Johnson invaded the Mohawk Valley by way of lake Champlain and Crown Point, and made an effort to repossess himself of the old homestead at Johnstown. It was in connection with this expedition that the name of the celebrated Seneca chief Cornplanter, is first mentioned. He is said to have been the leader, or one of the leaders, of the Seneca warriors in that expedition; and it was on this occasion, that the incident in regard to the taking of his father a prisoner as related in the life of Mary Jemison occured. It is stated that the residence of the father, who was a white man of the name of O'Bail, was in the vicinity of Fort Plain. Repairing with a detachment of his warriors, to his father's house, he made the old man a prisoner, without letting him know who his captor was. After proceeding ten or twelve miles, the chief stepped before his sire, and addressed him as follows:

"My name is John O'Bail, commonly called Cornplanter. I am your son, you are my father, you are now my prisoner, and subject to the usages of Indian warfare; but you shall not be harmed, you need not fear, I am a warrior, many are the scalps which I have taken. Many prisoners I have tortured to death. I am your son, I am a warrior, I was anxious to see you, and greet you in friendship. I went to your cabin and took you by force, but your life shall be spared. Indians love their friends, and their kindred, treat them with kindness. If now, you choose to follow the fortunes of your yellow son and to live with our people, I will cherish your old age with plenty of venison, and you shall live easy. But if it is your choice to return to your fields, and live with your white children, I will send a party of my trusty young men to conduct you back in safety. I respect you, my father, you have been friendly to Indians ; they are your friends."

The old man chose to return. His son true to his word, furnished him a suitable escort, and he was conducted back to his home in safety. This story is probably without any foundation in fact, although Col. Stone who copies it in substance, endorses it, and says in a note :

"This anecdote related by Mary Jemison, may be true. In every instance in which the author has had an opportunity of testing the correctness of her statements by other authorities, they have proved to be remarkably correct."

He had forgotten his own contradiction of Mary Jemison's statement, that it was Lieut. Johnson who courted and married Miss Moore. The name of Cornplanter's father was John Abeel ; we find the name in the public records as a citizen or merchant of Albany, in 1692. This was probably the father of John Abeel, the father of Cornplanter, as he must have been a man somewhat advanced in years, and a trader. He also appears to have held offices at different times in the municipal government, and to have been connected with Indian affairs. John Abeel the father of Cornplanter, is spoken of about 1755–6, as an Indian trader, and is complained of by the Senecas, for bringing rum into their country, and when forbidden to do so, declared his determination to persist in it, for " every quart of rum was as good to him as a spanish dollar." It would seem that he began his career as an Indian trader as early as 1748, and was taken prisoner by the French while among the Senecas; and in a negotiation between the English and the French for an exchange of prisoners, John Abeel is said to have a child among the Senecas. This child, was undoubtedly the embryo Indian chief, Cornplanter, who must have been born about 1730.

John Abeel does not seem to have borne a reputation for the strictest integrity; about 1756 he came down from the Senecas country with a canoe load of skins, said to be "fraudulently obtained" in that country.

According to this computation, the age of the chief at the time of this expedition in which he was engaged, must have been over thirty years. He not only became a warrior of distinction, but he also became noted for his ability as a statesman and orator. The three things in which according to Indian estimation, true greatness consists. Perhaps no individual had more influence in all the negotiations of the Six Nations with the whites from the period when he became connected with public affairs, than Cornplanter. It is true he lost his standing in a measure with the Indians before the close of his life, by a supposed, or real sacrifice of the interest of his people, for a consideration received by himself in lands upon the Allegany, the place of his residence. That he was a man of extraordinary ability, we have abundant evidence in numerous letters and speeches of his which have been preserved and published ; although a straight, active, athletic man when young, he became in his old age quite infirm, and could not stand erect.

He had not the standing among the Indians that some of his cotemporaries had, and his character seems to have been that of a shrewd diplomatist, rather than that of an open, frank, ingenuous man. There is no doubt that he was at heart in the British interest up to the period of Wayne's victory over the combined forces of the British and Indians in 1794 ; his speeches and letters all show this. He seems to have acted in concert with Brant, during the period of the Indian troubles in Ohio, after the close of the Revolutionary war. The speeches of Cornplanter, Half-Town and Great-Tree, published in the American state papers (Indian affairs, vol. 1,) have generally been attributed to Cornplanter, whose signature stands first in order.* But it is more probable that these speeches, or more properly communications, were the joint production of the three, or perhaps of Great-Tree who was celebrated as an orator, which, strictly speaking, Cornplanter was not.

The curious letter of Cornplanter, written in 1794, to Lieut. Polhemus, who was then in command of Fort Franklin on the Alleghany, is characteristic of Cornplanter, and is an index of the temper of his mind and disposition. It is as follows :

Ginashadgo, 24 May, 1794.

SIR :—I have returned home safe. I wrote a letter to you, (hope you have received it,) in regard to the British sending a man to Catarogaras & he sent for me—I went

*See Appendix.

to see him, n'ot him alone, but likewise the Moncyes respecting the man that was killed at French-creek as you wrote to me concerning that business.

Brother this man that sent for me to Catarogais wanted to know what we were about, it seemed to him as if we were hiding ourselves. I spoke to him, & told him the reason of our hiding ourselves—that the white people think that we are nobody—I have told him everything from the beginning. That the Six Nations could not be heard by anybody. This was all passed between this British man & myself—his name is William Johnston.

Brother then I spoke to the Moncyes in regard of your writing to me to help you, and I asked their minds as the tommyhawk was sticking in their heads. Then the Moncys spoke & told me they was not drunk about this affair. As you writ to me, and told me you wanted to make our minds easy about this affair.—As you writ to me that you wanted our minds easy—it shall be so—this is all I have to say this present time about it.

As I went there everything happened right, & you will hear a little what Bears-Oil chief said as he was sent there by the chiefs of Conniatt, (Conyaut.) I send you three strings of wampum given to me by Bears-Oil chief and his words were that God almighty had mad day and night, and when he saw me it appeared to him as if it was daylight—Brother, says Bears-Oil my mind is very uneasy when I live at Conneat every summer and I see the bad Indians and always tell them not to interupt our friends this way.

Bears Oil says his mind is very uneasy and the reason is, that he cannot hardly keep these western nations back any more, as they the white people are making forts in their country and another thing our worriors & children are very uneasy. They say that they cannot go out of doors to ease themselves for fear of spoiling Genl. Washingtons lands—and that may (which must) be the reason we will or can (are to) be killed. Bears Oil speeks and says he was sent by all the chiefs, and they looked out which was the best way for him to go; by water their was a lake that God almighty had made for everybody and he hoped that Genl. Washington would have nothing to say if he went by water.

Now Brothers says Bears Oil to the Six Nations I have com to know your minds and if you want me to com down hear to live, I shall com, and I send you five strings of wampum as his speech on that head—I spoke to Bears Oil chief for Wm. Johnston to help him, as the white people thinks nothing of us, then Johnston spoke and told him he would help him, and for (told) him to go home and tell his worriors and children to go to work, plent corn and git their living—I then spoke to Bairs Oil myself to make his mind easy and go home, and if he see (saw) any of the western nations going to war, to tell them not to enterupt anybody about French-creek or anywhere in that country,* and if he should see them, to tell them to go back, to those that ware at war—I told Bears Oil afterwards that if you don't see any of them, and they do any mischief we cannot help it—then after that I considered and dispached runners to Oswego and to Bufflow-creek and to the Genessees for all the chiefs to rise and likewise Gen. Chapin Supiren't of Indian affairs.

---

*I wrote you last about stoping the troops—I hope you will till affairs is (are) settled.

Then Mr. Johnston spoke and said if the Six Nations went, he would go with them. Their is but eight days to com when they will meet at this place if they like what I have said—Brothers at French-creek if it should happen that they dont come you must not blame me, for it is not my fault, because you know very well I am almost tired of talking, because, none of you will hear me—it will be but a few days before I will know whether they are coming, and if they are coming, you will know it imeadeatly I am Your friend and Brother

his
JOHN ⋈ OBAIL
mark
(Cornplanter)

Lieut. John Polhemus Commandg F F

This letter was unquestionably dictated by Cornplanter, but evidently written by an unskillful amanuensis.

The following is the speech, or more properly the communication of Cornplanter and his associates, to Gen. Washington, already alluded to.

THE SPEECH OF THE CORNPLANTER, HALF-TOWN, AND THE GREAT-TREE CHIEFS AND COUNCILLORS OF THE SENECA NATION, TO THE GREAT COUNCILLOR OF THE THIRTEEN FIRES.

FATHER—The voice of the Seneca Nation speaks to you, the great councillor in whose heart the wise men of the thirteen fires have placed their wisdom. It may be very small in your ears, and we therefore entreat you to harken with attention, for we are about to speak of things which to us are very great. When your army entered the country of the Six Nations, we called you the town destroyer; and to this day, when that name is heard, our women look behind them and look pale, and our children cling close to the necks of their mothers. Our councillors and warriors are men, and cannot be afraid; but their hearts are grieved with the fears of our women and children, and desire it may be buried so deep as to be heard no more. When you gave us peace, we called you father, because you promised to secure us in the possession of our lands. Do this, and so long as the lands shall remain, that beloved name will live in the heart of every Seneca.

Father—We mean to open our hearts before you, and we earnestly desire that you will let us clearly understand what you resolve to do. When our chiefs returned from the treaty at Fort Stanwix, and laid before our council what had been done there, our nation was surprised to hear how great a country you had compelled them to give up to you, without your paying to us any thing for it. Every one said that your hearts were yet swelled with resentment against us, for what had happened during the war, but that one day you would reconsider it, with more kindness. We asked each other, what have we done to deserve such severe chastisement?

Father—When you kindled your thirteen fires separately, the wise men that assembled at them told us, that you were all brothers, the children of one great Father, who regarded also, the red people as his children. They called us brothers, and invited us to his protection; they told us that he resided beyond the great water, where the sun first rises; hat he was a King whose power no people could resist, and that his goodness was bright as that sun. What they said went to our hearts; we accepted the invitation, and promised to obey him. What the Seneca Nation promise, they faithfully perform; and when you refused obedience to that King, he commanded us to assist his beloved men, in making you sober. In obeying him, we did no more than yourselves had led us to promise. The men who claimed this promise, told us that you were children, and had no guns; that when they had shaken you, you would submit. We hearkened to them, and were deceived, until your army approached our towns. We were deceived; but your people, in teaching us to confide in that King, had helped to deceive, and we now appeal to your heart. Is the blame allours?

Father—When we saw that we were deceived, and heard the invitation which you gave us to draw near to the fire which you kindled, and talk with you concerning peace, we made haste towards it. You then told us, that we were in your hand, and that, by closing it, you could crush us to nothing, and you demanded from us, a great country, as the price of that peace which you had offered us; as if our want of strength had destroyed our rights; our chiefs had felt your power, and were unable to contend against you, and they therefore gave up that country. What they agreed to, has bound our nation; but your anger against us must, by this time, be cooled; and although our strength has not increased, nor your power become less, we ask you to consider calmly, were the terms dictated to us by your commissioners, reasonable and just?

Father—Your commissioners, when they drew the line which separated the land then given up to you, from that which you agreed should remain to be ours, did most solemnly promise, that we should be secured in the peaceable possession of the lands which we inhabited east and north of that line. Does this promise bind you? Hear now, we beseech you, what has since happened concerning that land. On the day in which we finished the treaty at Fort Stanwix, commissioners from Pennsylvania told our chiefs that they had come there to purchase from us all the lands belonging to us, within the lines of their State, and they told us that their line would strike the river Susquehanna below Tioga branch. They then left us to consider of the bargain till the next day; on the next day, we let them know that we were unwilling to sell all the lands within their State, and proposed to let them have a part of it, which we pointed out to them in their map. They told us that they must have the whole; that it was already ceded to them by the great King, at the time of making peace with you, and was their own; but they said that they would not take advantage of that, and were willing to pay us for it, after the manner of their ancestors. Our chiefs were unable to contend, at that time, and therefore they sold the lands up to the line, which was then shown to them as the line of that State. What the commissioners had said about the land having been ceded to them at the peace, our chiefs considered as intended only to lessen the price, and they passed it by with very little notice; but, since that time, we have heard so much from others about the right to our lands, which the King gave when you made peace with him, that it is our earnest desire that you will tell us what it means.

Father—Our nation empowered John Livingston to let out part of our lands on rent, to be paid to us. He told us, that he was sent by Congress, to do this for us, and we fear he has deceived us in the writing he obtained from us. For, since the time of our giving that power, a man of the name of Phelps has come among us, and claimed our whole country northward of the line of Pennsylvania, under purchase from that Livingston, to whom, he said, he had paid twenty thousand dollars for it. He said also, that he had bought, likewise, from the council of the thirteen fires, and paid them twenty thousand dollars more for the same. And he said also, that it did not belong to us, for that the great King had ceded the whole of it, when you made peace with him. Thus he claimed the whole country north of Pennsylvania, and west of the lands of the Cayugas. He demanded it; he insisted on his demand, and declared that he would have it all. It was impossible for us to grant him this, and we immediately refused it. After some days, he proposed to run a line, at a small distance eastward of our western boundary, which we also refused to agree to. He then threatened us with immediate war, if we did not comply. Upon this threat, our chiefs held a council, and they agreed that no event of war could be worse than to be driven, with their wives and children, from the only country which we had any right to, and, therefore, weak as our nation was, they determined to take the chance of war, rather than to submit to such unjust demands, which seemed to have no bounds. Street, the great trader to Niagara, was then with us, having come at the request of Phelps, and he always professed to be our great friend, we consulted him upon this subject. He also told us, that our lands had been ceded by the King, and that we must give them up. Astonished from what we heard from every quarter, with hearts aching with compassion for our women and children, we were thus compelled, to give up all our country north of the line of Pennsylvania, and east of the Genesee river, up to the fork, and east of a south line drawn from that fork to the Pennsylvania line. For this land Phelps agreed to pay us ten thousand dollars in hand, and one thousand a year forever. He paid us two thousand and five hundred dollars in hand, part of the ten thousand, and he sent for us to come last spring, to receive our money; but instead of paying us the remainder of the ten thousand dollars, and the one thousand dollars due for the first year, he offered us no more than five hundred dollars, and insisted that he agreed with us for that sum, to be paid yearly. We debated with him for six days, during all which time he persisted in refusing to pay us our just demand, and he insisted that we should receive the five hundred dollars; and Street, from Niagara, also insisted on our receiving the money, as it was offered to us. The last reason he assigned for continuing to refuse paying us, was, that the King had ceded the lands to the Thirteen Fires, and that he had bought them from you, and paid you for them. We could bear this confusion no longer, and determined to press through every difficulty, and lift up our voice that you might hear us, and to claim that security in the possession of our lands, which your commissioners so solemnly promised us. And we now entreat you to inquire into our complaints and redress our wrongs.

Father—Our writings were lodged in the hands of Street, of Niagara, as we supposed him to be our friend; but when we saw Phelps consulting with Street, on every occasion, we doubted of his honesty towards us, and we have since heard, that he was to receive for his endeavors to deceive us, a piece of land ten miles in width, west of the Genesee river, and near forty miles in length, extending to lake Ontario; and the lines of this tract have been run accordingly, although no part of it is within the bounds that limit his purchase. No doubt he meant to deceive us.

Father—You have said that we are in your hand, and that, by closing it, you could crush us to nothing. Are you determined to crush us? If you are, tell us so, that those of our nation who have become your children, and have determined to die so, may know what to do. In this case, one chief has said he would ask you to put him out of pain. Another, who will not think of dying by the hand of his father or his brother, has said he will retire to the Chateaugay, eat of the fatal root, and sleep with his fathers, in peace. Before you determine on a measure so unjust, look up to God, who made us, as well as you. We hope he will not permit you to destroy the whole of our nation.

Father—Hear our case: many nations inhabited this country; but they had no wisdom, and, therefore, they warred together. The Six Nations were powerful, and compelled them to peace; the lands, for a great extent, were given up to them; but the nations which were not destroyed, all continued on those lands, and claimed the protection of the Six Nations, as the brothers of their fathers. They were men, and when at peace, they had a right to live upon the earth. The French came among us, and built Niagara; they became our fathers, and took care of us. Sir William Johnston came and took that Fort from the French; he became our father, and promised to take care of us, and did so, until you were too strong for his King. To him we gave four miles round Niagara, as a place of trade. We have already said how we came to join against you; we saw that we were wrong; we wished for peace; you demanded a great country to be given up to you; it was surrendered to you as the price of peace, and we ought to have peace and possession of the little land which you then left us.

Father—When that great country was given up, there were but few chiefs present, and they were compelled to give it up; and it is not the Six Nations only that reproach those chiefs with having given up that country. The Chippewas, and all the nations who lived on those lands westward, call to us, and ask us: Brothers of our fathers, where is the place you have reserved for us to lie down upon?

Father—You have compelled us to do that which has made us ashamed. We have nothing to answer to the children of the brothers of our fathers. When, last spring they called upon us to go to war, to secure them a bed to lie upon, the Senecas entreated them to be quiet, till we had spoken to you. But, on our way down, we heard that your army had gone toward the country which those nations inhabit, and if they meet together, the best blood on both sides will stain the ground.

Father—We will not conceal from you, that the great God, and not men, has preserved the Cornplanter from the hands of his own nation. For they ask, continually, where is the land, which our children, and their children after them, are to lie down upon? You told us, say they that the line drawn from Pennsylvania to lake Ontario, would mark it forever on the east, and the line running from Beaver (Buffalo*) Creek to Pennsylvania would mark it on the west, and we see that it is not so. For, first one, and then another, come, and take it away, by order of that people which you tell us promised to secure it to us. He is silent, for he has nothing to answer. When the sun goes down, he opens his heart before God, and earlier than that sun appears again upon the hills, he gives thanks for his protection during the night; for he feels that among men, become desperate by their danger, it is God only that can preserve him. He loves peace, and all he had in store, he has given to those who have been robbed by your people, lest they should plunder the innocent to repay themselves. The whole season which others have employed in providing for their families, he has spent in his endeavors to preserve peace; and at this moment, his wife and children are lying on the ground, and in want of food; his heart is in pain for them, but he perceives that the great God will try his firmness, in doing what is right.

Father—The game which the Great Spirit sent into our country for us to eat, is going from among us. We thought He intended we should till the ground with the plow, as the white people do, and we talked to one another about it. But before we speak to you concerning this, we must know from you whether you mean to leave us and our children any land to till. Speak plainly to us concerning this great business. All the land we have been speaking of, belonged to the Six Nations; no part of it ever belonged to the King of England, and he could not

*Evidently a mistake in the interpreter; Beaver and Buffalo in the Seneca are similar in their pronunciation; the termination of both is the same.

give it to you. The land we live on, our fathers received from God, and they transmitted it to us, for our children, and we cannot part with it.

Father—We told you that we would open our hearts to you. Hear us once more. At Fort Stanwix, we agreed to deliver up those of our people who should do you any wrong, that you might try them, and punish them according to your law. We delivered up two men accordingly, but instead of trying them according to your law, the lowest of your people took them from your magistrate, and put them immediately to death. It is just to punish murder with death; but the Senecas will not deliver their people to men who disregard the treaties of their own nation.

Father—Innocent men of our nation are killed, one after another, and of our best families; but none of your people who have committed the murder, have been punished. We recollect that you did not promise to punish those who killed our people, and we now ask, was it intended that your people should kill the Senecas, and not only remain unpunished by you, but be protected by you against the revenge of the next of kin?

Father—These are to us very great things. We know that you are very strong, and we have heard that you are wise, and we want to hear your answer to what we have said, that we may know that you are just.

his
CORN ⋈ PLANTER
mark
his
HALF ⋈ TOWN,
mark
his
GREAT ⋈ TREE.
mark

Signed at Philadelphia, the 1st day of December, 1790. Present at signing, Joseph Nicholson, Interpreter, Tim'y Matlack.

The reply of Gen. Washington was couched in kind and conciliatory language, informing the chiefs that he was aware that their people had been led into some difficulty about their lands, but assured them that the government of the United States felt bound to protect them in all the lands secured to them by the treaty of Fort Stanwix, in 1784. He also assured them that John Livingston was not authorized to treat with them in regard to their lands, and that every thing that he did was null and void, and that the federal courts would afford them relief as readily and as effectually as any white citizen, and that it did not appear from any proofs in possession of the government, that Oliver Phelps had defrauded them. He advised them to be strong in their friendship to the government which was sincerely desirous of their friendship, upon terms of the most perfect justice, and humanity. He also assured them that an agent would soon be appointed to reside at some place convenient to them, to whom they might apply at all times for advice or assistance. They were then dismissed with handsome presents for themselves, and for other chiefs in their nation.

Cornplanter and his colleagues had complained of some of the provisions of the treaty at Fort Stanwix in 1784. That they were compelled to give up too much of their lands, and asked that the treaty might be reconsidered, and a part of their land restored. To this the President replied : "You seem to entirely forget that you yourselves, the Cornplanter, Half-Town, and Great Tree, with others of your nation, confirmed, by the treaty of Fort Harmer, upon the Muskingum, so late as the 9th of January, 1789, the boundary marked at the treaty of Fort Stanwix, and that in consideration thereof, you then received goods to a considerable amount. * * The lines fixed at Fort Stanwix and Fort Harmer must therefore remain established."

The delegation took their leave of the President on the 7th of February, 1791, in an address of which the following is a copy:

Father—No Seneca ever goes from the fires of his friend, until he has said to him, "I am going." We now therefore tell you, that we are now setting out for our own country.

Father—We thank you from our hearts that we now know there is a country we may call our own, and on which we may lie down in peace. We see that there will be peace between your children and our children; and our hearts are glad. We will persuade the Wyandots, and other western nations, to open their eyes, and look towards the bed which you have made for us, and to ask of you a bed for themselves, and their children, that will not slide from under them. We thank you for your presents to us, and rely on your promise to instruct us in raising corn, as the white people do; the sooner you do this, the better for us. And we thank you for the care you have taken to prevent bad men from coming to trade among us; if any come without your license, we will turn them back; and we hope our nation will determine to spill all the rum which shall, hereafter, be brought to our towns.

Father—We are glad to hear that you determine to appoint an agent that will do us justice, in taking care that bad men do not come to trade amongst us; but we earnestly entreat you that you will let us have an interpreter in whom we can confide, to reside at Pittsburgh: to that place our people, and other nations, will long continue to resort; there we must send what news we hear, when we go among the western nations, which, we are determined, shall be early in the spring. We know Joseph Nicholson, and he speaks our language so that we clearly understand what you say to us, and we rely on what he says. If we were able to pay him for his services, we would do it; but, when we meant to pay him, by giving him land, it has not been confirmed to him, and he will not serve us any longer unless you will pay him. Let him stand between to entreat you.

Father—You have not asked any security for peace on our part, but we have agreed to send nine Seneca boys, to be under your care for education. Tell us at what time you will receive them, and they shall be sent at the time you shall appoint. This will assure you that we are, indeed, at peace with you and determined to continue so. If you can teach them to become wise and good men, we will take care that our nation shall be willing to receive instruction from them.

his
CORN ⋈ PLANTER.
mark.
his
HALF ⋈ TOWN.
mark.
his
BIG ⋈ TREE.
mark.

Signed at Philadelphia, 7th Feb., 1791, in presence of Joseph Nicholson, Interpreter, Thomas Proctor, Tim'y Matlack.

Cornplanter and Brant had attended the treaty at Fort Stanwix in 1784, as the principal representatives of the Six Nations. The concessions of land made at that treaty had been a subject of dissatisfaction and complaint, on the part of a great majority of the chiefs and sachems, and Cornplanter had already began to feel the growing unpopularity of those, who were considered the authors of those measures, and it is not surprising that he should make strenuous efforts, to get the terms of that treaty so modified, as to make it less obnoxious to his people.

The condition of Indian affairs in the Northwestern Territory, was daily growing more and more threatening. It was the policy of the government, by every possible means, to conciliate the Six Nations. While on the other hand, the British were active in inciting, and encouraging them to join the western Indians, in the impending struggle. Johnson, Brant, and others, were active agents of the British, and soon after the visit of Cornplanter, Half-Town, and Big Tree, to their great father, President Washington, an agent was dispatched to visit Cornplanter, with a view to engage him, and through him, the influential chiefs of the Six Nations, to go on an embassy to the western Indians; particularly the Wyandots, in the vicinity of Sandusky. Accordingly, in March, 1791, Col. Thomas Proctor was appointed to proceed to visit Cornplanter, at his residence on the head waters of the Allegany river. As his journal is interesting, and relates to the condition of the Senecas, and their location in this vicinity, it will be inserted at length, in an appendix.

It has been stated that Cornplanter acted in concert with Brant at the Fort Stanwix treaty in 1784. It should be understood however, that there existed between these two chiefs, a personal dislike. It may be, that the results of that treaty heightened this feeling of animosity on the part of Cornplanter, for he never ceased to regret the acts into which he was drawn, or driven, at that treaty; and he refers to it on almost all occasions, either to complain of its terms, or, of the bad faith, in which its provisions had been observed on the part of the whites. He was a war chief of the Senecas. Brant held the same position among the Mohawks. It is scarcely possible that they should have been rivals. As a warrior, whatever may be thought, or said, by white men, Cornplanter, in the estimation of the Indians, who were their cotemporaries, was his superior. The Senecas were a nation of warriors, and it will be admitted, that they did most of the fighting for the Six Nations, during nearly two centuries of their history, with which we are conversant. From the time Cornplanter came on to the stage, (and he entered upon the war path early,) down to the close of the Revolutionary war, he had no superior, and few equals as a warrior. His other qualifications will be judged, by the record he has left, in his speeches, and letters, in the archieves of our State, and national government. After the war, he retired to the land given him by the State of Pennsylvania, where he continued to reside until his death, which occurred in March, 1836, at the age of over one hundred years.

APPENDIX.

NARRATIVE OF COL. THOMAS PROCTOR.

March 12th, 1791. Left the city of Philadelphia, accompanied by Capt. M. G. Houdin, under a heavy rain, fully evidencing our intention to stop at no difficulties, until we should gain the settlement of Cornplanter, alias Capt. O'Beel, one of the chiefs of the Seneca Nation, residing on the head-waters of the Alleghany river. * *

March 14th. Proceeded to Curaherstown, in company with Mr. Potts and Mr. Baird; the latter of which gentlemen informed me, that he was engaged to attend Gen. St. Clair to Fort Washington, whither the General was immediately to proceed, in order to prepare for a campaign against the Miami, and other Indians, who are daily committing of murders on the defenceless inhabitants on the frontier settlements.

15th. Set forward at daylight. The roads from Philadelphia hither, nearly impassible, occasioned by the heavy rains that had fallen for several days past; with some danger we forded the little Schuylkill; on this day's journey we crossed the Blue Mountains.

17th. Crossed the east branch of the Susquehanna. Lay this night at Berwick, a small town situate on the west side of the Susquehanna.

18th. Proceeded on our journey up the west side of the Susquehanna, above twelve miles; * * from thence we proceeded on the road for Wilksburgh, by the way of the mountain path, as dangerous for man and horse as was possible; and at 9 o'clock in the night we reached the first house in a settlement at Wyoming.

March 19th. Arrived at Wilksbugh about eleven o'clock, halted for the night in order to rest our horses. * * Spent the afternoon at our lodgings with Colonel Butler and Capt. Grubb. The former was an officer in the Connecticut line, and stationed here during the late war, for the protection of the frontier inhabitants against the British and Indians in which station he proved to be a vigilant and brave officer. The latter part of the evening I accompanied Col. Pickering, Prothonotary of the county, and late Adjutant General of the armies of the United States. Much snow fell while we remained at this place; weather extremely cold.

20th. This day we set forward for Capt. Waterman Baldwin's; arrived there in the evening, halted for him part of two days, as I had orders to take him with me to the residence of the Cornplanter, at which place he was intended to act as instructor to the Indian youth, as also a director in the mode and management of agriculture, for the use and benefit of the Indians. This gentleman was made prisoner by Cornplanter, during the late war, and was treated by him with remarkable tenderness, until legally exchanged. * *

22d. Passed the first narrows of Susquehanna; * * encamped this evening in the woods, thirteen miles from Lahawanock, on the waters of the Buttermilk Falls. * * This place I had the opportunity of examining minutely, when going on the expedition of Gen. Sullivan against the savages, in the year 1779. We landed, and I passed to the top of the mountain to review so great a curiosity.

23d. The Susquehanna being so extremely high, and all the waters leading thereto, compelled us to quit the river road, and go by that lately cut (though not cleared) by John Nicholson, Esq., Comptroller General of the state of Pennsylvania. The taking of this road which was cut about twenty feet in width, the trees lying across the same, and in every direction, was not a matter of choice, but necessity, for the river road was impassible.

24th. We were obliged to encamp early this afternoon under a very heavy storm of rain, thunder and lightning, and what is very remarkable, the snow was in general fifteen inches deep on the ground.

25th. We still travelled by the way of Nicholson's road, till we reached the one cut by Mr. Ellicott, geographer to the United States, which leads to the great bend on the east branch of the Susquehanna, and to describe the same, it is hardly possible, but to say the least of them, there is none can equal them for heigth of mountains, and swampy valleys. Encamped this night ten miles from Tioga point.

26th. We arrived at the ferry at Tioga Point, the river still very high. From there we proceeded on our way to Newtown Point. At Tioga Point I was compelled to purchase a pack-horse, as the route we had to take from the Painted Post to the Genesee, was not inhabited; which by computation was ninety-nine miles. Capt. Baldwin also purchased another horse, the better to enable him to carry on the farming business for the

Cornplanter. * * From hence I also took a guide named Peter, in his own language Cayantha, there being nothing but a blind path to the Genesee river, * *

Sunday, 27th. Halted for the night, reviewed the ground on which the British and Indians were entrenched for better than a mile, against the forces under the command of Major Gen. Sullivan. * *

28th. Proceeded to the Painted Post or Cohocton in the Indian language; dined, and refreshed our horses, it being the last house we should meet with, ere we should reach the Genesee river. Here I was joined company by a Mr. George Slocum, who followed us from Wyoming, to place himself under our protection and assistance until we should reach the Cornplanter's settlement on the head-waters of the Alleghany, to the redeeming of his sister from an unpleasing captivity of twelve years, to which end he begged our immediate interposition. On leaving the Painted Post, we entered the warriors path, lying on the north east side of the Tioga river.

29th. Continued our route by the aforesaid path this day. * *

30th. We began our journey before sunrise; * * the course of the warriors path gives a traveller a sight of the river Tioga, upwards of sixty miles. The next principal water we crossed is called, in the Indian language, Connesserago, from whence it is called twelve miles to the Genesee river.

31st. This morning I found myself in a settlement of Indians, called the Squawkey tribe, but a branch of the Seneca Nation. * *

April 1st. Mr. Horatio Jones, Indian interpreter, arrived this morning, and about eleven o'clock, there were thirty odd Indians collected ; and shortly afterwards I convened into council, and introduced my message by some prefatory sentiments, touching on the candor and justice of the United States. I read the message to them from the Hon. Secretary of War ; having ended the same, they signified their full approbation in their accustomed manner. Capt. Little Beard acquainted me that their great warrior, Capt. O'Beel, or Cayantawanka, in the Indian language, had arrived at Pittsburgh, from Philadelphia, and sent out runners from thence, to summon the chiefs and warriors of the Six Nations at Buffalo, where he desired that the great council fire might be kindled, and where he should lay before them all the business that had been done by him at Philadelphia, and the public papers and documents, which he had received for the Six Nations, from the President of the United States, the Secretary of War, and from the Governor of the State of Pennsylvania. This information induced me to prepare myself for going to Buffalo in the morning, instead of continuing my route to O'Beelstown, and urged it upon them in a very pressing manner, that they would accompany me on this deserving errand to Buffalo, as its design was big with advantages to every Indian on the continent. Five of them immediately offered to attend Capt. Houdin and myself, and chiefs of the first notoriety in this settlement, and accordingly appointed a sugar camp, eight miles distant, the place of meeting in the morning, where they must go and acquaint their people of this hasty departure. I now made the necessary inquiry whether it was easy to obtain a good interpreter at Buffalo, or otherwise: and being informed that there were no interpreters there but those under British pay and establishments, I conceived it a duty incumbent on me, to engage Mr. Jones, as being a proper person for my business, from the reputation he bore from inquiries I have made, and I accordingly agreed with him, in the behalf of the United States, to pay him the customary wages, so long as I should find occasion for his services.

April 2d. Departed from the council fire at Squawkey Hill, to proceed by the way of Tonawandy, to Buffalo—presumed distance between ninety and one hundred miles ; but, agreeable to my promise to the chiefs yesterday, I had to call for them at their sugar encampment. On my way thither, I stopped at the hut of Stump Foot, with the Black Chief, who accompanied me, just at the instant that a runner had arrived there from Buffalo Creek, who brought the information that the council fire at that place had been quenched, by direction of the chiefs who had lighted the same, at the instance of O'Beel's message to them, and was to be covered for one moon. Upon this sudden information to me, and their determination to continue as above directed, I determined to change my route from this place, and go for the Oil Springs, near which the Cornplanter has his residence, and of which intention of mine I immediately informed them, that should I be so fortunate as to find him at home, I would use every possible endeavor to bring forward to Buffalo, Capt. O'Beel and his chiefs, in order to rekindle the council fire. On these remarks we parted, and I proceeded with my people to a village eight miles distant, called Nondas, and halted for the night at the hut of a white woman, who had been with the savages from her infancy, and had borne to one of them nine children, all of whom were living. Two of her daughters I have seen, possessing fair features, bearing the bloom upon their cheeks, and inclining to the side of beauty ; and her second son had lately been adopted a sachem, and styled the promoter of peace.

Sunday, April 3d. Arrived this day at an Indian village called Carasedera, situated on a high bluff of land overlooking the Genesee river. It consisted of about thirty houses, and some of them done in a way that showed some taste in the workmen. The town was vacated by its inhabitants principally, save only one squaw, and a young girl, who were left as guards to the interest of others, who were out providing sugar for their general stock. This day we were compelled to swim our horses three times across the Genesee river ; and at one of the crossings, Capt. Howdin's horse took down the current with him, and could not steer him to the intended shore, having crossed the reins of his bridle at mounting, and were it not that he had left the horse to his own management, (by our entreaties,) and our Indian guide rushing into the water to his assistance, and the horse turning for him, the Captain must have certainly drowned in the current, which was excessively rapid a little lower down.

April 4th. This morning we again swam our horses over the same river. From this place we have scarcely the trace of a path ; and took up our encampment for the night in an old Indian encampment, where the covering of their wigwam served to shelter us from the inclemency of the weather.

April 5th. We gained an Indian settlement called Ohhisheu, situate on the waters of Oil Creek, the emptying of which, into the Alleghany, about two hundred yards below the huts. In crossing the Oil Creek, at a very steep shelving place, my horse fell back into the water. I disengaged myself from falling under him, but got wet through all my clothes. We encamped this night at the Great Bend of the Alleghany. This place was formerly called Dunewangua.

April 6th. This morning, having advanced about four miles, we met two Indian runners, with belts and speeches from the Cornplanter, alias O'Beel, to the Indians resident in the upper towns, at the head waters of the Alleghany, to inform them that several of the Delaware Indians were killed by the white people, said to be a recruiting party of Virginians, near Fort Pitt The said Indians informed us, that the Indians who had escaped the catastrophe, that their brothers had fallen into, turned their resentment for the injury their nation had received, on the white inhabitants who resided on the Alleghany, some miles above Pittsburgh, and killed and scalped seventeen in number ; that at the same time this mischief happened, Capt. O'Beel, the New Arrow Chief, and several other chiefs of the Senecas, as also the commanding officer of Venango, coming up in the garrison boat, and in canoes, from Pittsburgh, were overtaken by a party of militia, who threatened them with instant death, which was happily prevented, but (they) forcibly carried back the garrison boat and canoes, with all the property purchased by Cornplanter and his nation. Having at this time no path to go by, made the way lengthy and disagreeable. * * Our guide conducted us in safety, at about 10 o'clock, at night, to O'Beel's town. This town is pleasantly situated, on the north side of the river, and contains about twenty-eight tolerable well built houses; and the one which they had selected for me and my followers to reside in, was commodiously fitted up, with berths to sleep in, and uncommonly clean, and provided us for the night with plenty of provisions, such as boiled venison and dumplings. Matters were no sooner arranged, than I desired my interpreter to have the chiefs collected where I could speak to them. Upon which, we found that all the chiefs and warriors of the town were gone on to Venango, hearing that their head warrior, O'Beel, and their sachem, the New Arrow, were forced to take sanctuary in Fort Franklin, (one of our garrisons,) for the protection of their lives; that none remained in the town on this account, but three very old men, the women and children. * * I then desired that they would furnish me with a canoe and a guide, to conduct me to the place where I could meet with O'Beel and his people, being desirous of going forward immediately; and that I should, without doubt, be the instrument of bringing their chiefs and warriors to them in a few days. Upon which, they sent five miles to procure me a canoe, and by daylight, two young Indians attended me, with whom my interpreter and Capt. Baldwin, went for French Creek, distant about one hundred and thirty miles, and arrived on the 8th day of April, about four in the afternoon, as we worked our canoe by turns, all night.

I no sooner arrived at the garrison on French Creek, than I received a visit from Cornplanter, and those Indians that accompanied him at Philaadelphia, who professed the greatest happiness to see me, being under the greatest anxiety of mind, for the safety of the New-Arrow, who was carried in the Garrison boat to Pittsburgh in the forcible manner before related. * * I desired him (Cornplanter) without loss of time, to bring with him into the garrison all the head men of the nation then present, so that I might inform them of the message I was charged with from his excellency, the Secretary of War, to the Six Nations; * * upon this Capt. O'Beel left me, and soon after summoned the chiefs present, eleven in number, who met me in the garrison by permission of Lieut. Jeffers, and in the fullest manner I gave them the necessary information. I proposed meeting them again in their encampment over French Creek, early in the forenoon, and of which I desired that they might inform their people, so that none might be absent.

April 9th. I crossed French Creek to their encampment, about eleven o'clock, where I found them prepared to receive me about seventy-five in number, exclusive of women, children and youth; in the whole one hundred and eighty. I read first the message to the Seneca Nation from the Secretary of War, and after explaining to them the principles upon which it was founded, I read to them the messages from Governor St. Clair to the Wyandot and Delaware tribes, who were deemed and observed to be friends of the United States. Here I thought it my duty to explain to them the force of my message to the Indians, who were carrying on their wanton depredations and cruelties on the defenceless inhabitants resident near the Ohio. * * That with this present council it rests to save those misguided people on the Miami and Wabash, from the distruction that is just ready to fall and crush them; and the better to effect so laudable an undertaking, let there be selected from amongst you, any number of your chiefs and warriors, not more than fifteen nor less than five, to guide and accompany me to the Miami's, as by your going from hence we shall save the distance of four hundred miles, if not compelled to go to Buffalo Creek; and by this act you will fully complete the end of my message to the Seneca Nation; and for your services you shall receive ample reward from the United States, and due honor to your nation. * * We left them for about an hour and a half, when a chief came to inform me that they were desirous of seeing me again at their fire. I accordingly attended, and Capt. O'Beel was appointed to acquaint me with the determination of their council; which briefly was that they could not agree to my request of going directly to the Miamies, as they must determine on that business in full council of the Six Nations at Buffalo Creek. Seeing therefore, that I had no other alternative, but by going to Buffalo, I requested then, that they would prepare themselves to leave this place, and proceed for Buffalo on to-morrow, which they readily complied with; and for Cornplanter's address to me upon this occasion, see subsequent page. * *

April 10th. Agreeably to the arrangements made by me at the general council yesterday, we set out from French Creek to go up the Alleghany river with thirty canoes. * * Halted this night at Oil Creek, about eight miles from the garrison. Lieut. Jeffers came to us at this place about 12 o'clock at night, and brought with him certain letters that he had received from Pittsburgh that evening, with verbal messages he had received by express, by which means the Indians were informed that some of their canoes were plundered of what they contained, but the garrison boat was returning with their chief, the New Arrow &c., under the escort of Major Hart, with a proper guard. *

Monday, 11th of April. We silently began to load our canoes, and shortly after took up the line of march, O'Beel taking the lead. I held it proper to take my place next to his canoe to stimulate him to press forward on his journey. Ere we could reach Buffalo Creek, we arrived this evening at an old Indian settlement called Hog's Town; we had much rain this night and very cold.

April 12th. I was invited this morning to breakfast with Capt. O'Beel his squaw, &c. Our repast, boiled chestnuts, parched meal sweetened; his daughter made us some tea, also, which she put into an open kettle when the water was cold, and being boiled in that manner without any cover to the kettle, it became very dirty and disagreeable to the taste; but of the chestnuts I took sufficiently. * * This day about one o'clock we arrived at the Munsee settlement, where all the canoes came to at, in order to rest and prepare for our dinners. Immediately after we had landed, and what appeared very strange to me, several Indian women came forward with kettles full of boiled corn and bear's meat, and placed it before Capt. O'Beel, who they had heard was approaching with his people. This being done, each family of a canoe, (as in each were women and children) approached with their kettles, without any signal being made, to receive their stipend; and to do which, an old squaw was appointed to act as an issuing commissary, who dealt it out in proportions so justly, that each went away fully satisfied. Capt. O'Beel requested of my interpreter to inform me it was expected that I would partake of what was prepared; I did so accordingly, to prevent displeasure, but with the weakest appetite. * *

12th. At 9 o'clock at night Capt. O'Beel the Delaware chiefs and Senecas, when Capt. Snake's interpreter gave his speech as follows:

"Uncle, (for that is the term given by the Delawares to the Senecas,) God has been good to us this day; for we have each heard the good talk from the great chief of the thirteen fires; and we have ever said that we would advise each other of everything we heard that was bad, or was like to befall either of our nations. Now uncle, we have determined to go with you and our brother, who brings to us these good tidings, to Buffalo, and there meet our nations at the great council fire. Blood may fall upon us while we are going, but now we give you our hands as we promised, and we will lie down and will rise together." (Here a belt of wampum was given, consisting of five strings, which Capt. O'Beel viewed in his hand a short time, and then presented it to me.) Capt. Snake again repeated: "Uncle in three days we remove our women and children, and all that we have to your towns, they are to remain with your women until our return." In the course of his speech, he alse mentioned that their people expected to receive a stroke from the Massasaugas, a part of that nation who were led to war by their brothers.

13th. Our fleet set out from Hickorytown, and reached Logtrap Creek, ten miles distant, and encamped. Rained all night, and not a dry thread on myself or companions.

14th. Proceeded up the river to-day, took up our encampment near the mouth of Casyoudang Creek, it being the place where Col. Broadhead, in 1779, had fought against the savages; and in which action Joseph Nicholson, his interpreter, was wounded.

15th. Being very unwell this morning, and overtaken with rheumatic pains, and to such a degree that I was obliged to have assistance to convey me from my canoe to the fire ; at the same time it being cold and raining, I informed Cornplanter that I should leave his fleet, and proceed to his lower town, to procure some assistance ; and I arrived there some time in the night, after a very laborious day's work for the Indians ; * * the Indians whom I hired at Venango, to bring me to O'Beel's town, (there being two called by his name,) drew so nice a distinction, that they chose the first, or lower town, and insisted that this was the town they intended to come to, and not the other ; and should I require their assistance to go to the upper town, I must pay to each one dollar. The terms being agreed upon, we proceeded to the upper town, aforesaid. * * At this town I left Capt. Houdin, Indian Peter, the guide which I brought from near Tioga Point, also our horses, when I departed thence to Venango. * *

16th. At this town I met in company with Capt. Houdin, a French gentleman from Montreal, by the name of Dominick de Barge, who had followed the Indian trade in this country for six years past, and who lost by the same a considerable fortune, by the credits he had given to some of the Indians, &c.; with them I found also a Mr. Culbertson, a trader from Genesee, and it gave me pleasure to find that the Captain was not altogether alone, he seeming to have an aversion in general, to the company of Indians.

17th. This day, the canoes which left on the 15th, arrived here, and brought the news which they had received from an Indian runner, that on Wednesday last, the 13th, the New Arrow and his associates, with the garrison boat, had arrived at Fort Franklin ; having suffered no damage in their persons, nor loss of their merchandise, as was reported. * *

18th. An express arrived here from the New Arrow, advising that they must send down to him at Fort Franklin, a certain number of canoes, sufficient to carry the goods brought forward by Cornplanter from Philadelphia. * * This afternoon, the canoes which had waited on the way, arrived; and by which I was informed that the Delaware and Munsee Indians at Hickorytown, were moving with their stock, &c., to Cattaraugus.

19th. O'Beel and chiefs arrived here from the lower town, and ordered their conch shell to be sounded through the town, to summon the head men to council. Nothing more material this day.

20th. An express arrived from Buffalo Creek, informing that the fire of the Six Nations had been kindled by a number of chiefs and warriors, and they had been stirring it long to keep it alive, waiting for the sachems of the Senecas and their brothers, who were sent by the great chief of the thirteen fires, whom we want to hear speak with us. * * On receiving this public message, I was requested by O'Beel and the other chiefs, to write an answer, on their behalf, as hearing that Col. Butler and Brant were at Buffalo, waiting our coming. I complied with their request, and directed the same to the Farmers' Brother, Kayasatta, and Red Jacket, chiefs of the Six Nations, at Buffalo Creek.

21st. This morning, the whole of the town were preparing to have a grand feast, to return thanks to the great keeper of all men, for their being spared to meet once more together; several of the chiefs called on us to invite us to be present. In the evening, Capt. O'Beel and other chiefs, informed me that they would be ready to go with me to Buffalo Creek in the morning, if I thought proper; the information gave me the most heart-felt satisfaction, and I acquainted him that I was ready to depart, at any hour they should agree to go, as much precious time had been wasted since my arrival in this place from the Genesee country.

23d. We left O'Beel's town about twelve o'clock, and proceeded with a few chiefs and warriors, (the whole not being ready to depart with us,) taking the route for Buffalo through the village called Cattaragus, which we did not reach before the 25th, in the evening; and on our way thither, passed through a settlement of Delaware, or Munsee Indians, in which was about twenty houses.

26th. We took up our journey towards Buffalo, and in about five miles going from thence, we came in upon the verge of lake Erie, which had a beautiful appearance, it being a pleasant morning, and the waters were very serene, and looking over the lake, we could just perceive the land upon the other side. We traveled along the sandy beach for some miles, but were obliged, at three or four different places, to leave the shore, and take to the woods, the rocks having come bluff up to the deep water,

27th. We arrived at Buffalo Creek, having travelled through a country of exceeding rich land, from our last encampment, the extent of which I have not been able to ascertain. The pre-emptive right to this valuable country is vested in the state of Massachusetts, but at present the property of the Hon. Robert Morris of the city of Philadelphia, by a late purchase. The principal village of Buffalo belongs to the Seneca Nation, and in it the Young-King and Farmer's-Brother reside; as also Red Jacket the great speaker, and prince of the turtle tribe. On my entering the town there were numbers of Indians collected at the hut where we alighted from our horses, and on taking a general view of them, I found that they were far better clothed than those Indians were, in the towns at a greater distance, owing entirely to the immediate intercourse they had with the British, being but thirty-five miles distance from Niagara, and but six miles from Fort Erie, situate on the north side of the lake; from which places they are supplied yearly with almost every necessary they require, so much so as to make them indifferent in their huntings, and the chiefs who are poor in general, have to look up to them for almost their daily subsistence, not only of provisions but for apparel; for the Young-King was fully regimentaled as a Colonel, red, faced with blue, as belonging to some Royal Regiment, and equipped with a pair of the best epauletts. So that from his after conduct, it may not appear extraordinary where the King has thrown in his opposition to my errand, he being paid so well for his influence over the Indian Nations as to carry his favorite point in question. I had not been long in the village before I was invited to the great council house, with my companion, attended by Red Jacket, O'Beel and other chiefs. Just as we approached the porch they had a two pounder swivel gun, which had been loaded very heavy, having put into her an uncommon charge which the acting gunner being sensible of, stood within the door, and fired it from the end of a long pole which he passed between the logs; which being done, the explosion upset the gun and its fixture. This they said was done as a treat for our safe arrival through the dangers that we had encountered and for which they were thankful to the Great Keeper. The speech given by Red Jacket, being ended, he came forward to me to the seat I had been invited to in the centre of the council, and presented me with four strings of wampum, which he had held in his hands while speaking (for particulars of which see another page) Capt. O'Beel having been particularly named by Red Jacket, he rose and returned the compliment in behalf of us that were strangers.

Being just at sun setting, I apprised the council through my interpreter, that I had messages from Gen. Washington, the great chief of the thirteen fires, which were particularly addressed to the notice of the Six Nations, the representatives of which nations I presumed were principally present; but as it was getting late, I requested leave to postpone the introduction till the morning, which was consented to. Upon this, Red Jacket rose to remark that many persons had occasionally come into their country who said they had also come in by the authority of the thirteen fires, but of the truth of which they were not always convinced. This intimation opened the door that I expected; having been informed by a French gentleman, a trader amongst them, that these sentiments had fallen from Brant and Butler, about seven days previous to our arrival at this place, who desired of the chiefs in private council to pay no attention to what should be said to them by me; and as they knew the purport of my mission, from the chiefs whom I had held council with at Genesee river; the Colonels advised them not to assist me in going to the Miamies, as the consequences would be fatal to those that should attend me, and consequent death to me and my companion. From these suggestions which had fallen from Red Jacket, I mentioned in open council, that I was desirous that they might call forward any gentleman of veracity in whom they had confidence, to be present while I should deliver myself to them, and examine any writing that I was directed to lay before the Six Nations, as by that means proof would be made that my commission was founded on the authority of the United States of America. They then agreed upon sending for the commanding officer of Fort Erie, and dispatched a runner for that purpose. Soon after the council broke up, Capt. John of the Onondagas came to my hut, and informed me in a private conversation, that no scruple was made of the authority I came under to them, being well informed by the chiefs of the Genesee, who had given that information some considerable time before my reaching Buffalo. The reason, he said, they were so particular with me, was on account of a certain William Ewing, a resident from Connedesago lake, who had come in behalf of the Hon. Robert Morris, whom he called the second greatest man in the union; that he had convened a council the day previous to my arrival, informing those of the Six Nations present, that the pre-emptive right to the land in this country as belonging to the state of Massachusetts, were now the property of the said Robert Morris, whensoever the Six Nations of Indians were disposed to sell any part of the same; that the better to authenticate the business he had to perform, he produced his instructions under the hands and seals of the said Robert Morris, and the Honorable —— Ogden, both of the state of Pennsylvania, adding that now the chain of friendship now stretched between the said gentlemen and the Six Nations, the centre of which was to be supported by him; that in consequence thereof, he desired their permission to traverse the several courses of the lands granted by their agent, —— Livingston, of New York, to the said State of Massachusetts.

28th. The council being convened within the house, there appeared to be about one hundred and fifty in number. Mr. Ewing began to open, and continue his business, which he had introduced the day before; upon which I rose to inform him that he must desist from going any farther, as it was an interferance with my mission, that was of the utmost consequence to the United States, and to the Indians in general; and that as soon as the same was completed, agreeable to the purport of my coming here, that then I would lend him such assistance as was in my power, and through which I would evidence my respect for the gentlemen who sent him. The commanding officer of Fort Erie sent word this morning, that he could not leave his garrison without the express permission of the commandant of Niagara, (Col. Gordon,) but that he had sent Capt. Powell, of the Indian Department, as a suitable person to superintend their business. As a proper introduction to my mission, and by the consent and desire of O'Beel, I began by reading his address to the Governor, and council of Pennsylvania, as also his several letters to the President of the United States, and his Excellency's answer to them, in order, and a third letter to the same, from the Secretary of War. The reading of these several papers, and the deed from his Excellency, the President, for the restoration of their lands in the Six Nations, and the interpreting the same, took up the whole of the day, upon which I concluded to adjourn till to-morrow. * * I thought it proper to give the invitation to Capt. Powell, to take up his abode at my hut for the night, which he very willingly accepted. After we had taken a little refreshment, we entered into a general conversation, and spoke on many matters, the consequence of the late war. The Captain being free in conversation, gave me to understand that Col.'s Butler and Brant, himself, and several officers from Niagara and Fort Erie, had been at Buffalo some time, waiting my coming, as they had advice that I was on my way hither; that while there, Brant received private instructions from head-quarters, to set out for the Grand River, and from thence to Detroit. This business, Capt. Powell judged, was to carry instructions of some kind, to the Indians at war with the United States. It had the appearance, of what had fallen from the lips of Butler and Brant, some days since, with the chiefs of the Onondagas and Senecas, as it had the tendency of their joint advice, when they spoke in the great council, viz: that they would not determine on any matter of consequence with me, without their concurrence. These injunctions being laid upon them, (as I received it from my informant,) the British officers retired to their different posts.

Friday, April 29th. The business which I postponed yesterday, I opened in a much larger council, than had appeared before; and after I had read the Secretary of War's message to the Six Nations, I continued to read those also directed to the Delawares, &c., and closed the whole with an address to them. * * The reply of Red Jacket to the foregoing, as it will come more proper in its place here, I will insert it at full length:

"Brother from Pennsylvania—We have heard all that you have said to us, and by which you have informed, that you are going to the bad Indians to make peace with them, and that you are sent to us, to seek our assistance. Now we must consider the matter thoroughly, and to choose which way to go, either by land or by water. You likewise tell us that you have messages to the Wyandots, and to Capt. Snake of the Delawares, and that they are to take hold of you and us by the hands, and go to the bad Indian nations with us; and this also, we must consider of thoroughly, for we find that all our Six Nations are not present; and as our brother, Capt. Powell, of the British is here, and true to us, for he is here at every treaty, we must let you know that we shall move our council fire to Niagara with him, and that you must go with us to-morrow, as far as Capt. Powell's house. And as soon as we can know what time we can reach Niagara, we will send runners off to the Fort to acquaint the commanding officer of the garrison. And now the council want to have your answer." I did not long hesitate to make answer in what I deemed a very unwarrantable request. * * therefore I should decline accompanying them. * * A silence prevailed for some time in the whole council, after which, Red Jacket and Farmer's Brother, spoke to the council by turns; the result of it being that a runner must be immediately sent to Niagara, to request the attendance of Col. Butler, &c., to meet them in their council as soon as he could make it convenient.

[Continued in appendix to second volume.]

INDEX.

www.ingramcontent.com/pod-product-compliance
Lightning Source LLC
LaVergne TN
LVHW021130110826
845150LV00005B/982

* 9 7 8 1 4 2 5 5 5 0 0 4 2 *